Helmke provides his readers with a fascinating and multifaceted biographical study of Landgrave Philipp of Hesse, an important participant in and contributor to the sixteenth-century Reformation. He does so by placing the landgrave into his familial, political, and religious contexts. While Philipp is the chief focus, his time, place, and influential contemporaries are also explored. Helmke's portrait of Philipp is a paradoxical one since he presents the landgrave as a person who is both "heroic and scandalous." Thus Philipp's admirable as well as his less-defensible character traits and actions are examined incisively. The book can be a resource both for scholars and for casual students of the Reformation.

Kurt K. Hendel
Bernard, Fischer, Westberg Distinguished Ministry Professor Emeritus
of Reformation History, Lutheran School of Theology at Chicago

Has there been a more studied and discussed century in church history than the sixteenth with its Protestant Reformation and Roman Catholic Counter-Reformation? Probably not—and yet John Helmke has found a hole in the record concerning one of that century's major players, Philipp of Hesse. That said, we might expect a dusty tome replete with obscure details and foreign language footnotes. Helmke, though, has provided an accessible story that will engage all sorts of readers and reward them for the time spent.

Leonard Payton
Pastor, St. John Lutheran Church
Forest Park, Illinois

In accounts of the Reformation in the Western Church, Martin Luther casts a long shadow. Most of those who step into the light are his friends and foes whose concerns were correct teaching of the Christian faith. But political leaders on both sides did much to shape and to extend the reach of the Reformation. Along with Luther's noble protector, Frederick the Wise, Philipp of Hesse looms large. In sixty-three years crowded with passionate living, Philipp had a significant impact on the Reformation's development. It's a story worth telling, and here it is well told.

The Rev. Fred Reklau (retired)
Author of Partners in Care: Medicine and
Ministry Together *(Wipf & Stock, 2010)*

D1523153

Philipp of Hesse

Unlikely Hero of the Reformation

John E. Helmke

CONCORDIA PUBLISHING HOUSE • SAINT LOUIS

Published by Concordia Publishing House
3558 S. Jefferson Avenue, St. Louis, MO 63118-3968
1-800-325-3040 • cph.org
Text © 2018 John E. Helmke

Manufactured in the United States of America

Library of Congress Cataloging-in-Publication Data

Names: Helmke, John E., author.

Title: Philipp of Hesse : unlikely hero of the Reformation / by John E. Helmke.

Description: St. Louis : Concordia Publishing House, 2018. | Includes bibliographical references.

Identifiers: LCCN 2018020461 (print) | LCCN 2018032277 (ebook) | ISBN 9780758661975 | ISBN 9780758661968

Subjects: LCSH: Philipp I, Landgraf von Hessen, 1504-1567. | Reformation.

Classification: LCC BR350.P45 (ebook) | LCC BR350.P45 H45 2018 (print) | DDC
270.6092 [B] --dc23

LC record available at https://lccn.loc.gov/2018020461

1 2 3 4 5 6 7 8 9 10   27 26 25 24 23 22 21 20 19 18

TABLE OF CONTENTS

Preface

Martin Luther's call for reform addressed and appealed to quite a variety of people in sixteenth-century Europe who found their own longings for a better life than that prescribed by the Church's practices and preaching. People of all social levels, of differing degrees of formal education, of contrasting religious preferences and practices responded in a variety of ways to Luther's discarding the ritualistic, hierarchical approach to God that formed the heart of the piety of the late Middle Ages. His turning to an understanding of the Christian faith that taught that God comes to us, in human flesh and in His re-creative Word in oral, written, and sacramental forms, found favor among the people of central, northern, and eastern Europe for many different reasons.

Among the more colorful and vibrant of the personalities that rallied to Luther's cause was a young prince, already as a child blessed and burdened with the trappings and, to a certain extent, the exercise of power in German society, Philipp of Hesse. Philipp was raised in the consciousness that God was laying on him tremendous responsibilities for rebuilding the lands of his family, the principality of Hesse, in the middle of the German empire—for his father and uncle before him had let their lands decline in many ways. Philipp brought a determination and decisiveness to the tasks his bloodline imposed upon him that reflected the seriousness of his calling from God to govern his subjects for their benefit. That benefit embraced both their physical needs and their spiritual welfare.

As with many gifted individuals, Philipp could not exercise these responsibilities, given the shape of his personality, without offending some. Not only those who despised and dreaded Luther's reform found Philipp detestable and despicable. Other supporters of the Wittenberg reformer and his colleagues suspected Philipp of not sharing their view of the Lord's Supper and regarded his taking a second wife as reprehensible. They differed with him in policy and principle. Others have admired him over the centuries for his bold confession of his faith at the Diet of Augsburg in 1530 and in other situations in which the

Wittenberg Reformation faced the crises of its early years. At Augsburg, as he had earlier and would later, he placed his lands, liberty, and life at stake in the face of threats from a number of colleagues in the imperial college of princes, who deemed his promotion of Luther's reform a threat to both order in society and a proper understanding of the Christian faith. His interest in reading the Bible, a habit he had learned as a child, and his fervent desire to serve God and confess the message of salvation through Jesus Christ commended him to many in spite of his moral failings.

Equally comfortable in his suit of armor, on his horse, and in discussions of practical administration of the Church and even theological questions, Philipp of Hesse illustrates the broad appeal of the message that Luther and his Wittenberg colleagues—Philipp Melanchthon, Justus Jonas, and Johannes Bugenhagen—were proclaiming for some at every level of society, from princes to patricians and peasants. Philipp also embodies the struggles that Christians still encounter while embedded in their own callings in their homes and at work, in society, and in their congregations, even when their responsibilities do not match in societal impact those imposed by birth on Philipp. He exemplifies Luther's insight, gained from St. Paul (Romans 7), that Christ's chosen people are constantly experiencing—indeed, are unceasingly involved in—the struggle between the law of sin and the Law of God. His was indeed not only a life of outer conflicts of all kinds but also a life of inner conflict that he did not deal with lightly. Yet for most who have brushed up against his name in our day, he remains a cardboard figure, an image thinly sketched by those whose focus on the Reformation lies elsewhere and permits him only a bit part on the stage. John Helmke is determined to change that.

I have known John Helmke for over four decades. Throughout that time, Philipp of Hesse has had a hold on his imagination; the Hessian prince early on became a hobby and passion for him. Like a good detective, he wanted to know the facts of the landgrave's life and times, and he has striven to incorporate those facts into the larger panorama of Philipp's turbulent and tumultuous time in order to make him come alive for twenty-first-century readers. Separated from Philipp as we are by five centuries, by language, and by strikingly contrasting cultures, we find it hard to grasp what was really going on in his world and his own mind as we stumble across confusing social structures, inscrutable decisions, or inexplicable reactions. We easily presume that our ancestors thought in the manner we do until we delve a bit deeper into their times. Helmke builds bridges into the world of Martin Luther and Philipp of

Hesse, bridges that help us make sense of our heritage and put it to proper use. He aids us in avoiding a habit that plagues all reflection on the past: we tend so easily to disregard the unique features of another age and discard what does not fit into the patterns we presume must have governed their decision-making because they govern ours.

Helmke practices the trade of biographer in such a way that he tries to lead us away from letting our present presuppositions govern our reading of the past. When we do that, we are wasting our time, for history is of use when it guides us into new perspectives on our own inheritance from the past and our own experience of the present. Helmke helps us see the unfolding events in the life of Landgrave Philipp from his perspective and that of his contemporaries. He helps us learn why Philipp viewed life and faith as he did. Therefore, readers will find in these pages the special treat of getting to know someone quite different from themselves, but another human being and brother in the faith whose example, as Philipp Melanchthon pointed out in Article XXI of the Augsburg Confession, should be remembered in order to strengthen our faith (as a warning for the conscience and a model of trust in times of trouble), a reminder of God's faithfulness and goodness despite our sin, and in order to give us an example of how and how not to exercise our own callings from our Lord.

Robert Kolb
Wolfenbüttel, The Eve of
Festival of St. Barnabas 2018

Acknowledgments

Most likely this book would never have been written had not Dr. Robert Kolb, professor emeritus at Concordia Seminary, St. Louis, read in 2012 a 165-page prospectus I wrote in 1979 for my graduate studies advisor, Dr. Robert Fisher of the Lutheran School of Theology at Chicago. His comments prodded me to write this popular biography of Philipp of Hesse's life and rule. Dr. Kolb wrote, "Your study meets a great need. There is nothing in-depth in English that brings Philipp as a living personality for the broader audience. Your book can stand alongside Bill Wright's focus on Philipp's politics, etc., and give readers a fair balance. Go for it!" With these words echoing in my mind, I did "go for it," and most eagerly. The book you now hold is due to Dr. Kolb's generous support. Words fail me to thank him enough.

I soon purchased my own copy of Dr. Wright's book *Capitalism, the State, and the Lutheran Reformation*. We corresponded, and I enjoyed an informative afternoon conversation in his home in Chattanooga. He encouraged me not to hesitate to read difficult German literature on Philipp. "Just do it," he said. Dr. Wright has always responded helpfully to my email requests. For all his help, I am most grateful.

Dr. Kurt Hendel, author of *Johannes Bugenhagen*, an impressive two-volume work on Luther's pastor and confessor, has been my local source for Reformation knowledge. He opened for me the impressive resources of JKM Library at the Lutheran School of Theology in Chicago and helped me shape my thoughts in the challenging early stages of writing. I owe Kurt very much!

Special thanks to Anja Zimmer, a native Hessian, who shared much valuable information in our regular Facebook conversations and was a gracious, well-informed guide for my sister Ruth, my daughter Catherine, and myself in her lovely childhood home. She guided us on our five-day tour of Hesse.

Thanks to Augie Alesky of our local Century & Sleuths Bookstore, who invited me to join his historical book club and introduced me to the concept of narrative history (which I call popular biography for simplicity); to Marty

Philipp of Hesse

Breen of Klinck Memorial Library of Concordia University Chicago, who conducted numerous searches for obscure published works, usually with gratifying results; to Richard D. Clegg of Dominican University of River Forest, Illinois, who, in a one-hour evening conversation, opened windows of understanding to the importance of two women for the formation of independent Hesse in the thirteenth century, St. Elizabeth of Hungary and her daughter Sophie von Brabant.

My three editors at Concordia Publishing House of St. Louis, Laura Lane, Scot Kinnaman, and Alexa Hatesohl, patiently taught me much about the fine art of book publishing and clear writing. What a gift they are for a first-time author!

I dedicate this book to my wife, Nancy, who understood, with her own high level of excitement, that year after year I would be preoccupied with Philipp. In January 2017, Nancy became my first reader, followed by Dr. Natalie Jenne, professor emeritus at Concordia University Chicago, and two classmates from Concordia Seminary, St. Louis, Dr. Ralph Klein and the Rev. Frederick Reklau. The contributions from all four of them were invaluable. My heartfelt thanks to all of them.

John E. Helmke
On November 13, 2018
The 514th Anniversary of Philipp's Birth

Prologue

Some learn of Philipp of Hesse's bold political leadership of the Reformation in Germany and honor him as heroic. Others learn of his bigamy and despise him as scandalous. Yes, Philipp of Hesse was a bigamist. He married a second wife during the lifetime of the first. Then he fathered children by both wives.

English-language writers have treated Philipp superficially. Others, like the sculptor Ernst Rietschel, portrayed Philipp as Luther's second protector on his famous monument to the reformer in Worms, Germany. I see Philipp as a complex political leader who was both saint and sinner. I see Philipp as the *Unlikely Hero of the Reformation*.

My aim is to make my story of Philipp's life useful for students and teachers alike, entertaining for anyone who enjoys reading stories when the children are tucked off to bed, when commuting to and from work, or when waiting in the hospital for a family member or friend to return from surgery.

Philipp of Hesse has held my imagination captive since I was a teenager. It is for you, my reader, to determine whether Philipp's heroism outshines his scandals.

Philipp was born on November 13, 1504, eleven years after Columbus returned from the New World, when Martin Luther was a twenty-one-year-old university student. He would rule Hesse for forty-nine years and die in 1567 when most of the first-generation reformers had passed from the scene.

Of the significance of Philipp of Hesse's life and rule, the historian Hans J. Hillerbrand has written, "Without Philipp, Luther's cause may well have tumbled like a house of cards, while without Luther's cause, Philipp may well have remained an innocuous territorial ruler in sixteenth-century Germany."[1]

Martin Luther described a Christian as being, at one and the same time, both saint and sinner. Philipp dramatically personified that description. He was heroic in his promotion of the Reformation, but he could also be scandalous when ignoring the cautious advice of his friends.

Philipp of Hesse

At least twice Philipp scandalized his friends as well as his foes, but on at least one occasion he acted on his own and succeeded brilliantly. At that time, it took him only forty-eight hours to restore Württemberg (not to be confused with Wittenberg, Luther's town) to its hereditary prince. Even then, Philipp's foes labeled this heroic act as scandalous.

At least three of Philipp's acts reveal his personal sensitivity, faithfulness, and compassion. First, his marriage to Christine was arranged when he was four months old and Christine was not yet born. Unfortunately, their marriage appears never to have blossomed into love. Still, Philipp refused to divorce Christine, for he knew the suffering that would cause her and their children. Second, Philipp honored Martin Luther. His actions revealed him as the boldest political leader of the Reformation when, on the other hand, conforming to the dictates of the Church and the empire promised him greater power and wealth. Third, Philipp loved all his subjects, not just the obedient. Powerful friends pressured him to execute subjects that left his church. Philipp always said no.

Philipp of Hesse ruled one of the most powerful lands of the Holy Roman Empire, which was more a crazy quilt of German principalities than an empire. The line of authority in the empire was first the emperor, Charles V, and his deputy brother, Archduke Ferdinand, then the electors, and finally the dukes. Landgraves like Philipp were the rulers of territories inside the empire. Margraves were rulers of territories on the border (*Mark* in German) of the empire. Both were roughly the equivalent of English dukes and earls. The emperors were elected by seven of the most powerful rulers, called electors.

In addition to the German states, the Holy Roman Empire included the Netherlands, Austria, Hungary, Bohemia, and several lesser-known eastern lands. Emperor Charles V was also the king of Spain. This meant his responsibilities included the recently discovered Americas. As a result, he had the care of one of this world's largest empires, roughly half the size of the then-known world.

Charles had valuable holdings in Italy and took particular interest in the Netherlands, the land of his birth. He assigned the Netherlands to his aunt Margaret, who served as regent until her death in 1530. To succeed her, Charles appointed his sister, Queen Mary, who was the widow of Louis II, the king of Hungary and Bohemia.

Charles's Turkish problem is well known. Less well known is how his Italian possessions often caused him fierce, open conflict with the papacy and the king of France.

Upon his election as the emperor in 1519, Charles gave his brother, Ferdinand, deputy authority over Germany and its neighbors to the east. This made Ferdinand responsible for defending the empire, including Germany, against two perceived threats: the Ottoman aggression and the Protestant Reformation.

The archduke reported to Charles. Charles normally respected his brother's wishes. The two regents of the Netherlands, his aunt Margaret first and sister Mary later, served as referees when the brothers had disagreements that could not be settled without their help.

Germany in 1519 appeared to be little more than a smoldering hotbed in the empire. This was only two years after Luther posted his Ninety-five Theses, fanning the flames of the German Reformation. Though the reformer had been savagely attacked, the Reformation had not spread far as a movement. One year later, in 1520, the pope condemned Luther as a heretic. In April of the following year, the emperor condemned him as an outlaw. By the summer of 1521, Germany, that smoldering hotbed, had exploded into a raging fire.

Hesse's geography has changed little since Philipp's death in 1567. Its land area today includes Hesse-Darmstadt, Hesse-Kassel, and parts of Nassau, Fulda, and other smaller territories and is about the size of Massachusetts, 8,100 square miles (3,127 sq km). The distance from its northern to southern borders is approximately 120 miles (193 km); from east to west, approximately 61 miles (98 km).

A great challenge when writing is to select what needs to be written and what must be left unwritten. Regarding Martin Luther's life, I will treat only those events that involved Philipp and/or shed light on Philipp's political leadership of the Reformation. I will include more-detailed sketches of three female ancestors important to Hesse; Philipp's father-in-law, Duke George of Saxony; and his theologian, Lambert von Avignon. These persons are less famous than Luther, but they played important roles in Philipp's life.

In 1962, Alton O. Hancock prepared his unpublished doctoral dissertation, *The Reformation in Hesse to 1538: A Study of the Encounter of Differing Reformation Points of View.* In it he treated only Philipp's first thirty-five years of life, leaving his bigamy and final twenty-nine challenging years untreated.

In 1967, when the 400th anniversary of Philipp's death was being commemorated, Hans J. Hillerbrand published his thirty-seven-page English biography of the landgrave, which was quoted above. In addition to its brevity, it is disappointing to me that many quotes from Philipp are not translated. They are published in the challenging sixteenth-century German of Hesse. Simply transcribing them into modern German would have been helpful.

In 1988, Professor William J. Wright published *Capitalism, the State, and the Lutheran Reformation*. This is not a biography of Philipp but an important treasury of Hessian information including valuable insights on Philipp.

In 2001, Richard Andrew Cahill published an impressive scholarly work, *Philipp of Hesse and the Reformation*. Unfortunately, he treats only Philipp's first twenty-four years and ignores his most heroic and scandalous last thirty-nine years.

In 2015, Professor David M. Whitford published *A Reformation Life: The European Reformation through the Eyes of Philipp of Hesse*. This is an impressive cradle-to-grave treatment of Philipp including a chapter on his bigamy, which is rarely treated in English. It may be helpful as an introduction to Philipp's life, but it presents him merely as a witness to the Reformation.

Many terms that were common in the sixteenth century have become archaic today. I find three stand out as most important: *diet*, *recess*, and *estate*. They are confusing terms because they are still used today but with meanings quite different from their meanings at the time of the Reformation.

The word *diet*, as in "the Diet of Worms," is from the medieval word *dieta*, meaning "a meeting and its routine." Today, our closest equivalent might be the word *congress*, though membership of the diet was not elected. It was by appointment or inherited. There were two levels of diets, the territorial diets and the imperial diets.

The word *recess*, as in "the recess of the diet," is also from a medieval Latin word, *recedere*, meaning "to go back." By Philipp's time, it had taken on the meaning of withdrawal or departure and was applied to the document drawn up soon after a diet to report the work done there, similar to our written minutes of a meeting.

The word *estate* presents more problems. For simplicity, it is best to tell how the word was used in Philipp's time. When a prince needed to organize a diet in his land, he summoned his "territorial estates." These included the nobles, the towns, and the church, represented by its clergy. When a diet of the empire was needed, the "imperial estates" were summoned by the emperor. Here the estates included the princes, the imperial cities, the bishops, and the archbishops. (Seldom if ever did the title *prince* mean the son of a king in the empire. I have found the title *prince* to be used there in a manner similar to the title *ruler*.)

A fourth word, *Protestant*, also needs some clarification. Today, a Protestant is a Christian who is not Roman Catholic. During Philipp's lifetime, *Protestant* was the third name used to address those following Luther's teachings.

It was coined in 1529. I use the words *Lutheran* and *Protestant* interchangeably for variety, but I use the term *Evangelical* sparingly, for that term addresses a movement today that has grown out of the Reformed, not Lutheran, tradition.

Except when quoting other authors who use the English spelling Philip, I will often use the German spelling, Philipp, and the English equivalent of German proper names, like John for Johann.

Philipp's most heroic decade was the 1530s. I will dedicate four chapters to that decade. Most important are chapter 11, his treatment of the revolutionary Anabaptists of Münster, and chapter 12, his treatment of his own peaceful but dissenting Hessian Anabaptists. Without Philipp's promotion of Protestant expansion, described in chapter 9, and his attention to the economic, educational, and health care needs of the poor, described in chapter 10, the landgrave's heroic treatment of his Anabaptist subjects described in chapter 12 might have met severe opposition from the estates, who had rebelled against his mother twenty years earlier when he was a boy.

In his last will and testament of 1562, Philipp divided his land among his four living sons by Christine, instructing them to remain faithful to the Augsburg Confession and treat benevolently those who might leave the Lutheran Church. As a result, Hesse remained a safe harbor for Anabaptists and others of dissenting faith.

The Amana Colonies of Iowa are such a dissenting group that benefited from Hessian hospitality. In 1714, a German religious group began meeting and called themselves "The Community of True Inspiration." They were persecuted for their faith and found refuge in Hesse. In 1842, after 130 years of peaceful coexistence with the Hessians, the threat of a renewed persecution and economic depression convinced them to emigrate to America, where they settled in Iowa.

A promising area to study might be how Philipp's refusal to execute Anabaptists may have planted a seed for the formulation of the Establishment Clause in the American constitution; it reads, "Congress shall make no law respecting an establishment of religion, or prohibiting the free exercise thereof."

Now let us enter the exciting sixteenth century to meet this unlikely hero of the Reformation, Philipp of Hesse. He was an unlikely hero due only to his scandalous private life gone public and the embarrassment he caused for the Reformation. Should you find you dislike Philipp after you have finished reading about his life, you will not be alone. My purpose is not to glamorize Philipp. It is to tell his story with sympathy, showing how incomplete the histories of the Reformation are when they treat Philipp with little or no care.

Chapter 1

RECOGNITION 1518–24
A Mother's Outrageous Request

"Declare my son the Landgrave of Hesse." A widowed mother of two precocious children, Elizabeth, age 15, and Philipp, age 13, approached Emperor Maximilian I with this outrageous request. Hessian rulers were addressed as landgraves, and even in 1518, thirteen was too young to rule.

Her request was more outrageous for the fact that Hesse had been in political turmoil for most of the previous nine years. In 1509, the widow's husband, Philipp's father, Landgrave Wilhelm II, died, leaving his land in the hands of regents who now lacked a unifying ruler.

Still, Maximilian did not hesitate to grant this widow's wish, for she was Anna of Mecklenburg, who had opposed the rebellious estates and become the most powerful person in Hesse. On March 16, 1518, Maximilian declared Philipp to be the landgrave of Hesse. That was five months after Martin Luther published his Ninety-five Theses, igniting the Reformation. In the turbulent times that followed, Philipp ruled Hesse well for forty-nine years and outlived most, if not all, first-generation Reformation leaders.

Within five years, Philipp would be recognized for three decisive acts: a "kidnapping," diplomatic success at the 1521 Diet of Worms, and putting an end to the Knights' War by defeating Franz von Sickingen, the most feared knight in the German nation and the Holy Roman Empire.

A CONFUSION OF NAMES

We need time out to learn some names, for the names of Philipp's family members can be very confusing. There were three Wilhelms. His father, Wilhelm II, was called "the Middler" because he was for a time the second to rule only northern Hesse from the city called Kassel. His uncle, Wilhelm I, was called "Mad Wilhelm" due to a mental disorder caused by syphilis. Wilhelm III was a cousin of Philipp's father who ruled southern Hesse from Darmstadt until he died in a hunting accident in 1500.

Mad Wilhelm had ruled southern Hesse prior to 1493, when he was compelled to resign his position to Wilhelm III, having been judged incompetent to rule. Upon Wilhelm III's death, in a hunting accident, Phillip's father united Hesse. Mad Wilhelm, however, outlived Philipp's father long enough to raise serious problems for Philipp's mother.

Adding to the confusion of the men in young Philipp's life were confusing names of some of the women. There were two Annas and two Elizabeths. Philipp's mother was Anna of Mecklenburg. His aunt, the wife of Mad Wilhelm I, was Anna of Braunschweig. Elizabeth, Philipp's older sister, was born in 1502. His cousin Elizabeth, whose dates are unknown, was the second daughter of Mad Wilhelm and Anna of Braunschweig. Her part in young Philipp's story will be told later in this chapter.

PUTTING YOUNG PHILIPP TO THE TEST

Professor William John Wright describes five factors that prompted a new economic policy for the empire at the time of Philipp's rise to power. They were the rise of the territorial state, the Lutheran Reformation, the growing influence of capitalism, the crisis of feudalism, and population trends.[2]

In those changing times, many watched to see if young Philipp might fail. Watchers included Philipp's next-door neighbor Frederick III, the most powerful elector in Germany, who ruled Ernestine Saxony from 1486 until his death in 1525 and would become Martin Luther's protector. Frederick had been troublesome to Philipp's mother, Anna of Mecklenburg, for he was slated to inherit the rule of Hesse should Philipp die young.

Another next-door neighbor watching Philipp was Frederick's estranged cousin, Duke George of Albertine Saxony. He ruled from 1500 to 1539 and connived to unite Hesse and Albertine Saxony by signing a contract with Wilhelm II, legally committing to marriage four-month-old Philipp and George's yet-to-be-born daughter, Christine. By signing that contract, George and Wilhelm envisioned how the power and wealth of Hesse, when added to that of George's Albertine Saxony, might topple Frederick from power and seriously challenge the emperor.

Other close neighbors watching young Philipp were Frederick's brother John, who would one day rule Ernestine Saxony, and George's brother Henry, who also would one day rule Albertine Saxony. The story of the two Saxonies and their leaders will be told in chapter 3.

Other powerful princes of the empire were also watching, including Emperor Maximilian himself, who ruled from 1486 to 1519. Would Philipp prove too young to rule? Would he be tied to his mother's apron strings and ignore some of the pressing needs of the empire? Would he die young and would Hesse then unite with one of the two Saxonies against the empire?

As it turned out, Philipp's mother arranged a hearing of grievances posed by the estates for Philipp. At thirteen years of age, Philipp was well prepared by his mother and her supporters. He handled himself well. Throughout his rule, the landgrave never found it difficult to make hard decisions. He would rule Hesse decisively until what was then the ripe old age of sixty-three. By the end of his first six years as landgrave, though he would only be nineteen, Philipp would have revealed that he was one young prince of Germany to be recognized as a decisive ruler.

A KIDNAPPING

It might seem a stretch to call Philipp's premeditated and alarming act during the first months of his rule a kidnapping. We might call it today a matter of "protective custody," but history remembers it as a kidnapping.

As early as 1500, Anna of Braunschweig had objected to the unification of Hesse under Philipp's father. She was convinced that, with her help, Mad Wilhelm could resume the rule of the southern half of divided Hesse. Following the death of Philipp's father in 1509, this Anna's constant objections caused serious conflicts with Philipp's mother. Anna of Mecklenburg was fifteen years younger than her sister-in-law, but she refused to bow meekly to Anna of Braunschweig's wishes.

Earlier her conniving sister-in-law had arranged the marriage of her elder daughter (whose name and dates are unknown) to a lesser count without bothering to ask for the approval of the territorial estates (the nobility, the clergy, and the towns). By 1514, Anna of Mecklenburg presided over these estates as the confirmed regent of Hesse. The marriage of Elizabeth's older sister was an accomplished fact, but now the estates refused to allow Anna of Braunschweig to give her younger daughter to any suitor they might deem unworthy. This was no idle threat, for the estates gathered regularly in territorial diets, financed the cost of raising young Elizabeth in luxury, and were already providing her with a dowry.

Philipp of Hesse

Mad Wilhelm died in 1515. By this time, Anna of Mecklenburg had completely solidified her control over the estates, and she petitioned the emperor to grant her custody of her niece, Elizabeth. Philipp's mother threatened that if she lost her petition, Anna of Braunschweig would lose her widow's holdings (in German, her *Wittum*) if she allowed her daughter to travel outside of Hesse or gave her in marriage without the consent of the estates.

In autumn of 1516, Anna of Braunschweig left her daughter at Melsungen, in northern Hesse near Kassel, and disappeared to lodge a complaint at the Imperial Court. Philipp's mother took Elizabeth into the Hessian Court, ostensibly for her security. There, twelve-year-old Philipp met his cousin Elizabeth.

Anna of Braunschweig won her suit. Upon her return she took her daughter back to Melsungen, where they lived until the spring of 1517. Mysteriously, in that year she left Elizabeth, now thirteen, in the charge of the servants and disappeared once again. This time she was gone for an entire year. In March 1518, the same month that Philipp was declared of age to rule, the emperor suggested to Anna of Mecklenburg and the Hessian estates that Elizabeth should come to live in his court in Innsbruck. There she would be raised in luxury at the expense of the Hessian estates. To no one's surprise, Anna of Braunschweig welcomed the emperor's invitation. Anna of Mecklenburg and her estates rejected it.

On April 15, 1518, Philipp, having ruled as the landgrave of Hesse for only one month, took a bold, somewhat reckless step. He "kidnapped" Elizabeth. It happened at a baptism. Who was baptized is unknown. Elizabeth and Philipp's uncle, Duke Albrecht of Mecklenburg, were invited to serve as sponsors. Following the baptism, Philipp invited Elizabeth to return with him to Marburg. He promised to treat her to all the luxury and privileges a princess of her status deserved. He added that should she refuse, she could expect no more favors from him. Apparently Elizabeth did not object. Philipp ordered her custodians not to interfere and took her to his castle in Marburg.

Anna of Braunschweig appealed to the emperor, who ordered Philipp to appear at the 1518 Diet in Augsburg. This was the diet at which Martin Luther was ordered to meet with Cardinal Cajetan. Luther obeyed, but Philipp refused to appear.

Anna of Braunschweig was financially ruined by the cost of her suit, and the emperor formed a special commission to settle once and for all the conflict of the two Annas. Fortunately for Philipp and his mother, the chairman of the commission, named by the emperor, was their friendly benefactor, Duke George of Albertine Saxony.

The commission announced its decision in October. Philipp was to have custody of his cousin for one and a half years. Her mother was to be allowed visitation rights. Philipp was required to provide his cousin with food, clothing, and jewels befitting a princess of her status and to seek a suitable husband for her. If she were not married by the end of the eighteen-month period, her mother could resume custody under two conditions: that she would not take her daughter out of Hesse and that she would not permit her to marry without the approval of Philipp and the estates. Three months later, in January 1519, Emperor Maximilian I died.

A HUGE RANSOM IS EXTORTED FROM YOUNG PHILIPP

In the early sixteenth century, knighthood was losing its blossom. It enjoyed a brief resurgence under Emperor Maximilian I, who fancied himself as the last knight and relied heavily for support upon the empire's knights, the most powerful being Franz von Sickingen. He had awarded Sickingen great wealth and twelve castles on the Rhine due to his support. By 1518, most of the knights of Germany were little more than ferocious bands of robber knights (*Raubritter*). Sickingen was the most widely feared knight of his day.

In that time there were two classes of knights in the empire: territorial knights, who were nobles down on their luck and in service to other nobles, and imperial knights, who were nobles in service to the emperor. As imperial knights, Sickingen and his friend Ulrich von Hutten had personal scores to settle with the still-unchallenged landgrave of Hesse.

The sixteenth century was also a time of state building, replacing feudal society with a society of imperial peace, built on Roman law as it had been codified by the emperor Justinian in the sixth century. Maximilian enlisted the support of the rulers of Germany to enforce this imperial peace. Prosperous nobles had stated their grievances as recently as 1515, believing this movement would be a threat to their powers, which indeed it was. The clergy and the towns supported the nobles, feeling they had been getting along quite well under feudal society.

Three events came together within a fifteen-month period to signal the death of feudal society. First, on October 31, 1517, Martin Luther posted his Ninety-five Theses, kick-starting the Reformation. Second, on March 16, 1518, the emperor declared Philipp of age to rule. By doing this, he recognized the limits Philipp's mother had placed on the Hessian nobility and how she had successfully pursued her husband's commitment to rebuilding united Hesse under Roman law. Third, on January 12, 1519, "the last knight," Emperor Maximilian died.

Hesse had gained its independence from Thuringia in the thirteenth century. Since then, the Free Imperial City of Mainz and its archbishop had been a thorn in the flesh of the landgraves of Hesse. "Free imperial cities" were cities denoted as self ruling, represented in the imperial diets, and subordinate only to the emperor. In 1521, of the approximately four thousand cities and towns in the empire, eighty-five were designated as free imperial cities. Philipp's two closest free imperial cities were Cologne, not far from his northern border, and Mainz, on his southern border.

Bishop Albrecht of Mainz had been recently elevated to archbishop. The funds needed to cover the cost of his elevation, together with funds to be used for building the new St. Peter's Basilica in Rome, were borrowed from Augsburg banks. The plan was to repay this huge loan by the sale of Pope Leo X's promises of release from the pains of purgatory, called indulgences. That sale motivated Martin Luther to post his Ninety-five Theses on October 31, 1517.

Both Philipp and the archbishop of Mainz claimed control of an area along the Rhine River. It was inevitable that the prince of the land and the prince of the Church would not see eye to eye.

Philipp inherited an unwritten feud between the archbishop and Wilhelm II that had not been settled since 1505, when Philipp was less than a year old. The land along the Rhine was famous for its fine Rhenish wine. At the Imperial Diet of Cologne in 1505, Emperor Maximilian granted Philipp's father the right to impose a road tax on Rhenish wine. This imposition, added to the customs fees already on wine, the tolls on Rhine River traffic, and the fact that Wilhelm II had taken some of the territory for himself earlier that year, caused a virtual feud by the archbishop against Wilhelm II that Philipp would inherit thirteen years later. Young and untested, Philipp presented an easy target for Franz von Sickingen, who supported Archbishop Albrecht.

It was September 7, 1518, and harvesttime was fast approaching, so Sickingen felt certain he could quickly make the entire area respect his power by laying siege to Metz, an important city located northwest of Hesse. He threatened the livelihood of Metz by announcing that unless they surrendered immediately, he would destroy their livelihood, chopping down their vineyards. Metz quickly surrendered. Sickingen allowed little time for the news of his victory to spread throughout Hesse. He wrote Philipp an official "letter of feud."

Sickingen's letter stated that he would allow forty days' notice to the city of Darmstadt, in southern Hesse, to prepare for battle or surrender. Once he had seen to it that his letter of feud was delivered to Philipp, Sickingen felt certain he could not be charged with murder. For centuries, such procedures had been accepted as legitimate throughout Europe, even by the Church. Though Sickingen had not been harmed by Darmstadt and had been employed by the emperor to enforce the imperial peace, Sickingen was still masterful at twisting outdated feudal customs to his own advantage.

At that time, Philipp had ruled Hesse for only six months. He recognized the difficult position he was in, and he provided a representative with power of attorney to settle Sickingen's feud. However, Philipp and his representative had different ideas about how his power of attorney was to be used. A treaty was drawn up with eighteen points, all of them favoring Sickingen.

Philipp was outraged when he learned of this lopsided treaty, for it stated that he agreed to pay the huge ransom of 35,000 gulden Sickingen demanded. The gulden was Hesse's most valuable coin. It was the only Hessian gold coin, used primarily in foreign trade. One gulden alone was a priceless treasure compared with the silver and copper coins used by the common people in the shops of Hesse. This treasure was all that Sickingen really wanted. He called off his troops and Darmstadt was saved. However, for the next five years, Philipp would harbor his own unwritten letter of feud against Sickingen.

THE WISDOM OF SIXTEEN-YEAR-OLD PHILIPP AT THE DIET OF WORMS

Emperor Maximilian died in January 1519. During the hotly contested election between Maximilian's grandson, Charles V, and Francis I, the king of France, Sickingen gathered an army to protect Charles. Two years later, at the Diet of Worms in 1521, he would perform a similar service to make certain the emperor honored his pledge of safe passage to Martin Luther. During the sessions of that diet, Sickingen gathered his troops at the gates of Worms. They were prepared to rescue Luther if necessary. Fortunately, the emperor honored his safe passage, and Sickingen's troops were not needed. Later, twenty horsemen, allegedly provided by Sickingen, would accompany Luther's departure from the city.

All the princes of Germany had been summoned to the diet, so it is difficult to imagine that Philipp was not present to hear Luther's famous refusal to recant. Still, while the late nineteenth-century mural in the *aula* (auditorium) of the Melanchthon Gymnasium (high school) in Wittenberg depicting Philipp greeting Luther soon after his refusal to recant is impressive, it is probably a product of artistic license.

At that time, Philipp was very upset with his mother for marrying below her station two years earlier. In fact, he had been so upset that at one point he threatened to raise an army to attack his stepfather. One week after Luther's appearance, Elizabeth, Philipp's eighteen-year-old sister, negotiated a mother-and-son reconciliation.

When Philipp was declared of age to rule in 1518, Hesse had been hard-pressed for allies to defend it against an attack by Sickingen and others. In the following year, Philipp saw to it that Hesse was accepted into membership by the Swabian League, which had been created in the late fifteenth century for the mutual defense of the lands of southern Germany. Prior to this, border-land Hesse had not qualified as a land of southern Germany.

Philipp devoted much time and attention to strengthening Hessian ties with old and new allies at the diet. He even renewed the controversial inheritance alliance with Elector Frederick, formerly his mother's foe. By now, Frederick was Martin Luther's protector, who had negotiated the reformer's safe passage to and from Worms.

To Philipp's credit, he listened to his advisers though he was still only sixteen. In addition to the pomp and circumstance arranged for his impressive arrival in Worms, it was said that the young landgrave's best adornment was his many "beards," meaning his councilors, with whom he surrounded himself. By the summer following the diet, Philipp and his councilors had improved their relations with most of Hesse's neighbors.

One exception to Philipp's impressive run of successes at Worms was a challenge by two brothers, the dukes Henry and William of Nassau. They sued Philipp for control of Katzenelnbogen, a valuable section of land on the Rhine that had been a part of Hesse since the 1470s. Making matters more difficult for Philipp, Henry of Nassau had been Charles V's tutor, and after 1522 would live in the Spanish court as the emperor's lord chamberlain.

The brothers' demands were high. They would settle for nothing less than complete control of Katzenelnbogen. At one point, the emperor entered the negotiations and convinced Philipp to offer the brothers 110,000 gulden if they would drop their claim. The brothers refused.

How personally involved was sixteen-year-old Philipp with all these negotiations? A document in Philipp's own hand sheds light on that question. The document is a checklist of twenty-six items that Philipp intended to accomplish at the diet. The first thirteen dealt with foreign relations. As each item was completed successfully, he marked it with an *X*. One item indicates that Philipp himself acted as the negotiator between Brandenburg and Bavaria. Among the treaties that Philipp and his councilors drew up at Worms, one that was important for the solution of the Sickingen problem, as we shall see later, was a treaty for mutual defense with Louis, the elector of the Palatinate.

Philipp visited Martin Luther in his apartment in Worms on the day after the reformer's arrival. All that was recorded of their conversation is a brief remark by Philipp as they parted. It would be remembered differently by the Catholics and the Lutherans. Luther's followers remembered Philipp's statement as evidence he was not yet Lutheran: "If you are right, Dr. Luther, God help you." Catholics, like the papal nuncio Jerome Aleander, remembered Philipp's words as evidence that Philipp was already a Lutheran: "You are right Dr. Luther, God bless you." Philipp also gave Luther safe passage through Hesse for his return to Wittenberg.

PHILIPP SLAYS FRANZ VON SICKINGEN

Philipp was not yet Lutheran, contrary to what Aleander had reported. His defeat of Franz von Sickingen, a follower of Luther, would contradict the nuncio's report. Was Sickingen really Lutheran? There can be little doubt he was. However, his decision to turn Lutheran may have been little more than a matter of political opportunity for him. Still, there is evidence that even Luther was convinced Sickingen's profession to be a Lutheran was sincere.

Sickingen's friend Ulrich von Hutten revealed that Sickingen had one serious shortcoming: he was illiterate. Hutten corresponded with Luther on Sickingen's behalf. Hutten claimed that Luther's tracts were read at Sickingen's table and the knight listened to them attentively. Also, Luther dedicated his tract *On Confession* to Sickingen. In March 1522, he sent greetings to Franz and Ulrich, addressing them as "our friends in the faith."

While waiting at the gates of Worms in 1521, Sickingen had devised a plan to bring about an immediate reform of Germany and restore feudal law. Sickingen would seize the city of Trier and capture its archbishop/elector, Richard von Greifenklau. Since Greifenklau had supported the candidacy of the king of France in the imperial election of 1519, Sickingen expected that the emperor would reward him appropriately for capturing Greifenklau. Hutten accepted Sickingen's plan and urged him to act on it quickly.

In the meantime, the emperor was returning to Spain by way of the Netherlands. From there he would sail on to Spain, a much safer route than traveling through France, which was ruled by his enemy Francis I, or sailing the Ottoman-infested Mediterranean Sea, where Barbarossa was inciting terror. On his way, the emperor stopped in Speyer and summoned Sickingen to appear before him. There Charles commissioned the great knight to serve as a general in his war with Francis. Though Francis would later be held briefly as the emperor's captive, he would remain a constant source of trouble for Charles V and would rule France until his death in 1547.

Sickingen obeyed the emperor's orders. He took his troops to France and delayed his plans for a military reform of Germany. It would, however, be a mistake to conclude that Sickingen abandoned his commitment to his military reform of Germany. Sickingen may have believed that being an imperial general might make it possible for him to gather a larger, better-trained army.

Sickingen's remarkable record of military success faltered in France, for Charles's campaign proved to be a failure. The celebrated French knight Bayard forced Sickingen to retreat. The emperor had failed to provide him with adequate support. Sickingen returned to Germany eager to resume his campaign against Trier.

Richard von Greifenklau was known as a fighting bishop, serving both as an archbishop and as the elector of Trier. Sickingen would underestimate Greifenklau. On August 29, 1522, Sickingen's army attacked Trier. Hutten, down with syphilis, was unable to lend his friend any direct assistance. Still, he had powerful connections in Mainz, for he had served in the court of Archbishop Albrecht, and a relative, Frowin von Hutten, was the court prefect in Mainz. Hutten used his influence, causing Mainz to delay coming to the rescue of Trier. He also saw to it that Philipp and his troops were denied passage at the Rhine for a time. Frowin von Hutten had ordered an unauthorized blocking of the bridges.

For three weeks, Sickingen's armies laid siege to Trier. He was defeated for two reasons. First, Philipp set an ambush and confiscated vital supplies of gunpowder meant to supply the knights. Second, Sickingen apparently forgot that the archbishop was a "fighting bishop" and underestimated the loyalty of his subjects.

In what appeared to be Trier's darkest hour, troops burst out of the city, led by the archbishop himself. They engaged Sickingen and his armies outside the city wall, and Greifenklau prevailed.

Sickingen survived that battle, but at Oberwesel on September 29, 1522, Philipp convened a meeting with the electors of the Palatinate and Trier. That meeting would seal Sickingen's fate. He had escaped to his Ebernburg Castle, where Philipp was eager to attack him. The others convinced Philipp that doing so would court disaster; winter was coming, and the Ebernburg was considered impregnable.

In February the following year, the three princes met again in Frankfurt. Sickingen still controlled all of his twelve castles. The princes agreed to attack only the one where Sickingen was most likely to be found. On April 22, they met again in Kreuznach, where they learned that Sickingen was at Landstuhl, one of his more heavily defended fortresses. Philipp offered 500 gulden to anyone who would capture the feared knight.

The princes laid siege on April 29, 1523. Philipp took advantage of the late fifteenth-century development of portable cannons on wheels. Over six hundred cannonballs were fired on the first day. Philipp joined his troops, clothed in their military garb. At one point he fired a cannon himself. A misfire might have ended Philipp's promising career. On the third day of the siege, Sickingen foolishly stepped out to inspect the damage done to his fortress. During the short time he was vulnerable, a cannonball shattered a wooden beam next to him, and it impaled him.

The seriously wounded Sickingen was taken into the fortress, there to linger until he died. On May 6, he surrendered to the three princes, ending the Knights' War. The next day, Philipp and his allies went into the fortress, where they found Sickingen in a dark chamber. Philipp entered first and asked the knight why he had attacked him in 1518. Sickingen promised that if he lived, he would make it up to Philipp. After Philipp and his party left the room but while they were still in the hallway, word came to Philipp that Sickingen had died.

For Philipp, the insult of being compelled to pay that huge ransom five years earlier had been avenged. The news spread far and wide. Now the child prince of 1518 was recognized as a decisive leader for all to follow with confidence.

How can one account for Philipp's rapid rise to recognition at such an early age? One's heritage is a powerful but often ignored factor. Stories of our ancestors and their deeds told to us in our youth fill our adult memory and influence our adult behavior.

Philipp's heritage included two lines competing for his youthful attention, his masculine and his feminine lines. The masculine line of Brabant was represented by generations of Hessian landgraves extending back to the early days of independence from Thuringia in the thirteenth century. As we shall see later, at the age of thirty-five, Philipp would make the unwise decision to abandon his feminine heritage, making his masculine heritage his identity of choice for the remaining scandalous years of his life.

Philipp's scandalous resort to violence and falsehood when making that choice appears to be evidence of the power his female line of heritage had previously held over young Philipp. That line reached back to the years when the landgraves of Thuringia ruled Hesse from the Wartburg castle near Eisenach. It included three remarkable women. Their story will be told in the following chapter.

Chapter 2

HERITAGE 100 BC–1518
St. Elizabeth Sows Seeds of Hessian Independence

Philipp's pious mother taught him to appreciate his heritage, especially its feminine line. One feminine ancestor was declared a saint. Another was the mother of independent Hesse. A third preserved united Hesse from hostile intervention and division. All three had one thing in common: they were all remarkably strong women.

In the first century before Christ, a Germanic tribe called the Chatti occupied the land. Through usage, the name of the tribe became the name of the land, and Chatti became Hesse.

Religious faith was a vital part of Philipp's heritage. In the eighth century, the Benedictine monk Boniface received a commission from the pope to convert the pagans of Hesse, which was governed by the landgrave of Thuringia from the Wartburg castle near Eisenach. Boniface blanketed the land with his preaching and charitable work. He established a monastic cell on the River Ohm in southern Hesse and dedicated it to the training of native clergy.

In northern Hesse, Boniface cut down an oak tree sacred to the thunder god Thor. The natives expected him to be killed by a lightning bolt from angry Thor. When this did not happen and Boniface survived untouched, they redirected their devotion to the triune God Boniface proclaimed. Then he moved north to the river Werra to build a church there. The Hessian town in the area named Wannfried is reminiscent of Boniface's baptismal name, Winfrid.

Boniface and a party of converts were massacred in Frisia on June 5, 754. His wish was to have his bones transported to Hesse and interred in the city of Fulda. His gravesite there is a popular tourist destination.

Four and a half centuries later, on July 7, 1207, Elizabeth of Hungary, Philipp's ancestor, was born in Pozsony in the Kingdom of Hungary (modern-day Bratislava, Slovakia). Only a short account of her remarkable life is possible here. Valid questions have been raised asking how much of her story is pious myth. That does not concern us here, for at the time of Philipp's birth, St. Elizabeth of both fact and fiction was venerated in Marburg. From early childhood, Philipp was taught to pray, asking her to intercede for him with the wrathful Christ of contemporary theology. St. Elizabeth's Church and tomb were among the most famous destinations for pilgrims until 1526, when Philipp introduced the Reformation in Hesse; he scattered her bones (relics) thirteen years later.

Landgrave Herman I of Thuringia (c. 1155–1215) ruled Hesse from the Wartburg castle near Eisenach. At age 4, Elizabeth was brought to Thuringia's sumptuous court and betrothed to Hermann II, the elder son of the landgrave. Hermann died in December 1216, when Elizabeth was nine years old. She was then betrothed to his younger brother, Louis. The couple were married in 1221, when Elizabeth was fourteen and Louis was twenty.

In 1207, the year of St. Elizabeth's birth, twenty-five-year-old Francesco Bernard, of the Italian town of Assisi, heeded this visionary command: "Francis, go and repair My church, which, as you see, is falling into ruin." Previously Francis had dreamed of knighthood. Now he threw off the wealth and pleasures of his noble birth and took poverty as his bride. Soon multitudes were flocking to Francis. His fame spread over the Alps to Germany.

Francis made an early attempt to introduce his order in Germany. That attempt failed, for his missionaries were poorly trained and knew little German. He made a second attempt in 1221. This attempt was successful. The missionaries chose Augsburg as their headquarters. They divided into several groups that settled near the border separating Hesse from Thuringia.

Impressionable young Elizabeth could not be sheltered from the spiritual fervor of her time. When she was five, the Children's Crusade rambled through her area. She learned about a crusading ancestor who refused to wear his crown when entering Jerusalem, for Jesus had worn a crown of thorns there. At worship, Elizabeth refused to wear royal finery. Once, she set Wartburg tongues wagging when she prostrated herself, removed the royal crown, and placed it at the foot of the church crucifix.

Landgrave Hermann I had ruled Thuringia/Hesse since 1190. He died in 1217. Louis, Elizabeth's betrothed, succeeded him. He was quickly recognized as one of the most effective princes of Germany and became a close personal friend of Emperor Frederick II (ruled 1220–50). Elizabeth and Louis were married in 1221. Their marriage was blessed with three healthy children, Hermann III (1222–41), Sophia (1224–75), and Gertrude (1227–97). The year of their marriage, 1221, was also the year the Franciscans made their first permanent settlement in Germany.

The Franciscan brothers lodged with the Teutonic Knights[3] in Marburg, and Elizabeth, now the landgravine, made certain they were allowed to remain there. It is likely the brothers told Francis about Elizabeth's piety, her work among the poor, and her support for Franciscan ministry, for Francis often spoke of Elizabeth before he died in 1226. He recognized her difficult role as a wealthy ruler's wife struggling to live in poverty, chastity, and obedience. He sent her one of his own gray cloaks. She treasured this as her most precious earthly possession and wore it whenever she prayed.

Soon the friars discovered Elizabeth's eagerness to learn. They taught her stories of Francis (c. 1182–1226) and his co-worker Clare of Rivotorto (c. 1193–1254). Louis supported Elizabeth's interest in Francis's mission. He knew how difficult her chosen role was for her. She had no support from her court and little from Louis's mother, Sophia. Also, the landgrave's opportunities to support his saintly wife were limited, for he served valiantly in the wars of the emperor, which caused him long periods of separation from his growing family.

In the spring of 1226, Louis was called to the Imperial Diet of Cremona. During his absence, famine ravaged Thuringia. Elizabeth took control, opening the Wartburg granaries to provide bread for the poor. She also distributed alms. She even gave some of her precious state robes and ornaments to the needy so they might sell them to buy food. Most important, Elizabeth had a twenty-eight-bed hospital built below the Wartburg castle. Many complained, "The landgravine is mad; she will bankrupt the kingdom!"

Upon returning, Louis learned of Elizabeth's generosity. Instead of rebuking her, he rebuked her critics. For his piety, his support of Elizabeth, and for miracles reported later at his tomb, Louis is a beloved historical figure of Germany. He was never declared a saint, but informed Germans still call him "Our St. Louis."

Francis died in 1226. Two years later, the emperor called on Louis to accompany him on a crusade. In September 1228, Louis died of the Black Plague in the port of Oranto, Italy. The news of his death reached Elizabeth in October. Now Elizabeth had lost the love of her life. Left with three small children, she was mentally and emotionally crushed. She walked the halls of the Wartburg crying, "He is dead! He is dead! The world with all its joys is now dead to me!"

From then on, Landgravine Elizabeth found it increasingly difficult to live as a devoted follower of Francis and still fulfill the expectations of her court. She moved her family 62 miles (100 km) west to Marburg where she lived in poverty, earning her keep spinning wool. In time, she placed her children into the care of willing family members. Only two devoted friends remained by her side.

In moving to Marburg, Elizabeth fanned the sparks of Hesse's drive for independence from Thuringia. She had a hospital and Franciscan chapel built in Marburg. She arranged housing for herself in a small room in the hospital so she could care for the sick both day and night. At the altar of the Franciscan chapel, she pledged to do everything God might ask of her.

Elizabeth's hair was shorn, and she received the gray homespun habit, the cord, and the veil of the Franciscan Third Order.[4] A few months earlier, Francis had been named a saint (canonized), and his mantle of humble service now fell upon Elizabeth. Soon after her own death and canonization, she would be named the patron saint of the Third Franciscan Order.

Elizabeth died shortly after midnight on November 17, 1231. She was only twenty-four years old and would be mourned far and wide. She was buried in the chapel of her hospital, and the first miracle at her grave was reported the following day. It was the healing of a Cistercian monk who, it was claimed, had been out of his mind for forty years. The news spread like wildfire. The sick that could walk or be carried headed off to Marburg. Many reported they had been healed at her tomb.

In 1235, after Elizabeth was declared a saint, her body was disinterred and entombed at the altar of the not-yet-completed church of Marburg, which would soon be named in her honor. It still stands today, drawing Sunday worshipers (including this writer).

St. Elizabeth is one of the most popular Catholic saints. Who has never heard of, seen, or visited a St. Elizabeth Hospital? By the time of Philipp's birth, it is said the marble steps at the altar of St. Elizabeth Church had been worn thin by three centuries of kneeling pilgrims. Much of Philipp's childhood would be spent in the shadow of Marburg's St. Elizabeth Church and the Franciscan monastery.

SOPHIE VON BRABANT, THE MOTHER OF HESSE

Sophie, Elizabeth's second child, was born in the Wartburg castle on March 24, 1224. If St. Elizabeth's move to Marburg set in motion Hesse's drive for independence, her daughter Sophie became the mother of independent Hesse. Her memory would hold great meaning for young Philipp, who was raised to rule Hesse well and keep it united through some of the most tumultuous years of its history.

Sophie's story will be told only briefly here, though it deserves much more attention. She was three when her father died. Landgrave Louis's will provided that his younger brother, Henry Raspe, should serve as regent until a legitimate heir reached age 12, the age of maturity at the time. Earlier, Henry Raspe had opposed St. Elizabeth's generosity. Now he would cause problems for Sophie as well. In 1247, Henry Raspe fell from his horse and died. No adult male heir was left for united Thuringia and Hesse.

In 1239, Sophie married Duke Henry of Brabant. Their son Henry was born in 1244. An impressive statue in the marketplace of Marburg depicts the day when Sophie lifted high her infant son Henry for all the citizens of Hesse to see the future landgrave of independent Hesse. Sophie took control of the land when Henry Raspe died, and she ruled united Thuringia and Hesse with remarkable skill. She was opposed by her cousin Jutta, Henry Raspe's daughter, and by Hermon of Henneberg, the archbishop of Mainz, who claimed Hesse as a fiefdom of the archbishop. The estates of Hesse (the nobility, the clergy, and the towns) feared the power of the archbishop and supported Sophie. The dispute that resulted involved prolonged military skirmishes known as the War of Thuringian Succession. At long last, Sophie prevailed in 1264.

In 1256, when Henry the Child had reached twelve, the age of maturity, Sophie proclaimed him landgrave of still-united Thuringia and Hesse. His rule of Hesse is dated from that year, though Hesse did not become independent until 1264. Sophie retired from the scene in that year when she prevailed in the seventeen-year War of Thuringian Succession. She died eleven years later, leaving her son Henry to rule as the first landgrave of independent Hesse, while her cousin, another Henry, was declared the landgrave of Thuringia.

ANNA OF MECKLENBURG
PRESERVES THE UNITY OF HESSE

On the morning of Philipp's birth, who would have thought his mother, a young woman of nineteen, would successfully fight the estates of Hesse for the guardianship of its future landgrave and the preservation of Hesse's unity? It is necessary to tell her story in a bit more detail, for it is here that Philipp enters his heritage as an intelligent young witness to his mother's successful political struggle.

Wilhelm II, Philipp's father, devoted a month to mourning upon the death of his first wife, Yolanda of Vaudemont. Her death had left him childless, and he knew he needed to take another wife to provide a male heir for his land. He chose fifteen-year-old Anna of Mecklenburg, the daughter of the powerful Duke Magnus II of Mecklenburg. A healthy daughter, Elizabeth, was born on March 4, 1502. In her adult life she would serve as one of Philipp's most intelligent and devoted advisers.[5]

Philipp was five years old in July 1509 when his father died of syphilis. This scourge had been brought to the Spanish port of Palos by Christopher Columbus's crew returning from the New World sixteen years earlier.

By 1506, Wilhelm knew he was dying, and he drew up his last will and testament. Because his relatives were either too old, too busy, or too mentally impaired, he named five members of the nobility as regents over Hesse and guardians of his children and their mother.

Anna was expected to retire quietly to her widow's pension near Giessen, about 20 miles (34 km) from Marburg. She had no intention of doing that, for she was proud of her heritage as the daughter of the powerful Duke Magnus II of Mecklenburg, who had died within recent memory, in 1503. Later, in struggles with the Hessian estates, Anna could recall how her father had been eulogized for putting down his estates "with fire and iron."

In 1508, Anna and several council members persuaded Wilhelm to alter his will, naming her as the regent of Hesse and guardian of her children. With the landgrave's sudden death, the two different wills came to light. The shock of his expected but still sudden death provided time for the nobles to solidify their position. They were supported by Elector Frederick of Saxony. At the time, Saxony was divided between Albertine Saxony, ruled by Duke George, and Ernestine Saxony, ruled by Elector Frederick III who, a decade later, would become Martin Luther's protector. The important story of the division of Saxony and the enmity between George and Frederick will be told in the next chapter.

Anna was caught off guard by the sudden death of her husband. To protect her interests against the ambitious Elector Frederick, she asked the elector's estranged cousin, Duke George, to assist her with a hundred well-equipped horsemen. The duke granted her request, and a lasting alliance was formed between Anna and George.

Anna planned to read in public the will that favored her. To prevent the estates from uniting against her, she organized two readings, one before the estates of southern Hesse and the other before those of the north.

But the estates were prepared. Her plan was thwarted by the appearance of an envoy from Frederick to reinforce the estates' refusal to accept the terms of the second will. In the compromise worked out by the Saxon envoys, the cards were stacked against Anna. A preliminary government included eight representatives of the estates but only three of her own. It was also decreed that in all important matters, this government of eleven would be advised by a committee chosen entirely by the estates.

The estates met with Anna four months after the landgrave's death. Also present were the four dukes of the two Saxonies, Frederick and his brother John, and George and his brother Henry. Only Duke George and Henry supported Anna when she demanded that the current regency be deposed and she be given the guardianship of Philipp until he reached fourteen, the age of maturity in the sixteenth century.

In the following year, Anna petitioned the emperor for assistance. Maximilian had serious concerns about Frederick's growing power. The acquisition of Hesse by Frederick would have doubled the wealth and size of Electoral Saxony, challenging the power of the emperor. Still, the emperor did support Frederick and the estates.

One year after the landgrave's death, the estates scored another victory when they were given charge of Philipp. Anna was allowed to visit him, but only infrequently. She was also allowed only one representative at the annual rendering of accounts and discussion of important matters.

With this one-sided decision, Hessian winds started to blow in Anna's favor. Anna of Braunschweig, Philipp's aunt by marriage, entered the scene. She claimed that her husband's health had improved and demanded a share in the government he had relinquished in 1493.

The estates refused her demands. Elector Frederick and his brother John ordered the citizens of Hesse to swear allegiance to them, should Philipp die without leaving a male heir. The regents took this oath gladly, revealing Frederick's influence at the time.

Homberg on the Efze River was one of the few towns of Hesse that objected. Fearing the consequences of involvement with Elector Frederick, Homberg became a rallying point of resistance. For this resistance, the city was forced to pay a high price. Its leaders were surrendered to the estates. The town lost all its urban privileges. The keys to the city gates were stolen. Finally, Homberg was forced to take the despised oath of allegiance and pay exorbitant fines to Frederick.

Though the resistance of Homberg had been put down, this worked to Anna's advantage. Popular resentment over the harsh treatment of Homberg caused Emperor Maximilian I to intervene. The influence of the estates was permanently weakened.

Now, even the regents, who had been appointed by the estates, became discontented with the high-handed decisions of their leader, Ludwig von Boyneburg. His reliance on Frederick was unpopular with the people, for the elector had offended many, acting like he was already the ruler of Hesse and making political appointments upon the recommendation of the regents.

Anna acted quickly to exploit her opponents' weakness. Armed with the signatures of fifty-four nobles, she summoned a territorial diet to meet early in 1514. At that diet, she attacked Boyneburg while skillfully feigning support for the estates, whom she knew she needed if she were to overthrow Frederick's influence.

The estates cooperated by sending their own list of grievances to Frederick. Four weeks later, they ignored the elector's command forbidding another meeting and met a second time. In the showdown that followed, only Kassel and fifty-four small towns sided with Frederick and the regents.

Anna's star was clearly on the rise as she made an agreement with the majority of the estates. Though she offered them the power of the purse, this concession was only a temporary limitation to Anna's power. She knew it would be important for her to develop the strong base for opposition to Frederick that this agreement afforded her. Anna called another diet for March 1514. There the majority of the estates stood with her, and the regents were deposed.

In April, Anna called still another diet. This one met with no pro-Saxon, pro-regent group in attendance. The tide had turned entirely in Anna's favor. A new government was elected consisting of Anna and five noble councilors. Should disagreements arise, Anna was to decide. From that day forward, Elector Frederick's hold on Hesse was permanently lost.

Philipp was nine years old at the time of his mother's victory. Nine is a great age for an eager young lad to absorb much from his mother's impressive example of clever political maneuvering. Four years later, Philipp would be declared the ruler of an independent and united Hesse, thanks to his mother's remarkable political skill.

Following the emperor's declaration in 1518 that Philipp was of age to rule Hesse, Anna's problems appeared solved. Still, opposition quickly consolidated to test how much Philipp had learned by watching his mother. Homberg on the Efze again became the rallying point. This time Anna was forced to flee with her son.

But once again, Anna demonstrated her impressive political skill. She rallied loyal members of the nobility and arranged to have Philipp listen personally to the grievances of each one and adjudicate their cases. Philipp performed well in these encounters.

Philipp's father had been trained for the priesthood, and he promoted the moral reform of the Hessian clergy. In his last will and testament, he directed that his reform efforts should be continued after his death. It soon became evident that Martin Luther's reform was not what Wilhelm II intended. Anna remained a devout Catholic and supported the Franciscans of Marburg liberally. She did all she could to keep Philipp in the fold of Rome until their final correspondence, several weeks before she died in 1525.

In those early years of the sixteenth century, a division in the Franciscan Order threatened to overshadow the order's influence upon young Philipp. The Observants, or spiritual Franciscans, rigidly interpreted the teachings of Francis. The Conventuals took a more liberal view. Pope Leo X brought peace in 1517, recognizing them both as legitimate Franciscan Orders. On October 31 of that year, Martin Luther posted his Ninety-five Theses.

The Franciscan Order continued to dominate the spiritual life of Hesse for another decade. In Philipp's lifetime, the 300th anniversary of St. Elizabeth's birth, death, and canonization all passed uncelebrated. They were overshadowed by Philipp's introduction of the Reformation in Hesse.

Philipp shouldered well his responsibility as a ruler, revealing how much he had learned from his mother's example of skillful political leadership. In 1520, Anna resigned her regency and turned over complete rule to Philipp. The estates were divided. The instigators of revolt were removed. Philipp prudently refused to call another diet until October 1526. The stage was now set for Philipp's forty-nine-year rule of Hesse.

Philipp's heritage, the examples of these three strong women, prepared him well for that rule. Philipp learned much from the tales told him of these three. Soon he would extend his own political influence beyond the borders of Hesse, promoting Luther's Reformation throughout much of southern Germany.

Meanwhile, as we shall read in the following chapter, Duke George was dreaming of the power and wealth he expected would be his own through the marriage of his daughter Christine to the landgrave, Philipp of Hesse.

Chapter 3

CHANGES 1524–26
Two Weddings

At the turn of the year 1524, Philipp could look back to see how he had accomplished two goals with one victorious act. He had settled his score with Franz von Sickingen and put a swift end to the Knights' War.

Now, two big changes lay in store for Philipp. The first would be his marriage to Christine, the eighteen-year-old daughter of Duke George of Albertine Saxony. The second would be his own change of heart when he turned to become Martin Luther's powerful political promoter.

On January 31, 1524, Philipp and Christine were married. Both were not yet twenty. George and his wife, Barbara, were strong-willed individuals accustomed to getting their own way and did not hesitate to meddle in the newlyweds' life, causing them difficulties until both George and Barbara died in the late 1530s.

Two years earlier, in 1522, Martin Luther had sent students to preach in three Hessian cities: Kassel, Marburg, and Alsfeld. Philipp had banished them all. On the day of their wedding, everyone had good reason to believe Philipp and Christine would remain lifelong servants of the Catholic Church.

No description of Philipp and Christine's wedding has been found, but the wedding of the daughter of a wealthy duke like George was expected to be a sumptuous affair, and much time and effort would have been expended to assure the bride's financial security, should her husband die early. George and Barbara's own marriage, in 1496, was attended by over six thousand nobles. Four years later, in March 1500, George attended the wedding of his cousin, Duke John of Ernestine Saxony, to Sophie of Mecklenburg, Philipp's aunt.

A description of John's wedding has been preserved, and it would have set a high standard for George twenty-four years later. John and Sophie's wedding was held in Torgau. Guests numbering 11,500 arrived with 6,500 horses.[6] Duke John and Elector Frederick received George and his father, Albrecht, outside the gates of the city. They had arrived with an entourage of ladies, the bishop of Merseburg, numerous counts, and knights with 545 horses. The hosts had stocked food and drink in enormous amounts. George alone sent six barrels of wine and eighteen barrels of beer along with wagonloads of carp and pike. Frederick and John had three-tiered grandstands built in the marketplace for jousting and other tournament games. Tapestries, shields, and crests adorned the lodgings, the dance hall, and locations for the knights' tournaments.[7]

THE TWO SAXONIES

A clarification of the division of Saxony and its cause is needed for us to appreciate the source of the enmity between the two cousins, George's hatred of Luther, and his later disappointment with Philipp.

Before 1485, George's father, Albrecht the Brave, shared the rule of united Saxony with his older brother, Ernst. Saxony was a large, powerful, and richly endowed land, recently enriched by silver lodes discovered in its hills. The heartbeat of Saxony was German. This posed a serious threat to the imperial house of Hapsburg, which was Austrian and Burgundian. This threat was partially resolved by the fact that Albrecht was the emperor's highest field marshal and he was frequently absent from Saxony, on duty for the empire.

Ernst governed united Saxony in Albrecht's absence. For years this arrangement worked quite well. Still, it was only a matter of time before tensions arose. Ernst divided Saxony in 1485. This division fell along lines giving Ernst the silver mines. His land became known as Ernestine Saxony. The rest was left for Albrecht and became known as Albertine Saxony. The financial inequity of this division was a major factor causing the pot of their estrangement to frequently boil over.

George was born in 1471. He would rule Albertine Saxony from 1500 until his death in 1539. His devotion to the Church of Rome was enhanced by several years of study for the priesthood. He also had studied other branches of learning. This made George one of the better-educated princes of his day, better educated than his more powerful cousin Frederick.

Upon his father's death in 1486, Frederick became the elector of Ernestine Saxony. Electors were very powerful. Chosen by their peers, they were given the power to elect the emperor. Frederick became the leader of the six electors and therefore the leading prince of Germany. In time, he would become known as Frederick the Wise, Martin Luther's early protector.

In 1496, when Frederick was thirty-three and George, twenty-five, they negotiated for their marriage to the two daughters of the deceased Polish king, Casimir IV. Frederick sought the hand of Elizabeth and George sought that of her sister, Barbara.

Frederick's negotiations went nowhere. George was successful. He married Barbara in Leipzig on November 21, 1496. The two were devoted to each other until Barbara's death in 1535, and they were blessed with ten children. In that day of high infant mortality, only one of their ten children outlived George and Barbara—Christine, who would become Philipp's wife.

Upon his father's death in September 1500, George inherited title to the Duchy of Albertine Saxony. This meant George and Frederick had inherited not only the lands of their fathers but their fathers' distrust of each other as well.

A decade later, George would give Philipp's mother, Anna of Mecklenburg, military support to counter Frederick's growing influence in Hesse. That story has been told in chapter 2. Frederick never married, but he took a lover. Since she was below his class, they could not marry. This meant their eldest son could not inherit the land. George felt certain that should Frederick and Philipp die, he might unite Hesse and, with all of Saxony and Hesse under his rule, he might enjoy immense power and wealth, perhaps even challenge the emperor.

George held Albertine Saxony unchallenged, but friction between George and Frederick soon broke out. George needed money, for his father had left him with large debts. Frederick and George could never agree on the proceeds from the silver mines. George had his officials harass Frederick's wagons, diverting them from the Ernestine high road to the low Albertine road. In other ways, George repeatedly tested Frederick and John's patience. They still corresponded, but in Frederick's eyes, George was two-faced and malicious. Frederick could be heard saying with an exasperated sigh, "Ach, my cousin George."

Germany was a relatively literate land when Martin Luther posted his Ninety-five Theses. Luther originally wrote his Ninety-five Theses in Latin, intending them for scholarly debate. Soon they were translated into German. Whoever wished could read this and other German pamphlets by Luther. Some, finding they agreed with what they read, added their voices to a growing demand for reform.

At first, George showed remarkable restraint, including some guarded support for Luther. He even had a German translation of Luther's theses posted in Leipzig. For nearly two years, he agreed with much he read in Luther's writings.

THE LEIPZIG DEBATE OF 1519

It was the Leipzig Debate in the summer of 1519, the first year of Philipp's rule, that would fill George with hatred for Luther. John Eck, a thirty-two-year-old professor at Tübingen University, brought up the idea of a debate. He wrote to George in December 1518, asking him to arrange for the University of Leipzig to host this debate and asking to be invited as a participant. George was flattered by this request from the already famous Professor Eck. He shared Eck's wishes with the faculty, assuming they would share his enthusiasm. To his dismay, the faculty refused to have anything to do with the matter. They feared becoming involved in Luther's heresy and suggested that George should call a synod to decide the matter.

On December 30, 1518, George took matters into his own hands. Ignoring the concerns of the faculty, he sent Eck his personal invitation. Eck soon spread the word that he was going to Leipzig to debate Luther. The reformer responded that he would cross swords[8] with Eck at Leipzig. As George's plans developed, it was Andreas Bodenstein von Carlstadt (hereafter Carlstadt) that George invited, not Luther. He made that choice for at least two reasons. First, George was offended by Luther's assumption that he would debate Eck, and second, Carlstadt enjoyed seniority on the Wittenberg faculty and had earned two doctoral degrees, compared with Luther's one degree.

Bishop Adolph of Merseburg, who had jurisdiction over the area, tried to persuade George to drop his plans. George angrily held his ground, stating he believed the real reason for the refusal of the Leipzig University theologians was their gluttony, laziness, and fear of inferiority. He advised his theologians that it would be wise for them to adopt his plan and render an opinion on the outcome of the debate. If they refused, he warned them, the rendering would be left to others.

George also threatened that if the Leipzig faculty continued to refuse, he would conclude that his theologians were incompetent and ashamed to have such erudite men as Eck debate in front of them. At that point, he warned he would replace them with old women.

Eck received official permission in February 1519, and four days later, he wrote the Leipzig faculty asking it to schedule the debate for June 27. George ignored Luther's repeated letters asking to be recognized as Eck's opponent. By March 9, the Leipzig faculty changed its mind and asked George to give Luther permission to debate.

Luther sent more requests to Eck, asking the professor to recognize him as his opponent. He even apologized profusely for having announced prematurely that he would "cross swords" with him at Leipzig. Eck refused to answer Luther's letters and, in the end, George approved only Carlstadt. Still, he allowed Luther to attend, but only as an adviser under Carlstadt's safe passage. When the debate began, Luther had to sit in the balcony.

Luther was allowed to take the podium only after the debate had completed its first week. It is not clear whether George was present on that day. He was, however, present on the day when Eck attempted to confuse Luther by calling him a Bohemian. That was Eck's way of accusing Luther of being a disciple of John Hus, the Bohemian who was burned at the stake for heresy in 1415. George was alerted to Eck's charge and listened intently for Luther's response, for his maternal grandfather and his own mother had been Hus supporters, facts George preferred to ignore.

George reacted violently when Luther stated limited appreciation of Hus. Shaking his head and putting his hands to his side, George shouted so loudly it could be heard by everyone in the auditorium, "May the plague take him!"

The debate lasted seventeen days. It only ended because Elector Joachim I and the bishop of Brandenburg stopped in Leipzig on their return trip from Frankfurt am Main, where they had participated in the election of the deceased Emperor Maximilian's nineteen-year-old grandson, Charles, as the new emperor. They were in Leipzig to give their report. George's auditorium was needed.

Now George was faced with a vexing problem that would tax his patience. Who should decide the winner of the debate? The University of Erfurt objected to serving. The University of Paris held out for a time, but finally did agree. In the meantime, it was left for George to decide. He ruled that the judges should be theologians and canon lawyers. Luther objected to this, feeling they would be biased against him. He wanted some laity to be included. Eck objected to anyone who was not his equal. George's problems had only begun.

It was six months after the debate, on December 29, 1519, when the University of Erfurt absolutely refused to give a verdict. Eck wrote to an acquaintance in Paris asking him to influence the Sorbonne in his favor. He also wrote to King Francis I with the same request.

Meanwhile, the faculty of the Sorbonne in Paris wrote that too much was at stake for them to act quickly. George received a letter on December 26 stating that a committee of twenty-four members had been selected to prepare a decision. The university finally gave its official report to the diet meeting in

Worms. On April 18, the same day Luther refused to recant his writings, 104 of Luther's articles were declared heretical.

The effect of the Leipzig Debate upon George was profound. He would devote the remaining eighteen years of his life to blocking Luther's influence. This was George's anti-Luther spirit that Philipp, the future leader of Luther's Reformation, would need to deal with until George died, fifteen years later.

PHILIPP TURNS LUTHERAN

Philipp and Luther were gifted with quite different temperaments. Thought by many to be bold and courageous, Luther was, in fact, quite cautious both in temperament and theology. Unfortunately, it is Luther's violent outbursts that are remembered most vividly. Philipp was a firebrand whose reputation as a bold leader willing to throw dull caution to the wind would one day carry him through military defeat and years of captivity at the hands of the emperor. Luther would remark about Philipp, "When the landgrave burns, nothing can stop it."[9]

Left to his own devices, with his mother, Duke George, and his spiritual adviser, Nikolaus Ferber Herborn (hereafter Herborn; 1485–April 15, 1534), the guardian of the Fransciscan monastery in Marburg, all urging him to remain faithful to Rome, young Philipp might have remained faithful to the Catholic Church until his death. A third party was needed to help him take his stand with Luther. Another Philipp came forward, Luther's colleague and close friend, Philipp Melanchthon (hereafter Melanchthon, to avoid confusion over the two Philipps). As it would turn out, the two Philipps worked together well, promoting the Reformation until Melanchthon's death thirty-six years later.

If Luther, being twenty-one years older and more experienced than Philipp, might have seemed paternal to the landgrave, apparently Philipp came to appreciate Melanchthon, only seven years his senior, as a respected older brother.

Born Philipp Schwarzerdt, Melanchthon was the oldest son of George, a respected armorer, and Barbara, a daughter of a prosperous merchant. His education was monitored by his maternal great-uncle, the famous scholar Johannes Reuchlin (1455–1522). His German name, Schwarzerdt, meant "black earth." He changed his name to Melanchthon, Greek for "black earth," following the custom of many educated men of the day.

In 1518, when Elector Frederick was seeking a qualified candidate to teach Greek in his sixteen-year-old University of Wittenberg, Melanchthon was chosen upon Reuchlin's recommendation. In the following year at the Leipzig Debate, Melanchthon became Luther's lifelong friend and promoter of the Reformation and would become known later as "the preceptor of Germany" for his work organizing the German educational system.

A Latin memoir of Melanchthon's life was written by a close friend and fellow reformer, Joachim Camerarius. In it he describes the first meeting of the two Philipps. William J. Wright has provided a translation:

> Philipp was on the way to a crossbow shoot at Meidelberg in June [1524] when his party encountered Melanchthon on the highway through the romantic Odenwald. Pursuant to their roadside chat in Melanchthon's carriage, the professor agreed to prepare a small summary of true Christian doctrine and practice. This promise was kept and the little pamphlet called the *Epitome* [meaning a brief presentation or statement] was in the hands of the prince by late October of that year.[10]

Melanchthon's thought process may seem confusing to some today. Still, he skillfully designed the Epitome to meet well Philipp's current concerns. It is brief, written in Latin, crisp in style, and contains just enough theology to introduce Philipp to Luther's teaching, while including practical guidelines for this prince who was open to introducing the Reformation in his land.[11] He begins by introducing two topics of hot discussion at that time: "Wherein does Christian righteousness consist, and how does it relate to human tradition?"[12]

He reminds Philipp how at the end of Luke's Gospel "Christ enjoins that repentance and the remission of sins be proclaimed to all peoples."[13] From this he gathers that "the Gospel is the preaching of repentance and of the remission of sins."[14] He qualifies this, adding, "It is truly Christian righteousness when a confused conscience is lifted up by faith in Christ and feels that it receives the remission of sins for Christ's sake."[15]

Then Melanchthon skillfully explains the work of the Holy Spirit for Philipp:

> Accordingly, the Holy Spirit, after revealing sin and the judgment of God, strikes terror into our consciences by the preaching of repentance, and he lifts them up again through the Gospel, that is through the announcement of the remission of sins.

> Moreover, life eternal is that very righteousness by which the Gospel declares and which Christ places simply in the knowledge of the Father and of himself. Christian righteousness is not common to all, but it is the possession of the few whom God calls, as it were, out of this world.[16]

Now Melanchthon moves on to human righteousness: "Beside Christian righteousness there is human righteousness by which the wicked should be coerced . . . political righteousness is wisely to be distinguished from religion or evangelical righteousness, but many today are preaching evangelical righteousness in such a way that a new wickedness is being born."[17]

Turning to human traditions, Melanchthon wonders: "Although the former topic [human righteousness] is more obscure than the argument about human traditions, I still do not know why it is that this dispute incites greater disturbances in the world. . . . There are not a few who think that Luther is teaching nothing but contempt for human traditions."[18]

Approaching his conclusion, and with words that appear prophetic of Luther's meeting with Zwingli in Marburg four years later, Melanchthon challenges Philipp to defend Luther by reflecting on the growing radical opposition, including but not limited to Zwinglianism. He writes, "You see how the whole world is being afflicted with dangerous dissension. And, too, the contest is almost solely about ceremonies and human traditions in which, if the princes were to permit somewhat sane counsels, peace could be restored."[19]

Melanchthon wrote his Epitome in Latin. He was equally conversant in Latin and German. He might have chosen to write Philipp using either Latin or German, but he chose Latin, and he carefully crafted his Epitome to address Philipp's concerns. Is it likely Melanchthon would have written in a language his reader was unable to understand? Is it likely he would have entrusted the translation of Philipp's life-changing message to advisers who might be biased against reform?

Melanchthon's Epitome accomplished its desired effect. Less than a year after receiving it, Philipp published his decision to follow and promote Luther's teaching. On January 19, 1525, Philipp wrote a revealing letter to Herborn. In it he declared that truth was available in the divine Word through grace granted by God. He gave his opinion on three subjects: first, faith and good works; second, Mary as a mediator between God and man; third, whether or not the Scriptures should be given to the common people and theological matters discussed with them. On each item, Philipp revealed that he held the Bible to be God's Word and took his convictions from it.[20]

In April of the same year, Philipp wrote a letter to his mother to inform her of his conversion, for she feared he might be exposing himself to the emperor's wrath. On another issue she had raised, Philipp assured her he was not confiscating the wealth of the monasteries for his personal use but only to help the poor.[21]

In that same month, April 1525, "Philipp had little difficulty putting down the [peasant] uprising, and he did it without slaughtering masses of Hessian peasants." He raised a small army and "captured the four ringleaders, decapitated them, and fastened their heads to the tower in Fulda."[22] Then he joined Duke George of Saxony, his father-in-law, and on May 15, they slaughtered the peasants at Frankenhausen, bringing the Peasants' War to an abrupt end.

The Battle of Frankenhausen was Philipp and George's last military action together. George resented the fact that earlier Philipp had not come to his aid at Sonnenwalde. He also observed Philipp's regular visits to prostitutes and, most serious for George, he received firsthand proof that his son-in-law was now a "Martinian."[23] In deference to Christine, the two men carried on a troubled relationship. Their separation of 300 miles between Dresden and Marburg allowed them only infrequent visits.

Two months after the Battle of Frankenhausen, the Catholic princes of northern Germany, led by Duke George, met in Dessau and, on July 19, united to form the Catholic League of Dessau. Though Philipp was only nineteen, Lutheran princes met that autumn in Gotha in response to an invitation he sent them. Their meeting started negotiations for the defensive League of Torgau completed early the following year.

In the second half of 1525, Philipp set in motion preparations for his reform of Hesse. "Early in the year, he issued a directive for his officials to inventory the property of all churches, cloisters, and hermitages. He ordered a report of all jewels, rents, income, and treasures of all sorts sent to the local magistrate."[24]

Philipp's mother, Anna of Mecklenburg, died on May 12, 1525, just weeks after the two had corresponded.[25] In January the following year, Philipp and Christine would celebrate two years of marriage. They still were childless, but sixteen months later, on May 31, 1527, a healthy daughter, Agnes, would be born. She would be the first of ten children. Of the ten, nine survived to adulthood—remarkable in that day of high infant mortality.

By 1526 the Lutheran princes of Germany had been emboldened by Philipp's defeat of Franz von Sickingen in 1523 and the quick end to the Peasants' War two years later. The formation of the Torgau League had prepared them to stand united at the diet about to be convened in the city of Speyer. Philipp, age 22, was eager to assume leadership at that diet. As we shall see in the next chapter, things went well in Speyer and opened the door for Philipp's reform of Hesse.

Chapter 4

PHILIPP'S COMMENCEMENT 1526

Philipp Prepares for the Diet of Speyer

With the new year, 1526, Philipp was sure of himself. Still, it would take months of planning and a canceled diet for him to prepare for the Diet of Speyer (hereafter Speyer I, to distinguish it from Speyer II, the diet of 1529).

Speyer I would be Philipp's commencement, the recognition of his qualifications to be a powerful young Reformation prince. Already at the end of 1525, he could look back on four significant events that had enhanced his public recognition: his defeat of Franz von Sickingen; his marriage to Christine, the daughter of the powerful Duke George of Albertine Saxony; his meeting with Philipp Melanchthon; and his announcements to his mother, father-in-law, and spiritual adviser that he had become a follower of Martin Luther. Now, Philipp was prepared to assume leadership among the Lutheran princes.

For five years, Emperor Charles V's edict condemning Martin Luther had loomed as a dark cloud over Germany. That edict threatened with imprisonment—and likely, death—anyone who gave Luther aid, especially his publishers.

Three imperial diets had been scheduled for the five-year period following the Diet of Worms in 1521. Two met in Nürnberg, in 1522 and the following year. A third was announced to meet in Augsburg early in 1526. That diet was canceled due to lack of interest.

Charles V was absent from Germany in the 1520s, not returning for nine crucial years for the Reformation. His younger brother, Archduke Ferdinand of Austria (1503–64),[26] presided over the diets in Nürnberg. At both diets, the emperor's edict was affirmed, but the archduke's power was limited, for he knew he would have to curry the favor of the German people if he were one day to be elected as the German king and heir apparent to the emperor.

Ferdinand was a devout Catholic.[27] Luther's followers were by now calling themselves "Lutherans." Luther objected to this, suggesting they call themselves "Christians" or "Evangelicals," from a Greek word meaning "people of the Gospel." The Lutheran princes of Germany lacked the solidarity needed to effectively challenge Ferdinand's support of the Edict of Worms. That would change once they affirmed Philipp's leadership at Speyer I.

On the other hand, the Catholic princes of Germany looked to Philipp's father-in-law, Duke George, for leadership. George was convinced that Luther had been responsible for the peasant rebellion the previous year. Soon after their swift defeat of the peasants, George had called a meeting of like-minded Catholic rulers to meet in the town of Dessau. There they formed a defensive Catholic alliance which became known as the Dessau League.

Philipp took the creation of the Dessau League as his personal challenge to consolidate the Lutheran princes of Germany. He invited the new elector of Saxony, John, to a preliminary private meeting. Frederick had died in May of that year. Philipp and John met in the autumn of 1525 in the town of Gotha. The following February, they met with more Lutheran princes in the elector's favored city, Torgau. There they shared the plans they had made in Gotha with other princes. The defensive league they formed became known as the League of Torgau. By the time Speyer I convened, both the Catholics and the Lutherans were united into competing leagues.

Regarding the Lutherans in this period, Hans Hillerbrand concludes, "The adherents of the new faith . . . had braced themselves for the possible political consequences of their ecclesiastical position."[28]

Speyer, one of Germany's oldest cities, was founded by the Romans. It is located on the Rhine River and is approximately 120 miles (193 km) south of Marburg. Speyer was a busy river crossing in the sixteenth century. It was also one of the free imperial cities of Germany. During Philipp's lifetime, Emperor Charles V or his brother, Archduke Ferdinand, regularly convened imperial diets in Speyer. The two diets in the 1520s are best known for playing significant roles in the Reformation. A third diet would be convened there in 1544. Four years after that, a fourth Diet of Speyer would bring dire consequences for Philipp. That story will be told in chapter 16.

Duke George published the recess (closing document) of the 1523 Diet of Nürnberg. It confirmed the Edict of Worms. Five free imperial cities joined the Lutheran princes, refusing to follow the mandates of the Second Diet of Nürnberg.

Philipp promoted the Evangelical cause at a rump session of the Diet of Augsburg. Archduke Ferdinand had called that diet to be convened on November 11, 1525. Philipp's envoys were among the first to appear, arriving on November 26.

Only the electors of Trier and the Palatinate, three princes, and representatives of the imperial cities of Cologne and Aachen were present by December 11.

The imperial chancellor, Albrecht, the archbishop of Mainz, boycotted the planned diet. He had heard of Philipp's plan to form a strong alliance of Lutheran princes. He knew that if he did not attend, the diet would be adjourned prematurely and Philipp's plans would be dashed. That did happen. The princes returned to their lands, but Philipp remained and continued to develop his plans for Speyer I, to be held later that year.[29]

Though Philipp's alliance did not materialize at Augsburg, his work was not in vain. His envoys helped draw up a seven-paragraph recess of that canceled diet. This document called for another diet to be held in the city of Speyer in the summer of 1526. Until then, the princes were instructed to see to it that "the holy Gospel and God's Word would be preached in their lands according to the proper, true understanding, and the interpretation of the common Christian Church's accepted teaching."[30]

This sentence was a direct quote from the recess of the 1523 Diet of Nürnberg, but in this new context, they were a clever ploy by Philipp. The quote had been buried in the twenty-ninth article of the recess of that diet. By Philipp's placing it in a more prominent place in the recess of the canceled Diet of Augsburg, it empowered the Evangelical princes to attend Speyer I, confident they would be heard.

The recess also bore further evidence of Philipp's influence, for it urged the princes to attend Speyer I in person. This meant Philipp was now certain he would be supported by his Lutheran peers at Speyer I.

In November 1525, the members of the Catholic Dessau League had written to Duke George stating they would gladly unite with the Evangelical princes if that would assure them the peasants would not rise up again; but little came of their offer, for they refused to meet with the same princes if they insisted on negotiating Church teaching.

Late in December, the Catholic princes met in secret with George in Leipzig. They decided to ask Duke Henry of Braunschweig, who was in Italy supporting the emperor's sack of Rome, to solicit Charles's support should their conflict with Philipp and his allies turn bloody. The same Henry would face Philipp in battle twenty years later. That story will be told in chapter 14.

The Cathedral Chapter of the archbishop of Mainz also took measures to oppose Philipp and the Evangelicals. Complaining about the new sect, they prepared a document that became known as the *Mainzer Ratschlag*, meaning "the statement of Mainz." That document attributed the Peasants' War to Luther's teaching. It painted for Pope Clement a horrible picture of future attacks on civil authority if this heresy was not wiped out promptly.

In Rome, Pope Clement was well aware that the armies of Charles V were invading Italy and threatening papal lands, even the Vatican. In the Alliance of Cognac, signed shortly before Speyer I, the pope and the cities of Milan, Florence, and Venice agreed that they would join King Francis I of France, to expel Charles's army from Italy. With this threatening development, the emperor dared not leave Italy to preside at Speyer I.

The previous November, when John and Philipp met in Gotha, they had decided that John would reach out to the princes of northern Germany for support. Philipp would appeal to those of the south. Therefore, in the weeks leading up to Speyer I, John and Philipp gathered support for the Evangelical cause throughout all of Germany.

John was quite successful. He organized a meeting in Magdeburg in June. Six princes attended, including Philipp's uncle, Duke Henry of Mecklenburg, and Elector John's twenty-two-year-old son, John Frederick. These princes signed their names to the Torgau Pact, agreeing to take a common stance for the Gospel. Philipp was pleased.

It is remarkable to note that Philipp and his father-in-law, Duke George, were still convinced that each could convince the other to change. In late February, when Philipp and John were meeting in Torgau, word came to Philipp that George had instructed his preachers to preach according to the Scriptures. Philipp was overjoyed and wrote to George, asking if that report was true. George wrote to Philipp, stating that he had been wrongly informed. He declared that he followed only the Gospel according to "the Christian Church." Philipp wrote back asking his father-in-law to define his concept of "Church." George replied. Both Philipp and George quoted Scripture in support of their positions. After a month, Philipp felt he was making progress with his father-in-law. He wrote to Elector John, asking him to have Luther refrain from attacking his father-in-law. Luther complied, but only for a time.[31]

PHILIPP'S LEADERSHIP AT THE DIET

The recess of the canceled Diet of Augsburg had made it clear that religion should be the primary focus of Speyer I. On June 15, the princes met and decided that clerical abuses should be dealt with first. At this point, no one was present to represent Hesse. Philipp's envoy, Balthasar Schrautenbach (c. 1460–1529), arrived by June 30. Schrautenbach worked hard, openly representing Lutheran concerns. When Philipp's chamber secretary Eberhard Ruell (dates unknown) arrived, the two were described as dynamic supporters of the Evangelical cause at Speyer.

Philipp was well prepared for the diet. Though he did not appear on time, he shouldered the burden of leadership, happy that the recess of the Diet of Augsburg had placed religion at the top of the agenda. His main concern was how the Lutheran princes would behave themselves. In a letter to Duke John Frederick, Philipp declared he had heard rumors that the duke's father, the elector John, was misusing cloisters and evicting monks and nuns without compensation. He hoped this was not true. In his opinion, such behavior would not be Evangelical.[32]

He wrote another letter to John Frederick, who was known for heavy drinking. Philipp declared that their entourages should behave in a pious manor and avoid drunkenness and blasphemies, which would make a bad impression.[33]

Just days before the diet convened, Elector John sent word to Philipp that he would not be attending in person. As evidence of his growing self-confidence, Philipp wrote the powerful elector that he must attend, and he gave three reasons: first, other princes would be there in person; second, it would be an opportunity for John to dispel the rumor that he was becoming the leader of the rebel peasants; and third, he should stand up for his faith. If it were absolutely impossible for Elector John to come, Philipp concluded, he should send John Frederick in his place.

The diet was scheduled to convene on May 1. When Archduke Ferdinand arrived on May 18, he found he was one of the first to appear. By the end of May, when other rulers had not yet arrived, Ferdinand became angry over the waste of his time and money. He wrote to Philipp demanding that he appear within twelve days. Following Mass, with only Catholic princes participating, Ferdinand formally convened the diet on Monday morning, June 25, almost two months behind schedule.

When Philipp did arrive, he claimed he was late due to his fear of another peasant uprising in Hesse. In reality, he had plans for his dramatic late arrival at the diet. The estates (meaning the electors, the princes, the bishops, and representatives from the imperial cities) had begun to speculate that Philipp might not attend in person. On July 5, Philipp was informed that many members of the estates awaited his arrival and were putting much hope in him. At the same time a rumor was spreading that Philipp and other Evangelicals were preparing a specific garb to wear upon their arrival.

Philipp did skillfully stage his late arrival. For months he had been making plans with his uncle, Duke Henry of Mecklenburg, and Elector John to dress themselves and their entourages in a similar manner. Their main color was brown, and the acronym VDMA—for the Latin *Verbum Domini Manet in Aeternum*, meaning "the Word of the Lord Remains Eternal"—was sewn onto their sleeves. Their knights wore the same letters.

Philipp arrived on Thursday, July 12, with an entourage of over 250 horsemen. He was disappointed, however, for he was not received by the princes, as was the custom. They were out on a hunt near Heidelberg.[34]

Philipp arranged to be housed near Elector John. During the diet, the street that accommodated the two princes and their entourage became known as "Heretic Alley." Ferdinand claimed Philipp had three white flags with red stripes prepared and, as the leader of the Lutherans, planned to use them to rally support. His claim proved to be true.

Philipp's planning included more than wardrobes and flags. He promptly ordered an ox to be slaughtered in front of his accommodations. On the following day, a Friday, he and his entourage enjoyed an outdoor "barbecue" in defiance of canon law forbidding the eating of meat on Fridays. Philipp was not the first Lutheran prince to do this. Four months earlier, Elector John had ordered a buck slaughtered in Torgau, and he, too, ate the meat in public on Friday.

The archduke announced there would be no Evangelical preaching in Speyer. Philipp rejected the submissive attitude of other Lutheran princes. He insisted that his court preacher, Adam Krafft, whom he had appointed in August of the previous year, be allowed to preach. The city supported the archduke and refused to allow Krafft to use the pulpits of its churches. On the morning after his arrival, Philipp simply arranged for Krafft to preach from the balcony of his lodging surrounding a large open courtyard. A crowd, estimated to have been about four thousand, gathered to hear Krafft preach. That number was far more than could have possibly crowded into any one of the city churches. Throughout the diet, Krafft preached his open-air sermons to standing-room-only congregations once every other day and twice on Sundays.[35]

Obviously, Philipp's actions upset Archduke Ferdinand. He commanded the imperial commissioners to forbid any Lutheran preaching and breaking of the Friday fast. Philipp responded that he would not submit even if it cost him his head.

Philipp did his best to win several more imperial cities to the Lutheran cause. His contact was a man named Kress, a representative of the imperial city of Nürnberg. He asked Kress to communicate quickly with Nürnberg so they could conclude an agreement for the city to join the Torgau League before the diet adjourned. This time nothing came of Philipp's efforts, for Nürnberg was inclined to wait and see how the diet would conclude.

Philipp never trifled over breaking protocol. It was not common at the time for princes to seek the opinions of imperial cities. Still, on July 17, Philipp summoned the envoys of Strassburg, Augsburg, Nürnberg, Ulm, and Frankfurt to his accommodations. Philipp explained to these envoys that he and Elector John had vowed to stand by the Word of God at the diet, and they were seeking their cooperation.

Elector John rode into Speyer on July 20, 1526. Two Lutheran preachers, George Spalatin and John Agricola, were in his entourage. The elector had little choice but to follow Philipp's lead. His own clergy preached daily in the courtyard of his accommodations, and they ate meat on Friday in spite of the fast. By now it was apparent that twenty-one-year-old Landgrave Philipp was in charge, enjoying his commencement ceremonies. He had succeeded in emboldening the Lutheran princes and determining their public stance at Speyer I.

PHILIPP'S SUCCESS AT THE DIET

With Philipp and Elector John making such bold moves, other Evangelical sovereigns were motivated to do the same. Margrave Philipp of Baden, who had sent his Lutheran preacher home upon hearing the archduke's prohibition, now recalled him.

The charged atmosphere in Speyer by the middle of July is described by Richard Andrew Cahill: "The Catholic theologian, Johann Fabri, openly preached the virtues of the Catholic Mass. From the Evangelical side, Agricola openly preached against the Mass and Fabri's claims. Crowds were packing the courtyards of Philipp and Johann's accommodations to hear their preachers in 'Heretic Alley' while the Evangelicals called the street where Catholics resided 'Pharisees and Hypocrites Road.'"[36]

Written instructions from the emperor were published, but only after the diet had debated the matter of clerical abuses and proper faith for over a month. His instructions were explicitly Catholic: the diet was to "undertake, debate, name, and decide absolutely nothing which would be against or destructive to our holy Christian faith, or to the praise-worthy laws, or to the old-traditional teachings, ordinances, ceremonies, and practices of the Church."[37]

It was apparent that Archduke Ferdinand had withheld these instructions from the diet, for they were dated March 23, 1526, three months before he opened the diet. Facing the opposition of the Lutheran princes now made bold by Philipp, Ferdinand felt his back was against the wall. He needed the support of his powerful brother, Emperor Charles V.

Fearing the emperor's wrath, Philipp's colleagues were split. Philipp suggested they ask the archduke and the imperial commissioners how, in the light of these instructions, the grand plenary committee could deal with abuses.

Philipp felt this would be a good time for the Evangelical princes to reveal that they were aware of the contents of the *Mainzer Ratschlag*, the instructions from Albrecht, the archbishop of Mainz, mentioned earlier. He believed this document could prove it was the so-called "spiritual [i.e., Catholic] rulers" who were to blame for the Peasants' War the year before, for it was in Catholic cities like Mühlhausen, not the cities of Saxony and Hesse, that the rebellion was most severe.

On August 21, Philipp was the first prince to leave the diet, returning to Hesse before it was adjourned. He secretly rode out of Speyer at night with only a few horsemen in his entourage. No one knows why he left in such a manner. Some insisted he had left on good terms with the archduke. The recess of the diet was being written. It seems likely Philipp saw no reason to remain. His envoys could complete his business and sign the recess in his absence. He also had restless peasants and his first-time pregnant wife to keep an eye on in Hesse.

In response to the demand for the enforcement of the Edict of Worms, the recess of Speyer I read, "Every State shall so live, rule and believe as it may hope and trust to answer before God and his imperial Majesty." This language, adopted unanimously by those still present on August 27, was seen as ambiguous and was welcomed by Lutheran sovereigns as tacit permission to proceed with the reform of their territories.

For Ferdinand, the diet accomplished little. For Philipp, the diet filled him with confidence. Philipp left Speyer confident, ready, and well prepared to turn his attention to reforming Hesse. Little did Philipp know what challenges he would face in the coming year. That story will be told in chapter 7. First, we must turn to Philipp's recruitment of a theologian at Speyer and his leadership of the reform of Hesse in the town of Homberg on the Efze River.

Chapter 5

LAMBERT OF AVIGNON 1526–30
Philipp's Felt Need for Another Theologian

Philipp was no theologian, but his commitment to Luther's Reformation was sincere and would endure years of humiliation by the emperor. He had employed Adam Krafft, his court preacher, to administer the progress of the Reformation in Hesse. Still, he felt the need for his own systematic[38] theologian, believing it would be essential to formulate Luther's theology to fit the needs of Hesse as he understood them. Philipp would preside over a meeting he would convene to reform the land. Adam Krafft was serving well and could not be spared. Philipp was aware of the possibility that in his search for another theologian, he might introduce matters not in full agreement with Luther, but he would make what he believed to be the best choice offered him.

At the Diet of Speyer earlier that summer, Philipp spent time finding this theologian. There he met with Melanchthon and two leaders of Strassburg, the politician Jakob Sturm (1489–1553) and the theologian Martin Bucer (1491–1551). They introduced Philipp to a runaway monk, Francis Lambert of Avignon (1487–1530).

Lambert was French, not fluent in German. In spite of this, Philipp and Lambert found common ground. Most likely, it was the fact that Lambert had spent fifteen years as a Franciscan monk, while Philipp had been raised in the shadow of the Franciscan monastery and church in Marburg and his ancestor was St. Elizabeth, the patron saint of the Third Order of the Franciscans. Lambert had spent over a year with Luther in Wittenberg, a point that must have made him attractive to Philipp. The two must have conversed in Latin, the language familiar to both of them.

Upon returning to Hesse, Philipp employed Lambert to compose the opening theological address and program for the meeting at which he planned to begin the reform of Hesse. He provided him living quarters and space for writing in the Carmelite cloister of Kassel. Lambert named his Latin document the *Paradoxa*, hinting that some matters under discussion in this meeting might at first appear illogical, but, when understood as addressing the life of the Church and its people, they would be revealed as very important.

LAMBERT'S PILGRIMAGE TO WITTENBERG

Avignon, France, where Francis Lambert was born in 1487, was a city of the popes. There Pope Clement V (1264–1314) established his official residence in 1309, starting what came to be known as the "Seventy-Year Babylonian Captivity of the Church." That was a trying period in the history of the Catholic Church, when there was a pope in Rome challenged by a pope in Avignon; and later, a third pope entered the fray in Pisa.

Of the Avignon popes, John XXII (1316–34) was the financial wizard who profoundly influenced the city of Avignon. The construction of the Palace of the Popes was begun in 1316, during his pontificate. It was completed in 1370. Roy Lutz Winters[39] describes the palace: "To this day this Palace remains a symbol of the Luxury and splendor of this period. Situated on the crown of a hill within the city, surrounded by boulevards and enclosed with battlements and towers, the ecclesiastical establishment at Avignon manifested that power and mystery which characterized the medieval church. It dwarfs the Romanesque Cathedral located beside the Palace."

It was in such regal surroundings that Lambert's father was appointed to serve as the private secretary to the papal legation, which remained in Avignon after its pope left in the late 1370s. Young Lambert was allowed to visit the palace. There he was allowed to see the dignitaries. The atmosphere of the place must have moved him.

At the age of twenty, Lambert entered the monastery of the Observant Franciscans. He served there as a monk for fifteen years. During that time, he was recognized for his gifts and promoted to the role of apostolic preacher of the order. In that role, he traveled to instruct the people in the countryside.

Lambert felt he needed to read the Scriptures to make him more effective when preaching. He studied the Psalms, Jeremiah, and Job. Then he focused on the New Testament. He turned to Paul's Letter to the Romans and the Book of Revelation. His familiarity with and enthusiasm for the Bible caused people to gather from the surrounding countryside to hear him. His success, however, aroused the envy of his fellow monks.

Eventually Lambert began to doubt he was meant to be a monk. He longed to join the Carthusians, an order of men and women founded in 1084 in the Chartreuse Valley of France, 154 miles (248 km) from Avignon. There Lambert felt he might be encouraged to spread the Gospel by the printed word.

Casting aside this longing, Lambert remained a Franciscan. He was already unpopular with fellow monks, but matters grew more difficult for him in 1521, when he started quoting some of Martin Luther's writings that had filtered into Avignon. Lambert was happy to learn that Luther had the courage to deal openly with ecclesiastical perversions. He commented, "More of really sound theology is contained in Luther's books than in all the writings of all the monks who ever were from the beginning."[40]

Lambert was thirty-five years old in 1522 when he left Avignon, supposedly on an errand for his monastery. His real destination was Wittenberg, which entailed a journey of about 1,346 miles (2,166 km). On the way, he traveled through Switzerland, where he met with Swiss reformers claiming to be disciples of Luther. He believed that visiting them would prepare him for his meeting with Luther.

Lambert preached in the city of Geneva June 8–15. He had already traveled about 637 miles (1,025 km) from Avignon and was nearly halfway to Wittenberg. From Geneva, he followed the northern shore of Lake Geneva, which led him to Lausanne. All was still calm in Lausanne, for word of Luther's reforms had not yet arrived. From Lausanne, he traveled through Bern to Zurich, another 127 miles (204 km).

In Zurich, Lambert met Ulrich Zwingli (1484–1531). He and Zwingli discussed cardinal doctrines of the Church. Once when Zwingli was listening to one of Lambert's sermons on the invocation of the Virgin Mary and the saints, a subject on which Lambert could still preach with conviction, Zwingli interrupted the sermon, shouting, "Brother, you are wrong!"

Thereupon Lambert challenged Zwingli to a disputation, which took place on July 17. Zwingli was well prepared. By the end of their long discussion, Lambert was convinced that Zwingli was right. He left for Basel, which is 59 miles (95 km) west of Zurich, the next day. There he hoped he might meet the great humanist Erasmus. I have found no evidence they met.

In Basel, John Oecolampadius was known for his zeal for reform. Whether Lambert met with Oecolampadius or not, he could hardly have avoided being influenced by reports circulating about this well-informed theologian. That same year, Oecolampadius had been appointed lecturer on the Holy Scriptures at the University of Basel. He had supported Luther at the Diet of Worms in 1521 and became so zealous for reform that the bishop of Basel refused to allow him to lecture and preach.

During Lambert's two-month visit in Basel, he met with at least three other theologians. The first was Wolfgang Capito (c. 1478–1541), a disciple of Erasmus. As early as 1512, Capito was teaching that many of the Church's ceremonies and usages could not be supported by the Bible. The second theologian was Conrad Kürsner (1478–1556), better known by his Latin name, Pellicanus. The third theologian Lambert met in Basel was Telamonius Limpurger (dates unknown), a professor at the University of Basel. Later, Luther would write that Pellicanus and Limpurger had given Lambert "a beautiful testimony."[41] Upon Lambert's arrival, Luther's teachings were only beginning to be accepted in Basel.

In less than nine months after leaving Avignon, Lambert had traveled through France and Switzerland, a distance of 860 miles (1,384 km). He had left Avignon on an errand for his monastery. His cowl was still the symbol of his continued devotion to Rome. Two months later, as he left Switzerland, he left his cowl behind, and with it, his devotion to the old ways. On his way to meet Luther, Lambert had fallen under the spell of some of the most dedicated and persuasive early leaders of the Swiss Reformation.

Lambert left Basel in September and headed north on a 320-mile (515 km) journey through Germany to Eisenach. On his way through Germany, Lambert took an alias, John Seranus. Most likely he did this to protect himself from the monks of the monastery who might still be hunting for him. His new name had special meaning. *Seranus* comes from the Latin word for "wood saw." Lambert's objective in changing his name seems to have been to present himself as one who had sawn himself off from his monkish past.[42]

Lambert arrived in Eisenach in November 1522 and was greeted warmly by Jacob Strauss (c. 1480–c. 1530), a local clergyman also from Basel. He claimed to be Lutheran but was influenced by radical Anabaptist teachings, especially their critique of loaning of money at exorbitant rates of interest (usury). Nine months earlier, Luther had ended his stay in the Wartburg castle near Eisenach. The town, with a population of approximately 5,000, was polarized. Many of the clergy were suspicious of Luther's new teachings, while most of the common people welcomed them.

The months spent in Eisenach were busy months for Lambert. He gave expositions on the Gospel of John, speaking only in Latin. Despite this limitation, his lectures were well received. He also preached in surrounding communities. There Lambert penned 139 theological opinions, which he called his theses, and he planned to defend them in December. This did not happen, for no one dared to dispute him. Then he sent a copy to Wittenberg as evidence of his sympathy for the Reformation.

Strauss encouraged Lambert to write Elector Frederick of Saxony and request his permission to travel to Wittenberg to visit Luther. Lambert, who must have been impatient after his long trip, had to wait for more than a month before he received Frederick's permission.

LAMBERT IN WITTENBERG

Meanwhile, in Wittenberg, Luther was wary of entertaining this monk from Avignon who had sojourned with Zwingli and other Swiss theologians. Less than a year had passed since radicals from Zwickau had stirred Wittenberg crowds during Luther's absence in the Wartburg castle. Could Luther trust this wandering French monk?

Lambert found an advocate in Luther's friend George Spalatin (1484–1545). Spalatin was the court preacher and personal secretary of Elector Frederick. He wrote to tell the elector that Lambert was a "man of uncommon erudition." He also sent two letters to Luther urging him to welcome this French exile. Finally, on December 26, Luther wrote to Spalatin telling him he would receive Lambert, but he would not trust him.

Lambert arrived in Wittenberg in January, having traveled another 166 miles (267 km) from Eisenach. Lambert's total six-month pilgrimage from Avignon to Wittenberg was 1,358 miles (2,185 km), revealing a very serious commitment and the depth of his desire to meet Luther.

Wittenberg was a town of 3,000 residents and 350 houses when Lambert arrived. The University of Wittenberg had been founded by Elector Frederick twenty years earlier. The university and Frederick's famous collection of relics in the Castle Church were the two centers of town life.

Still going by his alias, Lambert met with Luther sometime before January 20. He told Luther his life story, disclosed his true identity, and soon was given the same cordial reception in Wittenberg he had received in Switzerland and Eisenach.

Following that meeting, Lambert wrote to the elector, "I believe I was called to Martin by the Lord Himself so we may build together a strong fortress, the one brother giving assistance to the other."[43] Lambert's pride is evident, for though he had not yet matriculated as a student, his words reveal he felt he was Luther's seasoned comrade in arms, not just another immature student.

On the following day, Luther wrote George Spalatin, describing his favorable impression of Lambert: "Concerning the integrity of the man there is no question. The man appeals to me in every respect and I have tested him with sufficient care, in fact as well as a man can be tested; and I conclude he is worthy of a modicum of support and assistance from us in his exile."

Then Luther asked Spalatin to point out to the elector how "he may be lending to Christ in charity twenty or thirty florins which are to be given him [i.e., to Lambert] until he can support himself either by gifts from his countrymen or by his own income from his labors."[44] This was an optimistic request on Luther's part, for a gold florin was worth approximately $140 (116 EUR) in today's currency.

Lambert also wrote to Spalatin on January 20, stating that he planned to teach at the university and translate Luther's writings into French, his native language. In February, he was given permission to lecture on the prophet Hosea. Spalatin recorded in his diary that Lambert lectured "before an audience of goodly number."[45]

In that same month, Lambert wrote a tract describing his experience in the Franciscan monastery in Avignon and his reasons for rejecting the monastic habit. Lambert wrote this tract before he was accepted by the university as a student. It seems that he was very ambitious and possessed of an inflated self-image. On April 13, 1523, he matriculated with two other French exiles, a knight of Rhodes, and a nobleman. In May, Elector Frederick entertained the three Frenchmen on Pentecost Sunday. Now Lambert expanded his course offerings. He lectured on the Psalms, the Gospel of Luke, the Epistles, Ezekiel, and other prophets.

The elector took his time before acting on Luther's request for financial support for Lambert. On February 25, Luther wrote to Spalatin a second time. Now his request was more realistic: "I am not asking for a stipend for him, but only that he be assisted occasionally."[46]

By now Lambert was thirty-six years old, and he began to think about marriage. On June 24, he was betrothed to a baker's daughter named Christina. They were married on July 13. The elector was pleased with Lambert's decision to marry. He presented the couple with a gift of venison. Luther was not pleased, but circumstances changed things. Within two years, Luther, himself a former monk, would marry the former nun Katharina von Bora. At the time, Lambert's fellow exiles were not pleased to see him marry either. They still believed celibacy was the more sacred estate. Lambert responded by delivering lectures on the biblical Song of Solomon.

Late in the summer of 1523, Lambert decided to leave Wittenberg. He gave two reasons for his decision: his dire financial straits and his desire to further the Evangelical cause in France.

On December 4, Luther wrote to a friend in Strassburg, Nicholas Garber, asking him to help Lambert find a position.

In the months that Lambert had sojourned in Wittenberg, he translated some Evangelical works into French, which he exported to France by way of the German port of Hamburg. He left Wittenberg in the last days of February 1524, having tarried there for thirteen months. He had achieved his ambition to meet Martin Luther and to drink deeply from the waters of Lutheran reform. Still, Lambert's taking on such a heavy teaching load while he was in Wittenberg raises the question: How much time and energy did he have left for concentrated learning from Luther?

EIGHT MEMORABLE DAYS IN METZ

From Wittenberg, Lambert traveled on to Metz. Though Metz was located in the Lorraine area and its population was predominantly French, it was still part of the empire. Lambert arrived in March and stayed there only eight days. Still, dramatic events made those days in Metz memorable.

Why did Lambert choose Metz? It is not on a direct route from Wittenberg to Strassburg. Two factors may have influenced Lambert. First, the Reformation was winning converts in Metz due to the bold leadership of John Castellan and, like Luther, Castellan was an Augustinian doctor of theology. Second, perhaps Lambert felt he could assist Castellan, who was under attack about the time he arrived. Castellan would be burned at the stake for heresy on January 12 the following year.

Regardless of the hostile atmosphere in Metz, Lambert still sought and received permission to preach there. He planned to hold a public disputation on religious matters. He prepared 116 theses, which he offered to defend against anyone who would accept his challenge. He added that the basis for the disputation would be only the Holy Scriptures. Because the case of John Castellan was causing great conflict, Lambert was not allowed to conduct his disputation and was attacked himself. It was only through the efforts of the city council that Lambert was not arrested. He escaped from Metz eight days after he arrived.

OPPORTUNITY AND RISK IN STRASSBURG

When Lambert arrived in Strassburg late in March 1524, the city had been a center of reform for over thirty years. Johann Geiler (1445–1510) arrived there in 1489. He attacked the corrupt practices of the Church. Luther's Ninety-five Theses were posted on the doors of every church and parsonage in the city. Luther's other writings were opposed, but without enthusiasm, for the city censor was Sebastian Franck (1499–1543), a noted humanist freethinker who was privately sympathetic to reform.

Matthew Zell (1477–1548) was the first outspoken advocate of Lutheran reform in the city. In 1518 he was called to become the people's priest at the Chapel of St. Lawrence. For his first three years, Zell was careful not to publicly reveal his Lutheran convictions. By 1521, there was no doubt where Zell stood, and the chapter refused to let him use the cathedral pulpit. His admirers built him a rostrum and carried it into the cathedral whenever Zell intended to preach.

In March 1523, Wolfgang Capito had come to Strassburg from Basel. Martin Bucer arrived soon after. By this time, there had gathered a party of reformers who, as Winters states, "were probably not surpassed in Europe for brilliancy of intellect, fervency of zeal, and unity of purpose."[47] Lambert arrived during the formative days of this group, was welcomed, and soon became well known.

Those were also years in France when the Reformation had a sympathetic voice at the throne, the sister of King Francis I, Marguerite of Angoulême. Even Jacques Lefèvre (c. 1455–1536), a pre-Luther voice for reform in France, came to Strassburg escaping persecution. In Paris, his translation of the Bible had been burned. Lefèvre's student, William Farel (1489–1565), who would become the senior colleague of John Calvin in Geneva, followed Lefevre from France to Strassburg. Winters concludes, "The presence of these progressive preachers in this noted city during the sojourn of Lambert gave him a splendid opportunity to become acquainted with the leaders of religious thought in his own country."[48] It is also likely that Lambert's reverence for Luther began to fade in Strassburg.

There was opposition in Strassburg. Thomas Murner (1475–1537) was determined to defend Catholicism. Though he was a humanist who had attacked the immorality of the clergy, Murner forsook his reform efforts when other reformers assailed the doctrine and polity of the Catholic Church.

The reformers conducted a series of lectures in Strassburg: Bucer on the Psalms, Capito on Jeremiah, and Lambert on Ezekiel. Murner, defending the Catholic Church, offered his own expositions on I Corinthians. He became so unpopular that he was insulted on the streets. Finally, he sought redress from the city council. In 1526, he was given a pension on the condition that he would leave the city and never return or attack it in any way.

Martin Bucer began a series of lectures in Latin. They were well received. Within a year he was given a salary and an assistant. On one day, Capito offered expositions on the Old Testament. The next day, Bucer offered his own on the New Testament. As the student body grew, classes were moved from Capito's house to the Carmelite cloister and from there to the Dominican monastery. When Lambert arrived, course offerings were increased again. From these humble beginnings the University of Strassburg grew, and it still thrives today.

As Luther had feared, Lambert's income did not meet the needs of his growing family. A son was born in November 1524. The city fathers in Strassburg could only promise they would not let his family starve.

From Strassburg, Lambert traveled on to appear at the Diet of Speyer in the summer of 1526. There, as mentioned earlier, he was approached by Philipp, accepted the landgrave's offer to teach at a university still in the planning stage in Marburg, and prepared for the landgrave's meeting to reform Hesse in Homberg on the Efze River. (Five years later, Lambert died of the plague in Marburg.) Philipp and Lambert returned from the diet to announce and prepare for the reform of Hesse about to begin in October.

Chapter 6

THE REFORM OF HESSE 1526–27
Philipp Asks Wittenberg for Advice

While Lambert was writing his *Paradoxa* in early September 1526, Philipp corresponded with Luther and Melanchthon, asking their advice.[49] This letter reveals him, a young man of twenty-two, as both sensitive and well informed. It is one of the earliest writings preserved from Philipp's pen. The letter reveals Philipp's thoughts while preparing to introduce the Reformation in Hesse. He lists six concerns. Philipp writes:

> Grace and peace in Christ, gentlemen, dear Martin and Melanchthon!
>
> I have received your writings and am grateful for your genuine concern and will follow you as God gives me grace. But I have a trifling concern which St. Paul called an indifferent matter in his Letter to the Philippians [1:8]: what is meant there, that Christ would be preached in all ways, whether it is in truth or in pretense (I take it exactly as it appears), and there also, at the same time Christ speaks to his apostles, who said to him, "Someone is said to be driving out devils in your name, and the disciples were disturbed over this, but Christ would not have them forbid him" [Mark 9:38]. I am writing on this matter because you have advised me not to allow schismatic preachers. Although your advice is satisfying to me, still the foregoing statements and this following disturb me, for Christ speaks in a parable [Matthew 13:30] that one should allow the tares and the wheat to grow together until the time of harvest, so the Lord will better separate the one from the other. Surely you will share your opinion with me.
>
> For another matter, I do not completely understand you, Philipp [Melanchthon], regarding the Mass. There you write that

one should observe such things in the ancient manner. Now, I cannot understand what you mean by "in the ancient manner." I have concluded you must have meant the manner of the apostles and pious people, and certainly not the papal manner, but I am still asking you to clarify your position.

In the third place, I am asking advice from both of you. Will you set me straight on this: When I do as you have advised me, and the monks or priests or even my own officials do not conduct themselves in an upright manner, or avoid disputations, how should I carry on? I want to do the right thing before God and the neighbor as one in authority should do.

In the fourth place, I desire your best advice. Now addressing you, Melanchthon, according to what you have written to me, I should seek peace, as peace is precious. For my part I am so inclined. That which I am able to promote with the princes, lords, and the emperor, as I have written to you earlier, and as God wills, I will do that which may praise and honor God and serves for the peace of both the mortal and spiritual man.

Still the real point at issue here is that person under my rule, my brother and minister of the Gospel, should I have to remove him. Concerning that I seek your counsel. How should I carry it out? I know well that I should never act in my own self-interest, but on behalf of my subjects and the brother who is in need of such counsel. Although I know it, that certainly is not to say that I should defend my subjects in an announced cause against my own interests. How should I carry out my responsibility as ruler when my subjects will take and suppress the Gospel and on that account be punished in body and goods? Therefore, I am requesting your advice from the Scriptures.

In the fifth place, I see that in the cloisters there is great wealth in goods and everyone seeks to use them for his own needs. Some, who can in no way be called Evangelical, yet are eager to take these spiritual goods. Also those who would be called Evangelical like me and my comrades, they may be just as eager to have these goods as the others. Just about everything is being done to get these goods. I think that for the most part it would be best that they be applied to the common need rather than for those things by which they would be eaten up.

I have considered therefore, in my own discretion and feeble understanding, that it would be well that one should retain those who would stay in the cloister. One should allow them to remain there and give them the usual provision. Those who would not remain there, however, who would come out, one should also give them an income. On the other hand, all monasteries should be supervised so that those who remain may not observe publicly the godless ceremonies that would offend the neighbor and so that the ones in authority might not pick a fight with a landgrave, a noble, or a commoner.

That same person would live there with an income and be responsible for it. For those who would leave, he would give them their dismissal. Concerning that which is left over, that should be placed in a common chest and when an area or a ruler comes in need, whether it is a war or something else, that supervisor should hold onto that chest, for it could happen that the one in need may not value the poor. The chest should be for high needs so a noble could never approach the chest without the approval of the landgrave. Otherwise the goods would be used up and neither the noble nor the land would be in any way improved.

In an area where a person may wish to have either a teacher or a school for men or women, wherein children could learn discipline, honor, and especially the Word of God, one could also do that with the goods, still observing the aforementioned measures. I request your advice on how this plan appears to you. Should you have a better plan, please describe it to me and give me your answer to the aforementioned articles.

In the sixth place, don't forget Zwingli and Oecolampadius. Publish something against their new error [an apparent reference to Zwingli's controversial position on Holy Communion published the year before]. If you have already done so, send it to me. If I am able to render any service to you, I would be pleased to do so. I will help Hesse [Heinrich Hesse, a Wittenberg student from Hesse].

Commend yourselves to God who always arms us, that we may remain in the right and that he may move in us such a faith that we all stand in need of, when the flesh is of no avail and which our spirit does not help, as we say in the Lord's Prayer, "Lead us not into temptation."

> Given at Kassel [the date is illegible]. Being in haste my hand-writing is very bad.

By including this final statement, Philipp assured the reformers that he did not dictate but personally wrote this letter.

This letter is a blueprint of Philipp's concerns for reform, and he would do his best to carry out these concerns through the remaining years of his forty-nine-year rule, even in his years of captivity, when a simple recantation would have resulted in his quick release. If Luther and Melanchthon responded, their letter has not been preserved.

HOW REFORM HAPPENED
AT HOMBERG ON THE EFZE RIVER[50]

Less than two months after Philipp wrote to Luther and Melanchthon, at least 2,000 clergy, nobility, and laypersons filled St. Mary's Church of Homberg on Saturday, October 20, 1526. The synod convened at seven in the morning and adjourned two days later. Philipp was the first Lutheran ruler to act upon the permission they felt they had received in the ambiguous language of the recess of the 1526 Diet of Speyer. The three-day meeting would pit Philipp's former spiritual adviser Herborn against his landgrave himself in a most heated debate.

Homberg on the Efze River was a small city in 1526, located midway between Marburg and Kassel, which before 1500 were the two capitals of divided Hesse. Homberg had been a convenient meeting place for divided Hesse, for it was near the common border of Upper and Lower Hesse. Territorial meetings called diets had met in Homberg in 1508, 1509, 1514, and 1518. Earlier, Eugene Ungefug, a Wittenberg student, had preached reform in the area.

The summons to the synod was sent twice, on October 5 and 10. Friday, October 19, was the day set for arrival. Philipp; his counselors, John Feige and Balthasar Schrautenbach; his court preacher, Adam Krafft; and his theologian, Francis Lambert; all arrived early. The historian Wilhelm Schmitt states, "Local residents and guests filled St. Mary's Church of Homberg to capacity at an early hour. Landgrave Philipp, his councilors, court preacher, prelates, abbots, deans, pastors, monks, priests, counts, knights, mayors, council members, and citizens found themselves in a conference such as the walls of Homberg had never before seen."[51]

The three-day meeting was organized much like a tournament. Day one was the day of challenge, day two for conflict, and day three for cleanup. Much of the conflict turned out to be little more than overheated sparring. Philipp intended to act as a judge or referee, but soon found he was drawn into the fray.

Upon receiving a signal from Philipp, Chancellor John Feige opened the meeting. Feige was a graduate of the University of Erfurt and widely regarded as one of the most well-informed men of his generation. An edict was circulated that Schmitt calls "a feather in Feige's hat." The edict stated Philipp's desire to be impartial, for each party maintained that its outlook was right and was branded by its opponent as false and godless.

The agenda for the meeting, Lambert's lengthy *Paradoxa*, contained twenty-three titles.

1. All abuses must be abolished and how to do it
2. Through whom the amendment of abuses must take place
3. Who is to judge in spiritual matters
4. Of the Church of God and the synagogue of Satan
5. Of the keys of Christ and His Church
6. Of the true priesthood
7. Of the all-sufficient offering for the Church of God
8. Of the Eucharist and the Mass
9. Of the false and carnal priesthood
10. Of Sculpture and images or idols
11. Of the ministers of the Church, their authority, and the duty of believers over against them
12. Of the godless celibacy and holy matrimony
13. Of purgatory
14. Of ceremonies
15. Of the superstitious consecration of water, bread, the crops, and all such things
16. Of the temple altar, and consecrating of persons and anointing
17. Of burial
18. Of the confession of the divine name and the kind of psalms to sing
19. Of Baptism

20. Of true and false worship

21. That prayer may be made to God alone through the one and only Advocate and Mediator, Jesus Christ

22. Of faith, righteousness, and their fruits and the freedom of believers.

23. Of monasticism

Instead of attacking the *Paradoxa*, Herborn chose to attack Philipp, declaring that he had no right to call such an assembly on his own initiative and authority.

Feige responded. According to him, the example of the apostolic Church described in Acts 15 was their justification for calling this assembly: when confronted by a split over the demand of Jewish Christians that Gentile converts should be circumcised, Paul and the other apostles called a meeting in Jerusalem. There they declared their unanimous decision, which created unity of doctrine and conduct. Feige concluded that German rulers at the Speyer I the previous year had decided that each German territory should decide its own religious orientation, the German principle confirmed in the Peace of Augsburg in 1555. This is exactly what Philipp was doing. In the second part of his opening address, Chancellor Feige laid down three ground rules he expected the discussion to follow.

First, Lambert's *Paradoxa*, posted on the church door the evening before, should serve as the guideline for discussion. The purpose of this discussion would be to prove that the *Paradoxa* was identical to God's Word. Lambert was to read it in Latin, and Adam Krafft would translate it into German for the understanding of all.

Second, the free discussion that was to follow would be open to all, with one stipulation: objections could only be voiced if they were based on clear passages from the Bible. Those familiar with Latin were to sit near Lambert, while those who knew only German were to sit near Adam Krafft. They were to keep friendly and Christian order, to leave behind all invective and bitterness, and to speak in such a manner that all in the audience might follow the essential point.

Third, all who would speak should be equally familiar with all of the Scripture from beginning to end, not basing arguments on one or two isolated passages, but drawing equally upon the whole.

With Feige's opening address, Philipp had let the gauntlet drop. Though he was not a theologian, Philipp had a respectable knowledge of the Bible. Now, bristling with polemic zeal and peppered with biblical quotations, it was Lambert's turn to step forth to amplify Philipp's challenge in Latin. He appeared to be a good choice for leadership, for Philipp's opponent, Herborn, was the guardian of the Franciscan Order in Marburg, while Francis Lambert had been a Franciscan monk for fifteen years, and, being well educated, they were both fluent in Latin.

The balance of the morning was spent with Lambert reading and explaining in Latin his *Paradoxa*. As he droned on, one wonders: What did those untrained in Latin do to occupy themselves throughout the long hours crowded into a church with no heating or air conditioning in October, the month of unpredictable weather? History was being made in their presence. Still, they had to wait for Adam Krafft to explain in German the challenge Lambert was hurling at Catholic tradition. Philipp listened, absorbed in what was being said. He obviously had more than just a passing knowledge of Latin.

In the time left late that afternoon, Krafft explained what he considered the most important details of Lambert's Latin address. Then he closed his explanation by repeating the challenge expressed earlier by Philipp, Feige, and Lambert: "Show me from God's Word where I am wrong. State your objections." Herborn asked to be heard the following day. Philipp granted his request. With that, day one, the day of challenge, ended.

The assembly reconvened at seven the next morning. Though it was Sunday, the opening was conspicuous for its lack of a devotional period, a point that would be challenged soon after the meeting adjourned. Lambert started the day reading his twenty-three titles again. Everyone was eager for Herborn to stand up, certain that the wise old man would put up a good fight.

Herborn was wiser than others had thought. He had read the political winds of change and had been Philipp's confidant for at least four years.[52] He was especially close to Philipp's mother, Anna. Due to Herborn's influence, Philipp and his mother had generously supported the Franciscans in Marburg. When Philipp revealed his commitment to Luther's teaching, it was Herborn who, on Anna's behalf, wrote to Philipp urging him not to forget the religion of his ancestor, St. Elizabeth.[53]

Herborn was not a reactionary voice opposed to any change as a matter of principle. Herborn was a formidable theological power. The Franciscan Order in Hesse was benefiting from Herborn's moral and organizational reform. He had traveled widely, spreading those benefits elsewhere. Soon after this meeting he would travel again, not as a broken vagrant monk, as Lambert would claim, but as the moral reformer of more Franciscan monasteries. He would also write to urge mission work in Mexico when Emperor Charles V was enjoying their gold, a decade before the Jesuits sent missionaries.

That Sunday in Homberg promised to be interesting, but nothing turned out as planned. The *Paradoxa*, written as a guide for civil debate, was soon forgotten. Once again Herborn ignored Lambert and confronted Philipp directly. True to his character, the issue Herborn raised was basic: By what right had this meeting been called? Herborn insisted this was neither the time nor the place to decide matters of religion and life. That could only be done by the Church in council or by the pope. Discussion of Luther's heresy had been forbidden in Emperor Charles V's Edict of 1521.

Herborn claimed he had agreed only to act as an adviser to the meeting in matters of faith and ceremonies. Therefore, he would reply only to Philipp, not to Lambert. He promised that later he would address Lambert's *Paradoxa* in writing. Herborn added that should he fail to prevail, quoting the Bible, he would offer his body to be cut into a thousand pieces. He did respond later, but only when he had found refuge in Cologne.

As the conflict grew more heated, Herborn continued to address Philipp directly. He admonished the landgrave to remain faithful to the example of his ancestors. Herborn had more than St. Elizabeth in mind. He reminded Philipp that many of his male ancestors had been recognized by popes and councils.

He then referred to Feige's remarks concerning the abuses of the monastic life. He did not deny that there had been and still were abuses. He claimed that the right to reform the orders was the sole responsibility of superiors such as himself. Secular lords had no right to interfere.

Herborn spoke for approximately two hours. It must have been an impressive sight. Gaunt, sunken-eyed, fanatical in his zeal for the old tradition, Herborn did what few others dared to do. He challenged his powerful young ruler face to face and in public view! But Philipp was well prepared. Had he not been prepared, the reform of Hesse might never have occurred.

Finally, Chancellor Feige could take it no more. He interrupted Herborn. Speaking in defense of the landgrave's right to correct abuses in the monastic orders, Feige threw canon law back at Herborn, referring to St. Isidore of Seville, who died on April 4, 636, and was known in Catholicism as the last of the ancient Christian philosophers.[54] Addressing the situation in the Catholicism of his day, Feige described entrenched abuses, unspiritual pride, lust for honor and riches, and the cultivation of a false Christian faith. Then, as he had the day before, he referred to the example of the Early Church in the Acts of the Apostles.

Now Feige's defense of the landgrave turned personal. He endorsed Philipp as a man of faith. Feige stated that his landgrave was well enough trained in the Bible to know how to deal with error. He could encourage pure doctrine in Hesse and bring to order all that was contrary to good Christian order. Feige added that he would advise the landgrave in this matter, and he closed by repeating the challenge to anyone who felt able to question Lambert's *Paradoxa* on the basis of God's Word.

This Herborn refused to do—not because he was unable, as Lambert would later have his readers believe, but because he believed this was not the arena for him to speak against a teaching that had already been judged heretical by both the pope and the emperor.

Finally, the conflict reached its peak, and Herborn's attack on the landgrave grew still more personal. He had heard enough from the landgrave's lackeys. He confronted Philipp with two serious charges. First, he claimed it was Philipp who had disrupted the peace and caused discord, including the Peasants' War the previous year. Second, he claimed Philipp did this because he wanted to get his hands on the wealth of the monasteries.

Philipp remained quiet, listening to Herborn's accusation. Then he spoke for the first time that day. He reminded Herborn how often they had talked in private even after he had announced his decision "to promote the pure and true doctrine." Philipp stated that he felt obliged to offer his assistance so that false worship might be abolished and he and his subjects might be united in harmony with God's will.

Since Philipp and his mother had done much to enrich Herborn's monastery, the landgrave might have defended his decision to introduce the Reformation in Hesse by claiming to merely be taking back what was rightly his own. Still, he stated that the cause of the split was more important to him than all the goods of the monastery. With effective logic he reasoned that had he desired the goods of the monastery, he never would have bothered to call this assembly.

Concluding, Philipp urged Herborn to dispute with Lambert, reminding him to use the Bible as his source. He assured him that he could speak freely. Nothing would be held against him. He would listen "patiently and graciously."

Monday, cleanup day, was brief and anticlimactic. By now Philipp had emerged as both the director and lead actor of this religious drama. Still, there was one surprise in store for everyone. In the absence of Herborn, John

Sperber, a pastor from Waldau near Kassel, stood up to defend the old faith. Though he was not as well prepared or gifted as Herborn, Sperber felt that as a parish pastor, he could speak freely, unimpeded by considerations that weighed heavily upon Herborn as an official representative of the Franciscan Order. By now Philipp had taken complete control, and he engaged in direct exchange with Sperber.

Sperber urged Philipp not to allow the Evangelical mysteries to be shared with the laity, especially not with the peasants, who had demonstrated their unworthiness by rebelling the previous year.

Philipp replied quoting Habakkuk 2:4: "The just shall live by faith." Sperber might have brought up the invocation of Mary, for Philipp reminded Sperber there is only one Mediator between God and man, Jesus Christ. Concerning withholding the Gospel from the common man, Philipp reminded him of Jesus' command to preach the Gospel to all.

Philipp had struck the decisive blow. Sperber was silenced, and the representatives of the Catholic faith were vanquished. All that remained was to conclude the third day's session and provide for an orderly reform of Hesse. A committee, headed by Lambert and Adam Krafft, was assigned to draw up a plan for reform. The committee met. Within three days, it submitted the first portion of its document for Philipp's approval.

As soon as Philipp gave his approval, the committee completed its document, known in Latin as *Reformatio Ecclesiarum Hassiae*, "The Reformation of the Church of Hesse" (hereafter the *Reformatio*).[55] This was published in December, and Philipp sent a copy to Luther. On January 7, 1527, Luther rejected it as "such a pile of laws" and suggested that Philipp follow the example of the prophet Moses and introduce changes locally first. This Philipp did, and the *Reformatio* was all but forgotten.

PHILIPP'S UNIVERSITY IN MARBURG

The way was now cleared for Philipp's next move, the creation of his university in Marburg. In his Epitome, Melanchthon had recommended that the landgrave should tend to the educational needs of his subjects. At the Diet of Speyer (Speyer I), Philipp had served on the princes' committee and had demanded that children be taught in schools and that the empire should use a standardized Latin grammar.

Philipp had ample guidelines for founding his university. Two weeks before the Homberg Synod assembled, Melanchthon had encouraged him. Lambert's *Paradoxa* suggested that the authorities should close all monasteries and turn them into schools for believers. The *Reformatio* contained detailed plans for a university in Marburg and for the establishment of primary schools through-out the land.[56]

The need for a Hessian university was not only religious. Professor William J. Wright notes, "In the course of the sixteenth century, more and more state servants were individuals who had completed their university studies. By 1567 [the year of Philipp's death] the new University of Marburg was to supply most of this need, while foreign universities had filled the requirement before that."[57]

Marburg was chosen for its central location and because it had a monastery that, when emptied, could house the university. In the week between Christ-mas and the New Year, 1527, Philipp moved from Kassel to Marburg so that he might better supervise the creation of the university. First, he needed to empty the Dominican and Franciscan monasteries. Early in January, he had Lambert hold a disputation, hoping to peacefully win the monks' cooperation. The Dominicans cooperated and moved out promptly. The Franciscans resisted; they did not leave until April.

On January 16, Heinrich Hesse, a Hessian a student in Wittenberg, wrote to Philipp's senior aide, Balthasar Schrautenbach, stating that Lambert was remembered in Wittenberg as being "inconsiderate, inexperienced and selfish."[58] Philipp ignored this evaluation and listed Lambert as first among the three theologians on his faculty. Soon he would name Lambert as head of the department of theology. Lambert served in that position until his death in the plague of April 1530. The university opened with four departments: theol-ogy, law, medicine, and philosophy. Eighty-four first-year students enrolled.

Philipps University of Marburg is now a state institution with no religious affiliation. In 2005, it had 25,000 students with a staff of 7,500. At the same time, Marburg had a population of 72,000. Twentieth-century theologians associated with the university included Karl Barth, Rudolph Bultmann, and Paul Tillich. Among its former students of the arts were the composer Heinrich Schütz, the Brothers Grimm, and the poet Boris Pasternak.

At the end of 1527, Philipp's star was on its rise. At age twenty-three he was widely recognized as the impressive young hero of the Reformation. Who would have dared to predict the dark year of sorrow and scandal that lay ahead for Philipp and the Reformation?

Chapter 7

SORROW AND SCANDAL 1528
A Cauldron of Charged Emotions

As the page on the calendar of reform turned to January 1, 1528, no one could guess that the year would turn out to be a cauldron of charged emotions: hope and disappointment, boldness and fear, sorrow and scandal. The eyes of both friend and foe were upon Philipp. Friends trusted him as their young and bold new leader. Foes feared that the followers of Martin Luther might have found their political hero in Philipp. No one expected that by midyear, Philipp, of his own volition, would disappoint his Lutheran friends and delight his Catholic foes.

With the establishment of Philipp's university in Marburg the year before, the reformation of Hesse was showing great promise of expanding in an environment of trust. Luther may have been unhappy with Philipp's choice of Lambert for his theologian, but the reformer had little reason to distrust Philipp himself.

Still, beyond Hesse, clouds of distrust were gathering by early 1528. The Reformation in Electoral Saxony had enjoyed remarkable growth under the protection of its powerful elector, Frederick III, better known as Frederick the Wise. In the spring of 1525, that trust began to fade with the elector's death and the Peasants' War several weeks later. By calling upon the princes of Germany to vigorously put down the peasants, Luther had earned the distrust of the peasants.

Duke John, Frederick's younger brother, succeeded him. Unlike Frederick, who never publicly declared himself to be a Lutheran, John promptly declared his support for Luther. The emperor would never officially recognize John as the Elector of Saxony. Still, for his confidence in Luther and seven years of effective political leadership (1525–32), John would be honored by the German people and the world as Elector John the Steadfast.

There were, however, some voices asking whether this new elector could be trusted. Might not his candor, announcing his support for Luther, bring down Hapsburg wrath upon the Lutheran princes of Germany? If that were to happen, Duke George of Albertine Saxony, who had always despised his cousins John and Frederick, would gladly support Archduke Ferdinand and Emperor Charles V, hoping to take over the rule of united Saxony himself.

THE SORROWS OF THE SAXON VISITATIONS

Luther had received reports about the offensive lives of some in the Saxon countryside who were claiming to be Lutheran. He suggested to Elector John that a visitation of Saxony might be needed. Authorized churchmen had practiced visitations since the fifth century. Visitations were among the chief duties of the bishop and were felt to be in the fraternal spirit of the apostle Paul, who is recorded in Acts 15:36 as saying, "Let us return and visit the brothers in every city where we proclaimed the word of the Lord, and see how they are."

Visitations were neglected by the late Middle Ages. In the fifteenth century, Jean Gerson, an early French voice for reform and a spiritual mentor of Joan of Arc, declared that they should be revived, but his call was ignored. There were no Lutheran bishops in Electoral Saxony. Luther suggested to Elector John that he act as an emergency bishop and proclaim a visitation on his own authority. John agreed.

Luther joined at least one visitation himself. What he observed in the countryside gave him great sorrow. He wrote, "Dear God, what misery I beheld! The ordinary person, especially in the villages, knows absolutely nothing about the Christian faith, and unfortunately, many pastors are completely unskilled and incompetent teachers . . . they do not know the Lord's Prayer, the Creed, or the Ten Commandments! As a result, they live like simple cattle or irrational pigs and, despite the fact that the Gospel has returned, have mastered the fine art of misusing all their freedom."[59]

LOSING A CHILD
AND LEARNING ABOUT MARTYRS

Luther's marriage three years earlier to the escaped nun Katharina von Bora had been a surprising source of unexpected joy for him. A second child, a daughter, Elizabeth, was born on December 10, 1527. Her parents' joy at her birth was short-lived. Amid the turmoil of 1528, Elizabeth died on August 3. The happy parents had called her "little Elsie." Luther wrote, "We feel a great sadness, for with little Elsie died a piece of her father's and a part of her mother's heart."[60]

Added to the earlier causes of his distrust was a growing despair upon receiving reports of the supreme price two had paid as Lutheran martyrs. An early report had come from Denmark in 1525 reporting that Brother Henry Moeller had been burned at the stake for his support of the Reformation. Then on February 29, 1528, Patrick Hamilton, one of Luther's own students, had also been burned at the stake in Scotland. Luther could not help but question his own judgment. Because of him, good people were dying! His anguish was amplified to the point of despair, what Luther called his *Anfechtungen*, a word so significant for understanding Luther that Roland Bainton claimed it should be a part of our English vocabulary.[61] The Reformation scholar Kurt Hendel has recorded Luther's most serious experience of Anfechtungen that nearly caused his death on July 2, 1527.[62] Luther found solace in music and the Word, and in 1528 (or thereabouts), he wrote his powerful hymn of faith, "A Mighty Fortress Is Our God": "Though devils all this world should fill all seeking to devour us, we tremble not we fear no ill. They shall not overpower us."[63]

PHILIPP'S GROWING FRIENDSHIP WITH MARTIN BUCER

At the turn of 1527, Luther's trust in Philipp was threatened by his growing friendship with Martin Bucer of Strassburg. Luther and Bucer became friends at the Heidelberg Disputation of 1518. They had corresponded until 1524 when their trust was broken. What happened in 1524 made it nearly impossible for Luther to ever trust Bucer or, for that matter, his friend Philipp again.

It happened over the publication of two commentaries on the Psalms. One was written by Martin Bucer, the other by John Bugenhagen, the pastor of the Church of St. Mary, the city church in Wittenberg. Bugenhagen was also Luther's close friend and confessor. He published his commentary in Latin. At close to the same time, Bucer published his own commentary in High German. Bugenhagen and Bucer were friends. Bugenhagen felt his knowledge of High German was inferior to that of Bucer and asked him to translate his Latin commentary into German.[64] Bugenhagen gave Bucer permission to make whatever improvements to his commentary he felt might be helpful. Bugenhagen never dreamed how Bucer would betray this confidence.

When translating Bugenhagen's comments on Psalm 111, Bucer inserted his own Zwinglian interpretation of the Eucharist. Then he published his German translation of Bugenhagen's work in Basel without asking him to read it and give his approval. About six months later, bad news arrived in Wittenberg. Someone from Augsburg alerted Bugenhagen, telling him that people were saying that the University of Wittenberg agreed with Bucer's inserted Zwinglian comment.

Bugenhagen's first reaction was to laugh in disbelief. Upon further thought, he realized he had brought this upon himself. He had written, in his dedication to the memory of Elector Frederick, that he taught at Wittenberg University, and he included Luther and Melanchthon's letters of praise for his Latin commentary. All of this Bucer had included in his German translation. Bugenhagen wrote that it was "as if I too were a defender of the opinion of the sects who deny that in it [the Sacrament] the true body of Christ is eaten and his true blood is drunk by the believers."[65]

Bugenhagen might have been justified in suing Bucer for all he was worth, but he forgave Bucer, and for years to come, the two carried on a friendly correspondence. Still, the damage had been done. For the rest of his life, Luther found it hard to trust Bucer. When the reformer learned of the growing friendship between Philipp and Bucer, Luther's distrust of Bucer spilled over onto Philipp.

So, while the Reformation continued to win followers early in 1528, Luther's distress was also growing. It was kindled by the alarming spiritual conditions he personally witnessed in the Saxon countryside; the death of his daughter Elizabeth; learning of the martyrdom of two Lutherans, one in Scotland and the other in Denmark; and his estrangement from Martin Bucer, all of which gathered to cloud Luther's trust in Philipp.

THE SCANDALOUS PACK AFFAIR

How tragic that in this emotional climate, twenty-three-year-old Philipp would bring new distrust and scandal upon himself by ignoring the advice of his counselors! It would take less than three months in the spring of 1528 to destroy the reputation Philipp had spent ten years earning as the trustworthy young hero of the Reformation. Too quick to judge his neighboring Catholic princes, including his father-in-law, Duke George, Philipp lost the trust of many of his Lutheran friends as well.

On March 16, 1528, Luther received a message from Elector John summoning him to his court in Altenburg. There the elector informed him of a contract allegedly signed by Archduke Ferdinand, Duke George, and six other cosigners.[66] The contract revealed their supposed pledge to unite and to attack Lutheran lands.

Otto von Pack was a trusted vice chancellor in Duke George's court. He was very personable, hardworking, and apparently faultlessly loyal to the duke. Still, Pack had a tragic secret. Even his beloved wife, Margaret, was not aware of this secret. Pack was a gambler. Before 1528 ended, the events surrounding the revelation of Pack's secret would spell his eventual fate. In the meantime, Philipp would endure public scandal due to Pack's greed.

There were rumors in George's court that Pack might have Lutheran leanings. These rumors might have been what prepared Philipp to listen with sympathy and accept Pack's alarming revelation as true. Pack provided Philipp with a copy of a treaty that Catholic leaders, led by Philipp's father-in-law, Duke George, had supposedly drawn up and signed in Breslau that previous year. Unlike the earlier Catholic Dessau alliance, which was drawn up only for defense, this treaty committed its signers to attack Lutheran territories, reinstate the Catholic faith there, and divide the spoils among themselves, naming Hesse in particular.

It had been a long time since Philipp had trusted his Catholic neighbors. It is questionable whether he ever trusted Duke George. Now, however, he was far too eager to believe Pack's claim. After Philipp had paid Pack a steep sum, he was shown the document. He noticed that it was only a copy. He demanded that Pack give him the original. Pack replied that he had left it for safekeeping in Dresden with his friend the pharmacist, Valentin Kruel.

Philipp commanded Pack to retrieve the original document. Pack wrote to Kruel, asking him to give the original to his wife, Margaret. He also wrote to Margaret, asking her to pick up a package from Kruel and bring it to him in Hesse. Pack knew he was on very thin ice, only stalling for time. He had not given Kruel any document for safekeeping. Margaret, of course, could not deliver a nonexistent document.

About this time, one might expect that Philipp would have let the whole matter drop, but he had paid a princely sum and wanted to get his hands on what he had paid for. He even shut his ears to the advice of his counselors, Schrautenbach, Feige, and Krafft, when they pointed to evidence that the document was a forgery. Philipp failed to trust his most devoted friends.

Philipp's distrust in questioning Krafft's advice was somewhat understandable, for Krafft had only been in Phillipp's service for two years, but

Schrautenbach and Feige had served Hesse since Philipp's mother had been the regent of Hesse two decades earlier. Instead of trusting his counselors, impetuous twenty-three-year-old Philipp gathered his army.

On May 10, no one in Dresden had any reason to distrust Pack. He had taken advantage of their full confidence. Philipp's normally savvy sister, Elizabeth, was married to George's sole surviving son, John, and was living in the Dresden court. Pack convinced her to write to Philipp, warning him not to trust his counselors. Still, Elizabeth's letter did not convince Philipp to ignore his counselors, for the letter arrived too late. By May 28, when it arrived, Philipp and the elector's son, Duke John Frederick, were with their armies on the border of Catholic Würzburg.

Word spread quickly and far. Philipp's troops were rumored to be looting savagely, as they probably were. That's what attacking armies do. Archbishop Albrecht of neighboring Mainz, fearing that he, too, would be attacked, quickly surrendered his ancient claim to Hessian territory. Correspondence flew between George, Philipp, Margaret, Elizabeth, Pack, and Kruel. Fifteen letters were sent and received during the forty-eight hours of May 27 and 28.[67] It would not be long before the news reached the emperor's ear.

Soon, Archduke Ferdinand cleared the air by stating that Pack's Breslau Treaty was fraudulent. John Frederick withdrew his troops and Philipp reluctantly followed suit. George demanded that Pack must be returned to Dresden, where Pack knew he would be arrested. Philipp held Pack captive and refused to release him to certain death in Dresden. Instead, he released him to find his way to refuge in the Netherlands. George's search for Pack proved to be relentless. After nine years of uncertainty, Pack was finally arrested, brought back to Dresden, tortured, and put to death.

Philipp had learned a hard lesson. Never again would he distrust his advisers. Six years later, he would attack Catholic neighbors again. This time, however, he would not act on the impulse of youth, but only after painstaking preparation. Then he would succeed brilliantly, winning Württemberg for the Lutheran faith, and only his Catholic foes would call that scandalous.

As the year 1528 came to an end, Philipp had been beaten but not broken. He focused on rebuilding his heroic reputation, this time not as a warrior, but as a peacemaker. In Wittenberg Martin Luther fumed. Within two years, however, Philipp would recover Luther's trust and that of the Lutheran princes of Germany. That story will be told in the next chapter.

Chapter 8

RECOVERY 1529 AND 1530
Philipp and the 1529 Diet of Speyer

Having survived 1528, a difficult year for many, Philipp wasted little time on self-pity. For him, March 1529 would introduce his eighteen-month period of recovery. He knew that his reputation as the heroic political leader of the Reformation had stalled in the previous year. Now he set out to restart it.

The situation in the wake of the Pack Affair is described by Karl Brandi in his biography of Emperor Charles V: "The adherents of the Roman Church in the Empire had been for the first time seriously alarmed . . . their anxiety to defend their own interests enabled Ferdinand, acting as Charles's deputy, to adopt a far bolder attitude towards the Protestants."[68]

Archduke Ferdinand was determined that he would not make the same mistake he had made in 1526, when an ambiguous statement in the recess of Speyer I was interpreted by Lutheran princes as affirming that the rulers of the empire, answering to God, could determine the religion of their land. This had introduced three years of rapid Lutheran growth.

Born on March 10, 1503, Ferdinand was twenty months older than Philipp. The archduke and the landgrave had met by chance on the road to the Diet of Worms in 1521 and rode into the city together. Following that diet, the two traveled back to Hesse together, and they paused on the way to enjoy hunting.

In March 1529, they met again on their way to the second Diet of Speyer (hereafter Speyer II). This time, Ferdinand ignored Philipp. His unfriendly treatment alerted Philipp to the hard line Ferdinand was prepared to take at this diet.

When Ferdinand arrived in Speyer, he was determined to rescind the recess of Speyer I. He appointed a committee to draw up a formulation to do just that. The document the committee produced was blatantly one-sided. The Catholic estates were encouraged to keep up the good work. No less than six proscriptions were placed on Lutheran princes and imperial cities. They should:

1. Introduce no further changes.

2. In their territories no one should be forbidden from hearing the Mass or receiving Communion in one kind.

3. Other new teachings on the Sacraments were forbidden, including the emphasis on "believer's baptism" by Anabaptists. (Lutherans had no problem with this one.)

4. The clergy was to interpret the Gospel according to the standard authorities approved by the Catholic Church.

5. The government should implement book censorship.

6. The confiscation of Church or secular property was forbidden.

Six Lutheran princes, including Philipp, and fourteen imperial cities opposed the committee's draft.

Luther's colleagues Philipp Melanchthon and John Agricola (1494–1566) arrived at Speyer II with Elector John. Though the Lutheran voices were overwhelmed by the Catholic majority, it soon became apparent Luther had many powerful friends.

On April 12, 1529, Luther's supporters submitted a written declaration to the diet rejecting the committee's document and announcing they would not submit to the decision of the majority in matters of conscience.

By April 19, the committee's document had been rejected by the majority. The first protest of Lutherans followed. It was rejected. One day later a second protest was presented, repeating the previous day's arguments in greater detail and including a protest against five more points affirmed by the Catholic majority:

1. The binding nature of the Edict of Worms, which would prevent future acceptance of the Reformation by estates still loyal to the pope.

2. The "purification" of the ecclesiastical and liturgical status quo in the Evangelical territories. That would have thwarted the still incomplete development of new church structures.

3. The ban on new teachings on Communion.

4. The obligation to tolerate the Mass without toleration of Protestant worship in Catholic territories.

5. The binding force of majority decisions in matters of faith.

Philipp joined the Lutheran princes and imperial cities lodging a formal appeal before two notaries on April 25, 1529. This gave legal status to their protest. It was immediately printed and addressed to the emperor by a delegation of Lutheran princes. The emperor immediately rejected it. From then on, Lutherans would be called "Protestants," a name that today is applied to most Christians that are not Roman Catholic.

Philipp had stood in protest with fellow Lutheran princes and the Lutheran imperial cities. He returned from Speyer II emboldened to continue his pursuit of reform at home and Protestant political union throughout the empire. The historian John Michael Reu wrote in 1930 describing Philipp's influence at the close of Speyer II: "The Landgrave now seemed to be the leader of Protestantism and everything apparently hinged on the thought of a political federation."[69]

LUTHER'S OPPOSITION AT PHILIPP'S MARBURG COLLOQUY

Following Speyer II, Philipp devoted his attention to theological diplomacy. He prepared a three-day colloquy, a meeting of theological equals to discuss the different positions they held. At this colloquy, Philipp planned to feature four leading theologians of the Reformation: Martin Luther and Philipp Melanchthon from Wittenberg, and Ulrich Zwingli and John Oecolampadius from Switzerland.

Organizing and supervising the three-day colloquy in Philipp's castle in Marburg would be recognized later as the diplomatic and theological high point of his life. The fact that he was able to bring these strong-minded theological leaders together for a discussion was in itself an impressive diplomatic accomplishment.

For the colloquy, Philipp focused on the Lutheran and the Zwinglian interpretations of the Eucharist, seeking a possible reconciliation. Luther interpreted literally Jesus' words "This is My body. This is My blood." His view was that Jesus' body and blood are really present in, with, and under the bread and wine.

Zwingli took a rational approach. He interpreted the Sacrament as a feast of commemoration, focusing on Jesus' words "This do in remembrance of Me." According to Zwingli, the bread and the wine commemorate the body and blood of Christ, whose presence is spiritual, not real. Oecolampadius's spiritual view was slightly different from Zwingli's, but it still was not Luther's view of the real presence.

How did this breach in the Reformation develop? What follows is an attempt to shed light on that question by focusing on the background of Zwingli's and Oecolampadius's views.

A historian of the Radical Reformation, George Huntston Williams[70] traces the source of Zwingli's commemorative view of the Sacrament to the Netherlands and a monk named Tanchelm, who died in 1115. Tanchelm taught his many followers not to partake of the Sacrament of the priests, which he called a pollution. A milder and more devout form of the commemorative view was that of Wessel Gansfort (c. 1420–89), who left unpublished writings of his commemorative view of the Sacrament.

Cornelius Hoen (died 1523 or 1524), a lawyer at The Hague, emerged as an important formulator of commemorative theology, later called "sacramentarianism." He wanted to contact Luther in Wittenberg and give him Gansfort's manuscripts to read and, he hoped, publish, but he felt he was too old to travel. In his place, he sent Rode of Utrecht (dates unknown).

Rode arrived in Wittenberg early in 1521, shortly after Pope Leo X published his papal bull *Exsurge Domine*, excommunicating Luther as a heretic. Rode's timing was bad, for Wittenberg was alive with rumors that the emperor would summon Luther to recant his writings at the Diet of Worms the following spring. Luther ignored Rode's request.

On the other hand, Rode was received warmly by Andreas Bodenstein von Carlstadt, Luther's senior colleague on the faculty. By the winter of 1521–22, Carlstadt read and published some of Gansfort's writings while Luther was in protective exile in the Wartburg castle, having been declared an outlaw by the emperor.

During Luther's absence, Carlstadt introduced controversial practices in Wittenberg. On Sunday, December 22, Carlstadt announced that on Christmas Day he would distribute wine to the laity in the City Church. During this time, a radical group from Zwickau caused rioting in the streets of Wittenberg and destroyed sacred images.

Informed of this, Luther returned to Wittenberg and took control, preaching his famous eight sermons on the theme "Evangelical Freedom is Not a New Law," from March 9 to 16, 1522.

Carlstadt read the handwriting on the wall and resigned from his powerful position on the Wittenberg faculty. He moved to the parish church of Orlamünde. There he convinced the congregation to call him as their pastor, and he set about promoting his commemorative view of the Sacrament. He interpreted the wine as a reminder of God's covenant of forgiveness and the bread as a reminder of the promise of the resurrection of the body.

Luther could not allow such preaching and practices in Saxony. He attacked Carlstadt by publishing his treatise *Against the Heavenly Prophets* in early 1525.[71] He also convinced the new elector, John (Frederick had died in May), to banish Carlstadt from Saxony. Then Carlstadt traveled to Basel in Switzerland. There he sought the company of others holding his commemorative view, including John Oecolampadius, who would be one of Philipp's invited guests at the Marburg Colloquy four years later.

Oecolampadius (1482–1531), of Weinsberg in the Palatinate, was born John Husgen, the son of prosperous parents. He studied law at Bologna and theology at Heidelberg, Tübingen, and Basel. At Heidelberg the humanist Jacob Wimpfeling became his mentor. Under his influence John took the name Oecolampadius, a literal Greek translation of *Husgen*, meaning "hour light," "shining light," or "lantern."

John Froben of Basel was an influential publisher of Erasmus's and Luther's works. In 1515, Froben invited Oecolampadius to come and work for him in Basel. There, in 1516, he gained literary fame helping Erasmus finish the notes and commentary to his first edition of the Greek New Testament. Oecolampadius was allowed to add his own postscript.

In the autumn of 1516, Oecolampadius returned to Weinsberg. There he would be assisted by John Brentz (1499–1570), who would become the pastor of the St. Mark congregation of Schwäbisch Hall and the Lutheran reformer of Württemberg. In Augsburg the following year, Oecolampadius read some of Luther's writings. When a friend asked him how he felt about Luther, he replied, "Martin is closer to the evangelical truth than any of his opponents."

At this time, Melanchthon's great-uncle, Reuchlin, secured Oecolampadius a position on the Wittenberg faculty. Oecolampadius declined, stating his heart was in Basel. By 1522, thanks to the printers in Basel, especially Froben, Luther's writings were read widely throughout western Europe. Calls for reform were spoken in some of the Basel pulpits. At that time, Ulrich Zwingli became the leader of reform in Zurich, and Oecolampadius wrote to make his acquaintance.

The friendship that developed, as well as Oecolampadius's sound advice, tact, and diplomacy, contributed to establishing the Reformation in Switzerland by Zwingli. Still, his support of Zwingli did not cause Oecolampadius to turn his back on Luther. The two continued to correspond. Melanchthon, whose friendship with Oecolampadius was stronger, offered him refuge in Wittenberg, should it be needed. By late 1524, Oecolampadius had abandoned the real presence of Christ in the Sacrament. He favored a view similar to that of Carlstadt.

Ulrich Zwingli[72] and Luther were close contemporaries. Zwingli was born on January 1, 1484. Luther at Marburg would not face an eager-to-learn young student. He would face a very challenging peer.

Like Luther, Zwingli was raised in a family of comfortable means and was educated well for pastoral ministry. He attended the universities of Vienna and Basel. While continuing his studies, he served as the pastor in Glarus and Einsiedeln, Switzerland. There he was introduced to Erasmus and was influenced by the great humanist's writings. In 1506, Zwingli earned a master of arts degree from the University of Basel. He was ordained a priest in Constance, and on September 29, 1506, he celebrated his first Mass in his hometown, Wildhaus, Switzerland.

For ten years, Zwingli served as pastor in Glarus. It was there that he first became involved in politics. In campaigns of the Swiss Confederation, he took the side of the Roman See against the French and the Hapsburgs. Pope Julius II honored him with an annual income for services rendered. Zwingli traveled to Italy and was involved in several military campaigns, including the Battle of Novara in 1513. When the mood in Glarus shifted from favor for the pope to favor for the French, Zwingli moved to Einsiedeln to serve as their pastor.

A pivotal year for Zwingli was 1518, when he was elected to be the priest of the Grossmünster congregation in Zurich. He moved on December 27 and served there for the rest of his life. Zwingli organized two disputations in Zurich. The second one, in 1526, dealt with the Sacrament.

Meanwhile, in Basel, a tense situation arose between the Catholic city council and the Reformed craft guild. Their conflict made it impossible for Oecolampadius to conduct his own disputation to introduce the Reformation. That disputation would take place during the Peasants' War of 1525, the year that Carlstadt arrived in Basel and Oecolampadius published his own opinion on the Sacrament.

John Eck, Luther's opponent in the Leipzig Debate of 1519, now was judged victorious in another debate with Oecolampadius in May. Still, though he lost that debate, Oecolampadius was recognized as a theological leader of note. By then, all his theological ties with Luther had been broken. When Eck quoted Luther against him, Oecolampadius claimed he had never been a Lutheran.

Martin Bucer of Strassburg, another theologian that Philipp would invite to the colloquy as an auditor, now entered the scene. He advised both Zwingli and Oecolampadius not to forget their former love for Luther.

In February 1527, the city council of Basel proclaimed that matters of faith were the work of God and that the citizens should not hate each other for holding differing religious views. Later, the council hedged. It took some actions indicating it was moving in the direction of Zwingli's reform. On September 23, 1527, they greeted the new Catholic bishop warmly in the morning, but later that same day they turned on him, releasing the clergy from saying Mass and the people from attending Mass conducted by Catholic priests. In October, the council stood up to their new bishop, demanding that no one should be coerced in matters of faith.

Another disputation was held in 1528. The outcome favored reform. This brought little peace to Basel. In January 1529, the council, still hedging, called for a public disputation about the Sacrament and scheduled it for June that year.

Their call came too late. On February 9, the guilds, bent on reform, sent an ultimatum to the council. When the council hesitated to act, a crowd of approximately three hundred rioted. All the council members who still harbored Catholic sympathies were dismissed and replaced by those favoring reform.

Both the rioting and a confederation of Catholic cantons east of Zurich caused a tense social and theological climate in Zurich and Basel. It was at this time that Philipp's invitation arrived, asking Zwingli and Oecolampadius to participate in a colloquy with Luther and Melanchthon.

Philipp's dream of a theological confederation may well have seemed hopeless to both Zwingli and Oecolampadius. Luther's two catechisms, published earlier that spring, were best sellers, winning support far and wide for the real presence of Christ in the Sacrament. At the same time, Philipp's plan seemed hopeless to many, but for Zwingli and Oecolampadius the challenge was irresistible.

Martin Bucer had been the first to suggest such a colloquy at Speyer I in 1526. In the following year, Philipp suggested the idea to Luther, who flatly rejected it. Elector John entered the picture in 1529, urging Luther to accept Philipp's invitation. Bowing to the elector's wishes, Luther agreed to participate. He wrote to Philipp expressing a renewed confidence in the prince: "I am indeed absolutely convinced that Your Sovereign Grace is completely sincere and has the best of intentions. For this reason, I too am ready and willing to render my services in this, Your Sovereign Grace's undertaking."[73]

Philipp made certain that the colloquy was by invitation only.[74] False and misleading reports needed to be controlled. Carlstadt was not invited. According to Zwingli's later account, the number of guests was twenty-nine. Brentz claimed that nearly sixty were present. As physical evidence of the size of the assembly, its sessions were held in one of Philipp's large but still intimate personal living rooms, not in the large formal ballroom.

Only two princes were present—Philipp himself and Duke Ulrich of Württemberg, whose land had been taken by the emperor a decade earlier and who now was living as a guest in Philipp's castle. At least eight theologians were present. The remaining guests were dignitaries from Philipp's court and the city of Marburg.

The Swiss delegates sojourned for ten days in Strassburg, which, according to the historian Hermann Sasse, "offered an opportunity not only to prepare themselves for the theological discussion with the theologians of Strassburg [including Martin Bucer]. It also allowed them time to discuss the political situation with the authorities."[75]

Disturbing news arrived of an important peace treaty signed by the emperor and Pope Clement VII in Barcelona. This news was threatening; the emperor had been distracted from his German problem for almost a decade by frequent wars with the French and the pope. Now, however, with this treaty in force, he would be free to enforce his Edict of Worms against Luther and his followers.

Philipp invited Oecolampadius to preach in his presence during the days of waiting in Marburg. Luther arrived on Thursday, September 30. He was accompanied by Melanchthon and four or five other theologians. Arriving late were the Lutheran representatives of southern Germany, including Andrew Osiander (1498–1552) from Nürnberg, Stephan Agricola (1491–1547) from Augsburg, and John Brentz from Schwäbisch Hall. They arrived midway through the second session, on Saturday, October 2.

Sasse offers glowing approval for Philipp's hospitality at the colloquy, writing, "The courtesy and diplomatic skill of the host helped to create that friendly atmosphere which prevailed during the entire colloquy despite some serious moments during the discussions."[76]

Thursday, September 30, was devoted to what today we might call a "meet and greet" of theologians who previously had known each other only through their writings. Luther, remembering Bucer's insertion of his Zwinglian statement on the Sacrament when translating Bugenhagen's commentary on the Psalms, greeted Bucer saying, "You are a naughty boy."[77] Zwingli chose not to attend on this day.

Friday, October 1, was devoted to preliminary discussions between the four major theologians. Luther was paired with Oecolampadius and Zwingli with Melanchthon. Unfortunately, no records were kept, for it was decided these discussions were to be kept confidential. Sketchy passing references in later correspondence have not been very helpful.

The colloquy began on Saturday at six in the morning. It lasted all day with only one break for lunch. On Sunday, it continued with a morning and an afternoon session. It closed on Sunday evening.

Of Zwingli's influence on Swiss and some southern German worship practices, Sasse concludes, "Impressive as the liturgy of Zurich may have been, it was no longer the old Sacrament of the Altar but a new rite, a memorial of thanksgiving and joy not the *mysterium tremendum* of the Lutherans. The new liturgy has no catholicizing or even sacramental character."[78]

Are we to fault Philipp for attempting that which seemed humanly impossible, to bring to consensus two theological titans against their will? No option was suggested for them to part agreeing to disagree. That would have been unthinkable even for Philipp. Zwingli and Oecolampadius were no less inflexible when holding their position than Luther and Melanchthon were in holding their own.

Zwingli died in battle in 1531 and Oecolampadius died twenty-four days later. Their commemorative view of Holy Communion would continue to be promoted by Henry Bullinger, John Calvin, John Knox, and many others. It would be transplanted in the New World within a century and grow to become the dominant Protestant theology of the Sacrament in America today.

Luther and Philipp's theology of the real presence of Christ in the Sacrament is a critical teaching of the Lutheran faith. The body of its adherents would continue its remarkable growth, weathering multiple storms, until becoming today one of this world's largest Protestant denominations. From it would be born such a variety of historical talents as Johann Sebastian Bach, Søren Kierkegaard, and Dietrich Bonhoeffer.

PHILIPP AT THE 1530 DIET OF AUGSBURG

Three powerful rulers came to the city of Augsburg in the spring of 1530. Two came with their own agenda. The emperor came to settle his German problem once and for all. John of Saxony came demanding his right to be recognized by the emperor as the Elector of Saxony. Philipp came at the last minute. He had no apparent agenda other than to support the cause of Luther's reform.

After waiting eleven long years, Emperor Charles V had recently been crowned by Pope Clement VII. He would be the last emperor crowned by a pope. Now Charles was confident he could gather the lost German sheep of Rome.

The historian Roland Bainton has written about Philipp at this time: "A brand of Lutheranism began to emerge, political in complexion. The genius of the movement was . . . Philipp of Hesse. He was young, impetuous, and always active. He it was who had been on his toes in the Peasants' War when the Saxon princes were for leaving the outcome to God. Philipp was guided by three principles: he would compel no one to the faith, he would fight rather than suffer compulsion for himself, and he would make an alliance with those of another [Protestant] faith."[79]

Philipp ignored the emperor's summons until the last few weeks before the diet convened. When Philipp finally did appear, he claimed that family matters had detained him.

Duke John of Saxony came with a second cause, a serious confessional agenda that was not original to him. What was original was his desire to go it alone. Philipp suspected that John was doing this to strengthen his case for the emperor's recognition of him as the Elector of Saxony.

The idea of a union of like-minded Reformation leaders had first been suggested by the recess of the 1524 Diet of Nürnberg. There it was decreed that all estates that had control of one or more universities were to arrange for their "learned, reverent, experienced, and understanding doctors to prepare and extract all the disputed points in all the new doctrines and books." For the reform-minded leaders of Germany, these were taken as mild, somewhat confusing, but eagerly accepted words of encouragement.

By the time the diet convened in Augsburg on June 16, 1530, Luther's attitude toward Philipp had been softened by repeated appeals from Melanchthon, asking him to write and urge Philipp to come to the diet and to respect Duke John's confessional position.

Luther dared not attend, for he was a condemned heretic and outlaw. Elector John would have been powerless to protect Luther in Augsburg. John's first choice for Luther's residence during the diet was Nürnberg, which was about a three-day round-trip journey to Augsburg for a mounted messenger. Nürnberg refused, for reasons that were acceptable to Duke John. The Coburg castle was chosen, which was within John's borders, but this meant that correspondence to and from the diet would take about two weeks.

Melanchthon was still hoping for a reconciliation with Rome. His concern was somewhat similar to that of the emperor. Both wanted peace, but only at his own price. Melanchthon and Duke John arrived in Augsburg on May 2. While they waited for the emperor to arrive, Melanchthon wrote Luther several more times, urging him to correspond with Philipp.

Melanchthon was alarmed by the trouble brewing due to Philipp's growing friendship with Martin Bucer. At the time, he harbored little sympathy for a federation with Bucer and the Protestants of South Germany and Switzerland.

In the weeks spent waiting for the emperor to arrive, Landgrave Philipp and Bucer tested the winds and found the tide had turned in favor of John's confessional position. As a result, each one chose his own course. Philipp chose inaction. He had arrived among the last of the princes and would depart three months early, on August 6, without seeking the emperor's permission to leave. Bucer chose action and wrote his own confession of faith. He convinced four cities of southern Germany, Strassburg, Konstanz, Memmingen, and Lindau, to sign his confession, and he named it the *Tetrapolitana* after those four cities, *tetra* being the Latin word for the number four.

Later, the emperor, who had not yet arrived, would refuse to allow the *Tetrapolitana* to be read. The Lutheran princes rejected it for its Zwinglian position on the Sacrament. Following the diet, Luther did allow Bucer a cordial but unproductive visit in Wittenberg.

When the emperor arrived on June 16, he was received by kneeling Catholic princes, but defiant Philipp and Duke John stood upright. The same thing happened the following day. Charles decreed that during the diet, no Protestant preaching would be allowed in Augsburg. Philipp and John objected. Charles softened his demand, forbidding only polemic preaching intended to win converts from the opposite side. Philipp and John still objected, but now their objection won significant action. Charles banned all preaching during the diet, including that of his Catholic supporters. When Duke/Elector John wrote asking Luther's opinion on the matter, the reformer concluded that the emperor's decision must be obeyed and the reading of the Gospel would be good enough for all.

Charles commanded all Protestant princes to accompany him in the Corpus Christi procession the following day (*Corpus Christi* being Latin for "body of Christ"). In the Corpus Christi procession, the consecrated host was held high for all spectators to adore. Apparently, that is why the emperor delayed his arrival—to use the Corpus Christi procession to visually identify his Catholic supporters and the protesting Lutherans. As expected, the Lutheran princes refused to obey. They agreed with Charles that Christ is really present in the Sacrament, but they held that the procession was a form of adoration of the host that they would never agree to. In their opinion, it made an idol of the consecrated bread.

For the most part, Philipp kept a low profile at the diet. When he was given opportunity to speak, he declared before the emperor that only a council could decide matters of faith. Philipp's most significant contribution was giving Melanchthon occasional—but not too significant—advice on the wording of his confession, and then signing it along with six other Lutheran princes and two imperial cities.

Duke John was disappointed in his quest for imperial recognition as the Elector of Saxony. With apparent irony, he signed the confession "*Johannes, Herzog zu Saxony Elector* (John, Duke of Saxony Elector)." It is interesting to note that while Charles never officially recognized John as the Elector of Saxony, John is identified seven times in the recess of the diet either as the Elector of Saxony or simply as the elector.

All three rulers, Charles, John, and Philipp, returned from the diet disappointed. As he had done nine years earlier, Charles escaped from the chilly winds of Germany to return to the balmy breezes of Spain and the warm embrace of his beloved wife, Isabella.

Traveling by way of the Netherlands and from there by ship to Spain, the emperor made a stop at Speyer. There he learned of the death of his aunt Margaret, the archduchess of Austria and regent of the Netherlands. She had been Charles's, Ferdinand's, and their sister Mary's childhood guardian, and now in his years as emperor, she was one of his three most trusted advisers. Later, after he arrived in the Netherlands, Charles appointed his widowed sister, Queen Mary of Hungary,[80] to be Margaret's successor as the regent of the Netherlands.

For Philipp, the storm clouds of disillusionment and distrust that erupted in 1528 had vanished. Now entering the prime of his life, he was filled once again with heroic confidence, planning how he might accomplish great things for Hesse and the Reformation.

Chapter 9

HEROIC ACT ONE
Protestant Expansion in the 1530s

After his death in 1567, Philipp would be remembered as "the Magnanimous," a title he shares still today with his more cautious friend, Duke John Frederick of Saxony. Magnanimity includes many virtues, including large-mindedness, bravery, compassion, and wisdom. Another word for magnanimity might be *heroism*. The decade of the 1530s was Philipp's magnanimous, heroic decade.

At that time, the Reformation titles "Evangelical" and "Lutheran" were being replaced by the title "Protestant" earned by the protest of Lutheran princes and imperial cities at Speyer II in 1529. Philipp's and John Frederick's qualifications for the title "Magnanimous" would be suggested two decades later when they were both imprisoned simultaneously, isolated from each other. They would suffer five and a half years of captivity and still remain steadfast in their Lutheran/Protestant faith.

Philipp turned twenty-six in November 1530. People in the sixteenth century were given adult responsibility early, and by our standards, they aged quickly. If they lived to sixty, they were considered elderly, and they often died two or three years later. Martin Luther and Philipp of Hesse both died in their sixty-third year. In 1530, Philipp was entering the prime of his life. The 1530s would be his most heroic decade. It will take four chapters to tell the story of the heroic Philipp of Hesse in the 1530s.

There are at least three things that Philipp did simultaneously and well in the 1530s: his leadership of Protestant expansion, his care of his family and homeland, and his treatment of subjects who disobeyed the law by separating from the worship of the Lutheran Church of Hesse. Philipp was not a democratic ruler. He governed subjects, not independent citizens. Still, Philipp ruled with vigor, patient care, and remarkable understanding.

Philipp left the Diet of Augsburg on August 6, 1530, soon after the Catholic response to Melanchthon's Confession, called the *Confutation*, was read at the diet. He found the attitude of the emperor disappointing, and he felt justifiable pride standing strong with the Protestant princes and imperial cities. They had listened intently while Melanchthon's Confession was read by the two Saxon chancellors, Gregor Brück and Christian Beyer. Brück read the Confession in Latin, which all present, including the emperor and Philipp, understood. Then Christian Beyer read it in German in a voice loud and clear for many gathered outside to hear.

Philipp left, frustrated by the uncompromising attitudes of the emperor, the Catholic princes, and the leaders from Catholic imperial cities. He knew he was being called a heretic, for the emperor had given just six months for all Protestants to recant or face his wrath according to the terms he had laid down against Luther in the Edict of Worms nine years earlier. Philipp was prepared to share Luther's fate, and if it came to martyrdom, he prayed, as he had written to his mother in 1525, that he would do it well.

Charles V now was free to move against the Protestants, having signed a peace treaty with both the pope and the king of France. The news of the emperor's wrath traveled quickly to Wittenberg and distressed Luther. Now faithful followers like Philipp would share his fate. Protestantism was no longer his solo performance. Now a new confession of faith had been proclaimed, and with it a new community of faith had come to life. Since then, this day of the emperor's unfettered wrath, June 25, 1530, has been called the birthday of the Lutheran Church.

PHILIPP FORMS THE SCHMALKALD[81] LEAGUE

Philipp knew he needed to act quickly, and he sought Protestant colleagues, suggesting they form an aggressive new league. It would be defensive when attacked; but as the emperor's mistreated but still loyal subjects, the league would be devoted to preserving the peace and protecting the empire from the Ottomans while expanding Protestantism.

When it came to seeking allies, Philipp had no peer. In 1525, following the Peasants' War, he had met with Elector John of Saxony to form what would become the defensive League of Torgau. Four years later, Philipp convinced Martin Luther and Ulrich Zwingli to meet as his guests in Marburg, hoping to resolve their different positions on the Sacrament. This had turned out to be an impossible but still most worthy effort on Philipp's part.

Now, Philipp wasted no time. In November, once the recess of the diet threatening all Protestants was published, he signed an agreement with Elector John in the Thuringian village of Schmalkald. In February the next year, two northern princes, three northern cities, and seven southern cities added their signatures to the agreement, and the Schmalkald League was formed.

At the Diet of Augsburg, the emperor had made it clear that his brother, Archduke Ferdinand, should be his successor and the electors should bestow on him the title "King of the Germans," designating him as Charles's successor should he die first. Though the emperor's will was bravely resisted by Elector John's twenty-eight-year-old son, Duke John Frederick, the electors agreed to obey Charles's request. On January 5, 1531, they met to elect Ferdinand as their king.

Now the peace was broken once again by the Ottomans. King Ferdinand was occupied defending his lands. The Schmalkald League would play an important role in keeping the peace and supporting Ferdinand militarily for the next nine years. The Protestants had taken their stand. The emperor's threats had proved powerless. The Schmalkald League would survive to serve both the empire and the Reformation for a total of sixteen years.

This was possible because the Schmalkald League was something new. Previous attempts at mutual defense had been limited in scope. Even the Swabian League had included only the princes and the cities of southern Germany. The Schmalkald League would grow to reflect the empire itself in its geographical outreach. Its influence would extend from Strassburg in the west to Pomerania in the east and from Konstanz in the south to Bremen in the north. The Schmalkald League also had its own unique purpose. It was religious in scope. It was the first league established for the defense of the Protestant faith.

Still, the league had no written constitution until one was signed at Schmalkald on December 23, 1535. Even that constitution was superseded the following year. From 1535 on, the league was organized into two circles. The northern circle was led by Elector John, and Philipp led the southern circle. Operational command of the league's forces alternated annually between the landgrave and the elector. Duke Ernst of Braunschweig-Lüneburg (1497–1546) was delegated to make decisions in matters involving war.

Elector John died on August 10, 1532. His son, twenty-nine-year-old John Frederick, inherited his father's role as co-leader of the league with Philipp.

John Frederick was five months older than Philipp. For the first time the land-grave enjoyed the support of a Saxon elector from Philipp's own generation.

John Frederick, however, was no warrior. Philipp would write of him later, "He is not inclined to war. He will gladly help as best he can with words, but he cannot be brought to follow them with deeds."[82]

The Religious Peace of Nürnberg, also called the Standstill, was worked out in 1532. As the recess of Speyer I had allowed the Reformation to grow in peace from 1526 to 1529, so the Peace of Nürnberg now helped make it possible for the Schmalkald League to grow in peace and political strength until the outbreak of the Schmalkald War fifteen years later.

PHILIPP'S RESTORATION OF WÜRTTEMBERG

As early as 1519, Philipp had begun to dream of restoring Württemberg to its rightful ruler, his cousin, Duke Ulrich (1487–1550). When he became Lutheran, he realized that if he could fulfill that dream, the two of them, working together, would be able to extend the Reformation south to the northern border of Switzerland.

Ulrich was Philipp's cousin once removed and would adopt the Protestant faith during the eight years he spent as Philipp's guest. Early in his rule, Ulrich had shown promise as a military leader. When he was eleven, his uncle, Eberhard II, the ruling Duke of Württemberg, died, leaving Ulrich as the presumptive heir to the throne. Eberhard was the brother of Philipp's paternal grandmother, Mechtild. Ulrich was declared of age to rule in 1503, one year before Philipp's birth. He became a strong military supporter of Emperor Maximilian I.

In 1504, the year of Philipp's birth, Ulrich served with Philipp's father, Wilhelm II, supporting the emperor in the War of the Succession of Landshut. Later he also accompanied Maximilian on his attack on Rome in 1508,[83] and still five years later he marched into France with the imperial army.

However, by 1513, Ulrich had lost the support of his Württemberg subjects due to his extravagant lifestyle and repressive methods of taxation. In 1514, he put down a rebellion by the "Poor Conrad" peasants' leagues only by making important concessions to the estates in return for their financial aid. By then he had lost the support and good favor of the still-powerful Swabian League.

Ulrich married Sabina of Bavaria (1492–1564), a niece of the emperor. Their marriage was unhappy due to Ulrich's abusive behavior. One child, Christoph, was born to their union. Years later, upon his father's death in 1550, Christoph would become the ruler of Württemberg and an influential political leader of the Reformation.

Ulrich's wandering eye fell upon the wife of Hans von Hutten (1477–1515). Hans was a cousin of the famous writer Ulrich von Hutten. Duke Ulrich murdered Hans in 1515 during a heated altercation.

Ulrich von Hutten knew that the pen is mightier than the sword. He defended his kinsman's honor, mounting an effective writing campaign that undermined whatever support Duke Ulrich still enjoyed. In spite of his earlier military support of the emperor, Duke Ulrich fell twice under the imperial ban. Upon Maximilian's death in January 1519, the Swabian League deposed Ulrich and ceded his duchy to the newly elected nineteen-year-old Emperor Charles V.

Ulrich's activities for the next seven years remain a mystery. At Speyer I in 1526, Philipp met Ulrich and took him into his castle in Marburg, where he remained a guest for the next eight years, appearing at the Marburg Colloquy with Philipp.

Philipp did not ask for the support of the Schmalkald League when he planned his restoration of Württemberg to Duke Ulrich. It appears that, remembering the Pack Affair six years earlier, he felt the members of the league still might not trust him and would refuse to lend him their aid. John Fredrick urged Philipp not to attack.

Württemberg was ruled by the emperor's brother, King Ferdinand of Austria. If the land were recovered for Ulrich, Württemberg would enjoy an important role located as a buffer for Protestant growth between Saxony to the north and Switzerland to the south. As long as the area had been Catholic, it served Ferdinand well as his corridor to France to support the emperor in his wars against the French king.

Only one member of the Schmalkald League supported Philipp's plan and played an important role in the expansion of Protestantism in Württemberg. That was Jakob Sturm (1489–1553), the mayor of Strassburg. Sturm was born to a Strassburg family of political leaders and was educated and ordained for the priesthood. Forsaking the religious life, Sturm chose to take up the Sturm family business, political leadership.

During the Peasants' War of 1525, Sturm represented Strassburg as an envoy. At Frankenhausen, he witnessed the slaughter of the rebellious peasants. His reports brought him recognition in Strassburg. He became better known in 1526 at Speyer I. There he became a follower of Martin Luther and, together with Martin Bucer, played the challenging role of attempting to reconcile the Zwinglians and the Lutherans in Strassburg.

Sturm convinced the Strassburg city council to underwrite 10 percent of Philipp's expenses for his restoration of Württemberg. Francis I, the French king, saw the advantage of the area being taken from Ferdinand, and he willingly agreed to underwrite another major portion of Philipp's expenses.

Philipp's timing was perfect. To everyone's surprise, perhaps even his own, Philipp's attack prevailed with little or no bloodshed. The once-powerful Swabian League, which normally would have come to Ferdinand's aid, had collapsed. Ferdinand was not able to adequately fund his troops in Württemberg. His resources were devoted to the defense of Hungary, threatened once again by the Ottomans.

Philipp prevailed on December 27–28, 1533. Württemberg was ceded to Ulrich by the Treaty of Kaaden signed six months later, in June 1534. Ferdinand approved the treaty on the condition that Ulrich would swear fealty to the empire, which he did. The treaty covered those who adopted the Augsburg Confession, but not "Sacramentarians," namely, the Zwinglians and Anabaptists.

WÜRTTEMBERG TURNS LUTHERAN

Ulrich by now was a much wiser man than he had been fifteen years earlier. He devoted the remaining sixteen years of his life and rule to the expansion of Protestantism in Württemberg. The deaths of both Zwingli and Oecolampadius three years earlier had left a temporary vacuum of theological leadership in Switzerland. Henry Bullinger, Zwingli's successor in Zurich, was an effective leader, but in these these crucial years he was only one man replacing Zwingli and Oecolampadius. Twenty-five-year-old John Calvin published his first work, *Pschopanacea*, in 1534, but he had not yet risen to powerful leadership in Geneva. Still, Zwinglians were crossing the Swiss border to enter Württemberg and settle in some of its major cities. Philipp decided to adopt a policy of mediation between the Protestants and the Zwinglians. Ulrich bowed to his wishes.

To do this, Ulrich appointed two theologians, the Zwinglian Ambrosius Blarer of Konstanz (1492–1564) and the Protestant Erhard Schnepf, Philipp's Lutheran professor of theology in Marburg (1495–1558). Ulrich commissioned them to work out a compromise position for Württemberg.

The two theologians ignored the terms of the Treaty of Kaaden that rejected Zwinglianism. They patched together a compromise position on the Sacrament that became known as the Stuttgart Concord. Then they attempted to replace any clergy who refused to teach according to their Concord.

John Brentz, a devoted Lutheran reformer at St. Mark's in Schwäbisch Hall, was a prodigious writer of published works promoting Protestant reform in Württemberg. Brentz had been present to support Luther at the Marburg Colloquy and now played an important role in keeping Württemberg in Luther's fold.

Ulrich turned to Brentz for assistance. Brentz's catechism was added to the Württemberg Church Order of 1536. In the following year, he reorganized the University of Tübingen according to Protestant principles.

In 1538, Duke Ulrich was accepted into membership in the Schmalkald League. That same year, Blarer, the Zwinglian, resigned from Ulrich's service. Now the major remaining evidence of Zwingli's influence in Württemberg was a simplicity of church ceremonies and decor in contrast to the high church style favored at the time in Wittenberg.

THE WITTENBERG CONCORD

By this time, Philipp's leadership of the Schmalkald League and Ulrich's cultivation of Protestantism in Württemberg were well known in Wittenberg. This opened the door for the Wittenberg Concord, a remarkable new development that was totally dependent upon the aging Luther's approval and, in the eyes of many, was a feather in his cap.

Martin Brecht, Luther's biographer, has written of the concord, "The most significant development in the Evangelical camp during these years was the consummation of an agreement on the Lord's Supper between the southern German cities and Luther."[84]

At the time, Luther was gravely ill, certain he might die soon. He resolved that in whatever time he had left, he would do all in his power to leave his Reformation united.

Luther had good reason to feel his prospects for concord were bleak. The imperial city of Frankfurt near the southern tip of Hesse was also near Württemberg. As part of southern Germany, it was part of Philipp's Schmalkald League responsibility. At the end of 1532, Johann Cellarius (1496–1542), the Lutheran preacher in Frankfurt, had been dismissed. This alarmed Luther. Early the following year he wrote an open letter declaring that the remaining preachers of Frankfurt were not faithful to his teaching.[85]

The issue was, as it had been in Marburg, radically different interpretations of the Lord's Supper. Word of the Lutheran pastor Cellarius's dismissal led Luther to suspect that some preachers in Frankfurt were only pretending to accept the objective presence of Christ in the Supper, meaning that He is received in the Sacrament regardless of the recipient's faith or lack of faith. Luther suspected they taught that Christ is present only for believers. This, he proclaimed, was a devilish trick, concealing their commitment to Zwingli's commemorative view of the Sacrament.

In Wittenberg, Luther's genuine commitment to concord became evident in the way he handled an overture from the Bohemian Brethren. In the 1520s, he had parted company with them. In 1531, the Bohemians contacted him again, asking to renew their discussion. The following year, they presented him with a new confession, which they called *An Account of the Faith*.

Luther felt this confession still contained Zwinglian overtones. They submitted another confession at the beginning of 1535. Luther accepted it. He was, in fact, so pleased with it that he provided his own preface to indicate how, although they used different words, he was convinced the Bohemians agreed with his interpretation of the Sacrament. Reflecting his concern that death was not far off, Luther added, "One has to be patient until finally we are able to praise Christ identically and unanimously with one and same word and mouth."[86]

That was Luther's happy frame of mind when pondering concord with the Württemberg Protestants. Melanchthon had started the negotiations and Luther now felt motivated to support his younger colleague's efforts. Philipp of Hesse's involvement was political, not theological. Still, as the leader of the southern circle of the Schmalkald League, he was hospitable and deeply involved, even as he had been five years earlier at the Marburg Colloquy.

Luther had previously given little or no evidence that he might be open to the possibility of concord with the Protestants of Württemberg. He still distrusted Martin Bucer, the pastor of Strassburg, though Melanchthon had expressed approval of Bucer's efforts as early as March 1533. On September 1, 1534, Melanchthon offered to work with Bucer and proposed a discussion. When Melanchthon informed Luther of his desire, Luther replied that he was not unwilling.

Melanchthon shared this news with Philipp and asked for his support. On September 25, 1534, the landgrave wrote Luther asking him to support a concord. He believed the theological developments were promising and the

provisions of the Treaty of Kaaden made this concord politically necessary for
southern Germans. Then Philipp organized a meeting between Melanchthon
and Bucer and scheduled it for soon after Christmas in Kassel. Luther declared
on October 17 that he was prepared, for political reasons, to do whatever was
compatible with his conscience. [87]

The Kassel discussions took place in January 1535, seven months after
the Treaty of Kaaden was signed. Regarding the Sacrament, they settled on
a phrase that became known as "the Kassel Formulation": "With the bread
the body of Christ is essentially and truly received." The Augsburg clergy had
already agreed to this formulation, and Bucer was confident that because of
their support, the southern Germans would fall into line and accept it. Melanchthon was also confident that Luther would accept this formula. The
Kassel Formulation was considered preferable by far to Bucer's formulation in
the *Tetrapolitana*. There in 1530, Bucer had written, "Disciples of Christ partake
of his body and blood in a spiritual sense only."[88]

In the following month, Philipp wrote to Luther telling him he hoped he
would accept the Kassel Formulation. At the end of January, Luther referred to
the Augsburg Confession and Apology that stated that the body of Christ was
given and eaten. The reformer stated he could find no fault with the Kassel
Formulation as long as their heart was in it. "On February 3, 1535, Melanchthon could inform Bucer that Luther had a more charitable and affectionate
opinion of Bucer and his colleagues than before."[89]

Still, Luther advised caution when presenting the formula in southern
Germany. He wished to avoid their suspicion and advised that time and shared
positive experiences would go far toward overcoming their suspicion. Further
negotiations might still be needed to calm the troubled waters.

The city of Augsburg's clear change of attitude toward Luther provided a
breakthrough for concord with southern Germany. They sent to Luther a confession of faith that agreed with the Kassel Formulation. Luther was pleased.
It was said he shed tears of joy. Now his suspicions of duplicity on the part of
Augsburg and the cities of the south had been removed. Now Luther could die
in peace and leave a peaceful church behind him. Still, two of his supporters,
Amsdorf and Brentz, were not convinced.

The Wittenberg Concord was published in the major cities of southern
Germany. Bucer met with John Brentz in Stuttgart to discuss difficult points.
Their discussion included *manducatio impiorum*, the physical eating of Christ's
body, with the body of Christ being consumed by the unworthy as well as the

worthy. This posed problems for the southern cities. Bucer convinced Brentz to support the concord. By September 28, 1535, Luther reported to Elector John Frederick that the cities of the south were more favorable toward the concord than expected.

On October 5, Luther wrote to the clergy of Strassburg, Ulm, Esslingen, and Augsburg. He suggested the theologians meet in Saxony, but he did not propose a specific date for this meeting. About the same time, responding to a request from the city of Strassburg and not wishing to hinder the acceptance of the concord, Luther deleted his sarcastic references to the Sacramentarians from his collection of sermons that was about to be published. [90]

As 1535 drew near its close, Luther suggested to the clergy of Strassburg that the date for signing the concord should be set for soon after Easter the following year. On January 25, 1536, he wrote to Elector John Frederick that he should not invite "nervous geniuses" who could ruin the undertaking. Luther suggested Eisenach as the place of meeting. Though he was not a wealthy man, Luther offered to cover the expenses himself. [91]

On the first of February, Bucer met with Swiss theologians in Basel. The Swiss prepared their own confession that became known as the *First Helvetic Confession*. In it they stated they could not tolerate Bucer's esteem for Luther and preferred to remain faithful to Zwingli and Oecolampadius, who had died five years earlier.

Then, on March 25, Luther wrote to Bucer suggesting May 14 as the date for their meeting in Eisenach. He asked Bucer to share this news with the southern Germans, the Swiss, and especially the Protestants Brentz and Schnepf.

On May 1, the Swiss declined Luther's invitation, claiming the distance for them was too great. Most likely they feared that Luther would dominate the discussion. Melanchthon let Philipp know that some of the invited guests might foment more disunity than arouse improvement. He favored canceling the meeting.

By early May, Luther's health had deteriorated to the point that the meeting was postponed until May 21. The location was changed then to Wittenberg. Luther expressed fear that he now had little hope for the concord.

Still, the concord was signed, on May 29, 1536. Brecht describes the concord with these words: "In the sacrament there were two things, an earthly and a heavenly. With the bread and wine the body and blood of Christ were truly and substantially present and were tendered and received. There was no transubstantiation of Christ's body and blood. The bread was identified with the body of Christ by virtue of the sacramental union, and the body was present with the tendering of the bread, although not outside the eating. The unworthy receive Christ's body and blood, but because they receive it without true repentance and faith and thus abuse its intent, it works judgment upon them."[92]

THE SMALCALD ARTICLES[93]

Meanwhile, another event took place that was of importance to Philipp and the expansion of Protestantism: Luther's composition of his Smalcald Articles. In June 1536, Pope Paul III (1468–1549) called for a general council to meet the following year in Mantua, a city in northern Italy. The papal summons would be ignored by German Protestant princes. The pope, who feared a council, delayed it until 1545.

In 1537, Elector John Frederick felt it would be useful to have the aging Luther write another theological statement as his last will and testament. Luther agreed and on December 11, 1536, John Frederick commissioned him to assemble a group of theologians to assist him in writing this document: Nicholas Amsdorf (1483–1565), John Agricola (1494–1566), George Spalatin (1484–1545), and his Wittenberg colleagues Philip Melanchthon, Justus Jonas (1493–1555), Caspar Cruciger the Elder (1504–48), and John Bugenhagen (1485–1558). They met in Luther's ample home and assisted in writing what came to be known as the Smalcald Articles.

In February 1537, Luther's articles were read at a meeting of the Schmalkald League. That meeting was chaired by John Frederick. This was not Philipp's year to be in charge of the meeting. Still, he was present. Within seven years, Hesse would adopt the articles as an authoritative confessional statement.

Meanwhile, how were Philipp and his domestic administrators handling important matters in Hesse? The next chapter will address that question.

Chapter 10

HEROIC ACT TWO
Philipp's Care for His Family

On the home front, Philipp shared his growing reputation with those close to him whose opinions he valued highly. They included, but were not limited to, his chancellor, John Feige (1482–1543); his court preacher and superintendent, Adam Krafft (1493–1558); and his wife, Christine (1505–49), whose long-suffering virtues qualified her, too, as heroic.

Child mortality in the sixteenth century was extremely high, even among the nobility. Christine was the only child of ten who outlived her parents, Duke George and Duchess Barbara of Albertine Saxony. As it turned out, Christine was successful in delivering a total of ten children, born over a twenty-year period, from 1527 to 1547. Only one, Philipp, died early. The remaining nine outlived Christine. Eight outlived their father.

Agnes was the first to be born. She was three years old in November 1530 when her sister Anna was born. Five more children would be born in that decade. Wilhelm was born in 1532, Philipp died in his first year in 1537, Barbara entered this world in 1536, and Ludwig appeared in 1537, followed by Elizabeth in 1539.

By the end of the 1530s, Philipp and Christine had been blessed with six surviving children all under the age of twelve. Though the castle was large and domestic help no problem, home life in this large household must have been challenging to say the least.

Philipp and Christine proved to be excellent, loving parents. Years later, the children would support their father through Philipp's five years of humiliation and captivity under Emperor Charles V.

JOHN FEIGE AND ECONOMIC REFORM

Philipp entrusted with authority the counselors he depended upon. As a sixteen-year-old lad at the Diet of Worms in 1521, Philipp surrounded himself with wise counselors who some called his "beards." Philipp's chancellor, John Feige, was their leader. He had been the chancellor of Hesse since 1514, when Philipp's mother took over the guardianship of her children and the regency of the land. He would continue to serve in that high office until 1542 and he died the following year. Feige had been a fellow student with Martin Luther at the University of Erfurt. He became an important lay leader of the Protestant Reformation in Hesse. He also reformed the Hessian economy.

At the Synod of Homberg on the Efze River in 1526, Nikolaus Ferber Herborn, the guardian of the Franciscan monastery in Marburg, believed Philipp was strongly influenced by counselors who held Lutheran sympathies, especially John Feige. This no doubt was true, for the highest level of the Hessian bureaucracy of the day was dominated by burghers, that is, city and town leaders. According to the historian William J. Wright, "One finds what amounts to a cozy group of about twenty-five families. More than 70 percent of these families were related by marriage and tended to be personally connected through Johann Feige, Philipp's great chancellor."[94]

As we might expect, Philipp was ultimately responsible for all of his domestic problems, among them, control of the Hessian economy. He delegated this and other problems to the chancellor, and Feige's solution vindicated Philipp's confidence in him. The economic problem arose from the double standard of gold and silver in the world economy of the sixteenth century. The relative values of Hessian coins, the gulden, the albus, and the heller, had been set in a treaty of 1509 at about the time of Philipp's father's death. The gulden (made of gold) was used mostly in international trade. The albus (silver) and the heller (copper) were used by the common people in daily commerce. It had been declared in 1509 that there would be 26 albuses to one gulden and 12 hellers to one albus.

The price of silver changed little during Philipp's reign and did not become a problem until after his death in 1567. The change at that time was likely due to the mining at Potosi, the mountain of silver in South America. The problem for Philipp and Feige was the valuation of Hessian gold. The price of gold fluctuated with the world market influenced by the influx of gold from Mexico since the 1520s, among other developments, like transoceanic trade with far-off areas of the world. If the price of gold were fixed in Hesse while it rose elsewhere, speculators in Frankfurt would have bought up all the Hessian gold at bargain rates, leaving Hessians with no currency to use in their international trade.

Feige recognized this problem. He wrote an advisory note in 1527 explaining how useless it would be to attempt to control the value of gold coins in

Hesse. He indicated that one must be satisfied with regulating the value of silver at 26 albuses per gulden and 12 hellers per albus. He would allow the gulden to float with the international value of gold. Feige's solution turned out to be essentially the same standard adopted by the treaty of 1509.

ADAM KRAFFT, VISITOR/SUPERINTENDENT

Adam Krafft was active at the Synod of Homberg in 1526, summarizing in German Lambert's Latin address as Philipp's court preacher/practical theologian. He was born to Hans Krafft, a burgomeister (mayor) at Fulda, a town located near the eastern border of Hesse. Fulda is also the burial place of St. Boniface, whose story has been told briefly in chapter 2. Krafft earned the bachelor of arts degree from Erfurt University in 1514 and master of arts in 1519. That same year, in July, he attended the Leipzig Debate and became a devoted follower of Martin Luther.

During the Peasants' War in 1525, Krafft met Philipp, who appointed him to be his court preacher. His important role at the Synod of Homberg in October of the following year has been told in chapter 6. Soon after that meeting, Philipp appointed Krafft to be his "visitor" of the parishes in Hesse, a title that would be changed to "superintendent" in the 1530s. With these two important roles, court preacher and visitor/superintendent, Krafft became the major force administering the reformation of Hesse. His duties included the establishment and restructuring of schools, common chests for the relief of the poor, and support of the hospitals.[95] In 1527, Philipp also appointed Krafft to be a professor of theology in his newly created University of Marburg.

Adam Krafft, the practical theologian, and Franz Lambert of Avignon, the systematic theologian, were the two most important leaders of Lutheran theological reform employed by Philipp for the first five years of his Lutheran reform of Hesse. Lambert died in the plague of 1531, and Krafft assumed full theological leadership, adapting well to Philipp's growing reliance upon Martin Bucer, the theologian of Strassburg.

PHILIPP'S CARE FOR THE POOR AND INFIRM

The primary responsibility Philipp outlined for Krafft and the other visitors was to inspect and improve the care of the poor, the sick, and the children of the Hessian parishes. In later years, church discipline would be added to this list, due to the threat of the Anabaptist movement in Hesse and through Martin Bucer's influence.

In his last letter to his mother, Anna, in 1525, Philipp insisted that the wealth being confiscated from the monasteries was not for his own use but was to be used to care for the poor. In an order issued in 1532, Philipp confirmed this intent, stating that by using the wealth confiscated from the monasteries, he had established and endowed hospitals and poor chests for the good of the poor and sick orphans and widows of Hesse. Krafft worked in close harmony with another superintendent named Heinz von Lueder. Philipp ordered the two of them "to inspect each and every hospital and alms chest, get information about them . . . and thus equipped, to give order and measure to the same."[96]

According to Wright, "The superintendents were the central agents in charge of supervising the hospitals, as they were the watch-dogs of so many other projects of the Landgrave . . . for example, they helped in the nitty-gritty of preparing exemplary menus for the hospital poor."[97] Later, Wright adds more specifics: "If meat or fish was not available, then another vegetable should be substituted. Lueder and Krafft, however, were more realistic. They recommended meat three times a week."[98]

We conclude this section with another statement by Wright: "The point must be clearly drawn that the welfare system was successfully rationalized and personalized only because of the energetic supervision of the princely visitors, especially Adam Krafft and Heinz Lueder."[99]

PHILIPP'S ADMINISTRATION OF EDUCATION

Martin Luther wrote in his treatise *To the Christian Nobility of the German Nation* in 1520, "We handle these poor young people who are committed to us for training and education in the wrong way. . . . today the young people of Christendom languish and perish miserably in our midst for want of the gospel, in which we ought to be giving them constant instruction and training."[100]

Three years later, in *To the Councilmen of All Cities in Germany That They Establish and Maintain Christian Schools*, Luther published words that reveal the depth of his feeling on the matter. His words are all the more impressive when we remember John Feige's valuation of the coinage of Hesse, especially the gulden: "Even if only a single boy could thereby be trained to become a real Christian, we ought properly to give a hundred gulden to this cause. . . . For one real Christian is better and can do more good than all the people on earth."[101]

Then, in 1528, Philipp Melanchthon published, with Luther's approval, *Instructions for the Visitors of Parish Pastors in Electoral Saxony.* In it Melanchthon gives detailed instructions for the training of children. He states, "Because it is God's will then, parents should send their children to school and prepare them for the service of others."[102]

In the first statute of the University of Marburg, published on August 31, 1529, Philipp, age 25, agreed with the educational concerns of Martin Luther and Melanchthon. In some of his most eloquent words I have found, he wrote, "We have established a university with all studies, and thus a three language institution at Marburg. . . . Out of it shall go forth men 'full of wise counsel' as Homer called his heroes, not a few of whom shall distinguish themselves by their learning as well as their discretion and piety, that they may become administrators, part in the Christian Church, part in the direction of the state system. Indeed, the learned subjects can as little be set [aside] as the sun may disappear out of the great world. Without them no society, man, or manner of life can exist. And correct is he who calls the state fortunate in which philosophers rule and kings begin to philosophise."[103]

Luther had written that the education of the young was to prepare children for service to others. Philipp knew that society had been changing since the introduction of Roman law during the reign of his father. Family ties under the feudal system were being replaced by the penal system of the state judiciary. The growth of foreign trade was introducing a growing gap between the rich and the poor.

In the summary document of the Diet of Homberg of 1526, called the *Reformatio*, all the towns and cities of Hesse were called upon to establish schools for boys to prepare them for entrance to the University of Marburg, soon to be established. In these schools, the boys were to be taught elementary Latin, reading, and writing.

Girls also were to be in school. They were to learn to read, but only in German.[104] They were taught religion and skills such as punctuality and industry to qualify them to be good wives and mothers. Luther was among the earliest to recommend schooling for girls. Philipp followed his advice.

While Philipp was involved in the expansion of the Reformation and his care for domestic concerns in Hesse, the spread of Anabaptism loomed as a threat to his rule. The story of how Philipp handled this threat will be told in the next two chapters.

Chapter 11

HEROIC ACT THREE
The Anabaptist Revolution in Nearby Münster

By the mid-1530s, Philipp was confronted with a threatening development not far from his northern border. Anabaptists had taken over the city of
Münster, 124 miles (200 km) northwest of Kassel.[105]

This was not a tolerant age. Two and a half centuries would pass before the
religious liberty we enjoy today would be enshrined in our constitution. To
be an Anabaptist in 1530 was to be branded by the Church and the empire as
seditious, meaning undermining the unity of the state under one church, be
that Catholic or Protestant. To tolerate more than one church in one land was
unthinkable even for a prince as tolerant as Philipp of Hesse.

The Anabaptists of the sixteenth century renounced all state privileges.
They preferred to be known as "the Brethren" and rejected the name "Anabaptists" (literally "again baptizers"). "Believer's baptism" was their name for
the baptism of adults, the only baptism they claimed to have found in the New
Testament. Neither Catholics nor Protestants agreed with the Anabaptist use
of Scripture. The members of the Brethren were soon branded as Anabaptist
heretics. To be baptized again was seen by both Catholics and Protestants as
denying the efficacy of infant Baptism, a crime worthy of death.

PHILIPP IS INFLUENCED BY
THE PARABLE OF THE TARES

Thanks to the still-youthful forty-three-year-old Martin Luther, in 1526
a hint of tolerance was in the air when Philipp introduced the Reformation
in Hesse. One year earlier, Luther had preached on the Fifth Sunday after
Epiphany and published his sermon on Jesus' parable of the tares recorded
in Matthew 13. In that sermon he wrote, "Therefore this passage should in
all reason terrify the grand inquisitors and murderers of the people, where

they are not brazened faced, even if they have to deal with true heretics. But at present they burn the true saints and are themselves heretics. What is that but uprooting wheat, and pretending to exterminate the tares, like insane people?"[106] Philipp either read that sermon or was informed of its contents by his advisers. In a letter he wrote in September 1526, quoted in my translation in chapter 6, he asked Luther to clarify his understanding of the parable of the tares.

Jesus' parable of the wheat and the tares had served as a proof text for tolerance from the time of Pope Calixtus (c. AD 217). This interpretation was based on the words "Let them both grow together until the harvest." By the time of Augustine of Hippo, early in the fifth century, intolerance of religious dissent found its own biblical ground in the parable of the wedding feast of Luke 14. There the king tells his servants in verse 23 to go to the main roads and "*compel people to come in*" (emphasis added).

At Speyer II in 1529, the Code of Justinian was invoked by Emperor Charles V, making Anabaptism a crime of sedition punishable by death. Two years later, the theological faculty of Wittenberg University confirmed this decision. This was not a tolerant age. In the prevailing thought, including that of Luther and Melanchthon, the magnanimity of a prince and his tolerance of dissent needed to be counterbalanced by his concern for the political and religious unity of his people. Hell was very real to those people. Virtually all Christian leaders felt called to wrest unwary sinners from the gaping jaws of hell, using whatever means was at their disposal, including torture and the death sentence.

Luther in 1525 could be intolerant when attacking the teaching of Carlstadt and Zwingli regarding the Sacraments, for he held that the preached Word and the Sacraments of Baptism and Holy Communion are God's Means of Grace. Anyone rejecting the Means of Grace was not to be tolerated, for they were ignoring God's promise of grace and forgiveness administered through these means. This was a source of great comfort to Luther and his followers and still is today.

On all other matters, such as the use of liturgical vestments, Luther could be tolerant, declaring that wearing them does no good, but not wearing them does no harm. As a result, Luther was accused by his opponents, especially the Zwinglians and Anabaptists, of being too tolerant himself. They must have thought they could have it both ways. Years later, in Eisleben just days before he died, Luther preached on the parable of the tares once again. This time we find not a hint of a tolerance for others.

It was Luther's early interpretation of the parable of the tares that captured Philipp's attention and supported his tolerant treatment of the Anabaptists in Hesse. Still, Philipp threatened his Anabaptists in his so-called Harsh Ordinance of 1537, reminding them that if they persisted, he might respond to the pressure of his friends and be compelled to execute them unless they returned to the Lutheran Church of Hesse. Still, as it turned out, Philipp only ordered their hearth fires to be put out, meaning he banished them from Hesse.

Philipp's Anabaptists and those of the recently appointed Prince-Bishop Franz von Waldeck (1491–1553) of Münster were of two very different camps. Philipp's Anabaptists were peaceful. Those of Münster were seditious, posing the threat to Philipp that their seditious teaching and practice might spread to his peaceful Anabaptists in Hesse.

This chapter treats Philipp's support of Prince-Bishop Franz von Waldeck. The following chapter will focus on Philipp's treatment of his own peaceful Anabaptists.

MELCHIOR HOFFMANN

Melchior Hoffmann (1495–1543) was a furrier with no theological training who lived in the region of Livonia on the east coast of the Baltic Sea. He was born in Schwäbisch Hall. In the early 1520s, he was attracted to Luther's teachings, and by 1523, he was traveling in Livonia as a lay preacher, supported by his furrier trade.

There Hoffmann was involved in controversy, and he moved on to Stockholm, Sweden, arriving there in 1526. Again he was involved in controversy and was forced to leave that city. He moved on to Lübeck and stayed there for a short time before moving to Denmark, where he curried the favor of King Frederick I and was appointed as a preacher in Kiel. There he developed his Zwinglian view of the Eucharist and was banished from the city for refusing to retract this position. He made his way to Strassburg, where supporters of Zwingli welcomed him. It was in Strassburg that Hoffmann was rebaptized in April 1530, and he contacted Carlstadt two years later.

Hoffmann became convinced that Jesus would return in 1533. He began preaching that to prepare for Christ's return, his followers should purge the ungodly from their midst—a revolutionary message that was recognized as seditious and punishable by death.

When Hoffmann's prophecy failed and Christ did not return, John Matthys of Haarlem (c. 1500–34) and John Beukelsz of Leiden (c. 1509–36) supported him, claiming he was wrong only in the time and place of Christ's return. Münster, they claimed, was the correct location.

George H. Williams gives this description of Münster in 1531: "Münster had a population of about fifteen thousand. It was the chief city of a large princely bishopric. It differed from nearby Cologne in the relatively greater political power of its craft and merchant guilds which were fully represented in the [two] councils of the city. This fact, and the fact that the prince-bishop resided out of touch beyond the walls of the city, made radical changes possible at any time."[107] Philipp felt that Münster was too close to Hesse for comfort. He would need to keep a close eye on developments there.

BERNHARD ROTHMANN

The preaching of Bernhard Rothmann (c. 1495–1535), a self-ordained Lutheran pastor with little or no theological education, brought further unrest to Münster. Rothmann was supported by Bernhard Knipperdolling (c. 1495–1536), the leader of the powerful guilds. The guilds secretly raised funds to send Rothmann to study in Wittenberg. He decided instead to use these funds to briefly tour Wittenberg and travel on to Strassburg, known for its resident theologians, most if not all of whom claimed to love Luther but were influenced by Zwingli. In Wittenberg, he struck up a friendship with Melanchthon. While Rothmann was on tour, Philipp was managing his colloquy between Luther and Zwingli in Marburg. During his tour, Rothmann was treated to a taste of Luther and a plateful of Zwingli.

In July 1531, at about the time Zwingli was killed in battle and Oecolampadius died, Rothmann returned to Münster. His preaching disrupted the city. The bishop removed him from the cathedral pulpit. Still, the guild members continued to support him. On January 23, 1532, Rothmann published his own creed of thirty articles. His interpretation of the Eucharist was decidedly Zwinglian.

One month later, on February 18, Rothman chose to preach his first openly Zwinglian sermon in the yard of St. Lambert's Church outside the cathedral square. The city had two town councils and when the bishop objected, they both stood firm, reminding the bishop that they were the ones who traditionally enjoyed the right to nominate pastors for all six parishes of the town. Following this tradition, the councils appointed Rothmann as the pastor of St. Lambert's.

On April 10, the guilds rebelled, driving the priests out of all the remaining Catholic parishes. In that same month, this rebellion was reinforced by the arrival of a number of preachers expelled from Wassenberg, near Cologne and southwest of Münster. By this time, only the cathedral and the monastic churches in Münster remained Catholic.

The newly arrived pastors joined Rothmann, publishing a notice of sixteen articles against the Catholic Church that were surprisingly Protestant and moderate in tone. They stressed the real presence of Christ in the Eucharist, denied the sacrifice of the Mass, promoted worship services in the language of the people, and retained infant Baptism. In August 1532, the councils authorized a reformation along these Protestant lines. At just this time, Bishop Franz von Waldeck decided he must stop this movement.

PHILIPP HELPS BISHOP FRANZ VON WALDECK

On December 26, the bishop's priests were celebrating in nearby Telgt. A thousand armed citizens of Münster attacked and took them into the city as hostages. The bishop responded by raising troops, and Landgrave Philipp sent some of his own, hoping to prevent more armed conflict. Philipp also appealed for peace on the basis of the recently completed Peace (aka Standstill) of Nürnberg. On February 14, 1533, a treaty was drawn up through the mediation of Landgrave Philipp of Hesse,[108] enabling an election to be held the following month, which supported the Rothmannites and the guilds. The stage was set for Rothmann's Zwinglian phase.

In May 1533, more Anabaptists from Wassenberg arrived to support Rothmann, who grew still more outspoken and radical in his preaching. That summer, he boldly celebrated his own version of the Lord's Supper outside St. Lambert's, using ordinary bread sprinkled with wine. Now the Rothmannite movement in Münster was divided. There were still some conservative Protestants there who appealed to Philipp and the Schmalkald League for support. They were refused support by the league. As a result, the Rothmannites grew rapidly in number and influence.

Hoping they might still stem the growing tide of Rothmann's radical support, the Catholics and conservative Protestants held a disputation on August 7–8. Here the Rothmannites were, for the first time, publicly called Anabaptist. By October, the city councils, attempting to remain neutral, were compelled by sympathizers to reinstate Rothmann and his followers.

Then, on November 8, Rothmann and the Wassenberg Anabaptists composed their confession condemning infant Baptism. This caused the Protestants to unite with Catholics against Rothmann. The councils ordered Rothmann and his followers to leave the city and used armed guards to enforce their edict. Rothmann's followers prepared to fight. The Catholics responded by ordering all who had helped Rothmann and his followers, including the Protestants, to leave the city.

In December, the Protestants refused to leave. At that time, some important private negotiations consolidated their forces and, for a time, controlled all the city churches. By now, however, the city contained so many revolutionary citizens, including some followers of Melchior Hoffmann, that Rothmann remained free to spread his rebellious message.

While this was taking place, on November 15, Landgrave Philipp sent two of his theologians from Marburg to meet with Rothmann. Unfortunately, the Hessian emissaries Philipp sent had been influenced by Zwinglianism. One made a futile attempt but was ridiculed. They soon found little difference between themselves and Rothmann and only fed Rothmann's revolutionary fire. Philipp had seriously erred in choosing his emissaries.

The members of the two city councils were convinced they would have no peace until they expelled Rothmann from the city. Still, Rothmann was supported by the guilds. He continued to preach openly and the people continued to support him. He was in nearly complete control of the city by January 1534. The Catholics had lost everything but the cathedral. One of the two Marburg theologians stayed on to preach for Rothmann in St. Lambert's.

Meanwhile, from prison in Holland, Melchior Hoffmann published an injunction to suspend rebaptism for two years. John Beukelsz of Leiden (1509–36, hereafter John of Leiden) persuaded John Matthys (c. 1500–34, hereafter Matthys) of Haarlem to challenge Hoffmann's injunction. Mathys resumed the practice of rebaptism and ordained pastors to recruit people for their New Covenant. Twenty-four-year-old John of Leiden was among the first ordained. Then they moved to Münster, their city of hope.

More disorderly elements from the Netherlands continued to flock into Münster. For almost a year, Rothmann had preached his idea of stewardship, claiming it was the duty of all Christians to use their possessions for the common good. The leader of the guilds, Bernhard Knipperdolling, supported the influx of radicals.

JOHN MATTHYS AND JOHN OF LEIDEN

Within eight days of his rebaptism, Rothmann and his helpers had rebaptized fourteen hundred citizens of Münster in the privacy of their homes. More Anabaptists continued to arrive from the Netherlands, including John Matthys and John of Leiden. They claimed the right of true believers to execute those who refused to accept rebaptism. Matthys informed Rothmann that the time had come for a clear break with the old way.

The two town councils tried to regain control. Bishop Franz von Waldeck gathered an army near the city walls and offered to come to the aid of the councils. The citizens rallied around Rothmann and a settlement was reached, allowing toleration for all. They now called Münster their "New Jerusalem."

Catholics and Protestants began to leave the city in droves. When a new election of town council members was held on February 23, Rothmann's supporter Bernhard Knipperdolling was elected as the city mayor. By this time, the city was ruled by Matthys, who announced that on February 25, citizens who refused to join the Anabaptists by refusing to be rebaptized would be killed. Knipperdolling convinced Matthys to extend that date to March 2. By that time, all the Protestants and Catholics had left. Hubert Ruescher, who dared to call Matthys a deceiver, was slain on the spot by Matthys himself.

Bishop Franz called upon neighboring Cologne, Cleves, and Hesse for help in besieging the city. They threw up earthworks to seal off the city from more arriving supporters. The citizens fortified the city from within. The entire population, including women, was enlisted. The men of military age were divided into units. The boys were taught to shoot.

In Amsterdam, on March 21, 1534, the first uprising of revolutionary Anabaptists, calling themselves "the Covenanters," failed. Matthys invited them to come to Münster quickly. He instructed them not to bring any baggage, for he felt there was plenty for all in the city.

Matthys ruled for only six weeks. Still, in that short time, he introduced his own socialistic form of government. He did this by announcing the confiscation of all property and collection of all privately owned money. Householders were allowed to use what had been theirs, but the doors of their houses had to be kept open day and night with only a small grating allowed to keep pigs and fowl out.

Matthys was killed on Easter Sunday, April 4, 1534. He believed God would help him against overwhelming odds when attacking the troops of the bishop. John of Leiden took full control in Münster. He dissolved the city council, which had been elected only two months earlier. He chose twelve men to be his elders, or judges of the Twelve Tribes of Israel. The code they published decreed that to resist John of Leiden meant to resist God's order. "Sins punishable by death included blasphemy, seditious language, scolding one's parents, disobeying one's master in a household, adultery, lewd conduct, backbiting, spreading scandal, and complaining."[109] John of Leiden published his own confession of faith and sent a copy to Philipp of Hesse.

POLYGAMY INTRODUCED

On May 25, after they had repelled the bishop's full-scale attempt to storm the town and while the people's confidence was running high, John of Leiden established polygamy, even though the council of twelve first opposed it. He announced that all who resisted were reprobates in danger of execution.[110]

John soon gathered a harem of sixteen compliant wives. One was not compliant enough to suit him. When she dared to criticize him, he beheaded her in the public square as an example to others. It took little effort to convince Rothmann that polygamy was attractive for him as well. He preached on biblical precedents for polygamy for three days in the marketplace. Rothmann soon collected his own harem of nine wives.

Williams describes John's methods for gaining the acceptance of polygamy in Münster: "All persons of marriageable age were ordered to marry. Unmarried women had to accept as husband the first man to ask them. This led to disorder in the competition to see who could gather the most wives, and the regulation was finally moderated to allow women to refuse unwelcome suitors."[111]

Not all citizens obeyed. Heinrich Mollenbecke refused. On July 29, he raised a group of citizens who captured and imprisoned John of Leiden. Other citizens freed him. Mollenbecke was captured with forty-eight of his supporters. All of them were tortured and killed. Soon no one dared to oppose John of Leiden on this or any other matter.

Meanwhile, in the summer of 1534, strange as it may seem, Charles V decided he would add the Bishopric of Münster to his hereditary lands. The emperor's emissaries negotiated with the bishop, who rejected Charles's plan. Then the emissaries turned to Rothmann for help, but nothing came of that.

On August 31, the citizens of Münster repelled another severe attack, which caused the bishop's army many casualties. This filled the people with still more confidence and gave John of Leiden the victory he needed. In this atmosphere, he had himself crowned "King of Righteousness Over All."

Bernhard Knipperdolling claimed that while John was king according to the flesh, he himself was called to be the spiritual king. This was the only time John of Leiden is known to have shown clemency. After a few days of imprisonment, Knipperdolling was restored to office as second in command. John of Leiden had ruled Münster for fourteen months, from April 4, 1534, to June 25, 1535.

PHILIPP AND THE BISHOP STORM MÜNSTER

Two men betrayed their king by leaving one of the town gates open for attack by the bishop and his troops. After a fearful battle, the city was taken by storm on June 25. Most of the citizens were slaughtered. The historian Harold Grimm wrote in 1954 that Philipp of Hesse was personally involved at the time, and "After this brutal reprisal, Catholicism was restored in Münster and vigorous action was taken against the Anabaptists everywhere."[112]

John of Leiden, Knipperdolling, and a third man named Krechting were captured. For months they were exhibited throughout northern Germany. Then, on July 22, 1536, they were condemned and tortured with red-hot tongs for all to watch in public. Afterward, their seared bodies were placed in iron cages and suspended from the tower of St. Lambert's Church. There, above the tower clock, their remains could be seen until they were removed and finally buried in 1881.

Meanwhile, Philipp was also dealing with the peaceful Anabaptists of his land. That story will be told in the following chapter.

Chapter 12

HEROIC ACT FOUR
Peaceful Hessian Anabaptists

MELCHIOR RINCK

While supporting Bishop Franz von Waldeck's defeat of the revolutionary Anabaptist kingdom in Münster, Philipp was also taking great care to make certain his own Anabaptists, including their early leader, Melchior Rinck, remained peaceful.

The exact birth date for Rinck[113] is unknown. His parents were Hessian peasants. He studied at the University of Leipzig and probably became a humanist, for he was called "the Greek." We next learn of him in 1523, serving as a chaplain in Hershfeld, a few miles from the eastern border of Hesse. Jacob Strauss (1480–1530) of Eisenach had secured this position for him. As mentioned in chapter 5, Strauss was considered by Wittenberg to be a radical preacher with Anabaptist sympathies, though he called himself Lutheran.

Apparently Rinck's preaching was thought controversial already in 1523. On December 29 that year, Philipp, still Catholic, wrote to the city council of Hershfeld advising them to arrest Rinck for preaching rebaptism, an act that had been declared punishable by death by the Code of Justinian in the early centuries of the Church. Rinck escaped to Eckhardtshausen in Thuringia, where he married the daughter of Hans Eckhardt. It must have been an unhappy marriage for he did not stay there long. They lived together only one year, and Rinck would later complain that she had married him under false pretenses.

We do not know how Rinck met Thomas Müntzer (1489–1525), the leader in the Peasants' War. He admitted later to Eberhard von der Thann (1495–1574) at the Wartburg that he not only fought in the rebellion, but he had also served as one of Müntzer's captains.

Nothing is known of Rinck from May 1525 to January 1527. At that time, he appeared in Landau, where he struck up a brief friendship with the Lutheran pastor Johannes Bader (c. 1487–1545). Sometime between January 9 and 20, Rinck met the Anabaptist leader Hans Denck (1495–1527), who was passing through Landau. Denck rebaptized Rinck on January 19. The next day Bader and Denck held a public disputation, which Rinck attended as an observer.

Bader published the proceedings of this disputation. Rinck wrote his own response, which he called his *Widerlegung*, "opposition." Soon after, he produced a second article, his *Vermahnung*, "warning." Both manuscripts have been preserved. While both were written by the same hand, the second reveals less care, appearing to have been written hastily and under pressure.

It is possible that Rinck was one of the two Brethren, the name preferred by Anabaptists, involved in a debate at Worms on Pentecost Sunday 1527. By the summer of 1528, he was back in Hershfeld. There he was summoned to meet with Landgrave Philipp in Friedewald, one of his hunting lodges. Philipp gave him his choice of recanting or defending his position in a public disputation in Marburg. Rinck chose the latter, and the disputation was held August 17–18 with Balthasar Raidt (c. 1494–1565), a Lutheran pastor in Marburg, serving as Rinck's opponent. Following that disputation, Rinck was banished to western Thuringia. There, in Schalkhausen, on November 1, he rebaptized the Lutheran pastor Hans Hechtlein (dates unknown). By March 10, 1529, he was back again in Hershfeld.

Elector John of Saxony noticed Rinck's activities in Hausbreitenbach, an area ruled jointly by himself and Philipp and called a "condominium" (from the Latin, meaning "a joint dominion"). The elector had been alarmed by the disastrous Peasants' War. Adding fuel to his fire, in December 1527 an Anabaptist conspiracy had been uncovered in Erfurt. From that time on the elector was determined to watch for further suspicious activities, not only by his Anabaptists but by Philipp's as well. He wrote to Eberhard von der Thann on April 4, 1529, urging him to arrest Rinck. On December 4, he admonished Philipp to do the same.

Rinck managed to escape to Hesse, where he was arrested and held captive in the secularized monastery of Haina in northwestern Hesse. In May 1531, he was released, banished for the second time, and told never to return. Soon after that, Philipp decreed that anyone who had sworn not to return and broke his oath would be arrested and imprisoned for life. Rinck was arrested in Hershfeld on the evening of November 11, 1531. Philipp held Rinck prisoner for the rest of his life. One letter survives that indicates that Rinck's treatment was not severe. He may have been visited by Martin Bucer in 1540, for his conditions were improved upon Bucer's recommendation.

GEORGE SCHNABEL

Lacking Rinck's leadership, only the Anabaptists near the eastern border of Hesse, where Rinck was now being held, were silenced. Another group was still active near Marburg under the leadership of George Schnabel and three comrades. George von Kolmatsch, a high official in Marburg, wrote to Philipp on October 28, 1533, telling him Anabaptists had been arrested in Allendorf on the Lahn River. His letter identified George Schnabel as the Anabaptist leader.

Schnabel had been raised Lutheran and served in the administration of Philipp's common chest for the relief of poor Hessians. There he rejected what he saw as the landgrave's heavy-handed method of collecting funds for the chest. He objected that such tactics were against the simplicity of brotherly care in the Bible. In the landgrave's hearing, Schnabel was recorded as saying that he did not consider Philipp's Protestant Church to be Christian. When told he was about to be expelled from Hesse, he replied that as long as the landgrave would not allow him to live according to his convictions, he would gladly leave the land.

During the Münster revolution, Philipp found that his Anabaptists shared little in common with the Münster radicals. In 1531, he had written to his sister, Elizabeth, that he found more faith and piety in his peaceful Anabaptists than in many of his Lutheran friends. Pressure from all sides grew for Philipp to use the death sentence against his Anabaptists. This pressure included the imperial mandate of 1529, neighboring Catholic princes, and Philipp's friend and the elector of Saxony after 1532, John Frederick (1503–54).

The years 1535–38 provided Philipp with circumstances favorable to his tolerant policy. The emperor was occupied with the renewal of his war with France and the pope. Disharmony among the Protestants had not yet become a serious distraction.

On May 18, 1536, Kolmatsch wrote to Philipp again. This time he informed the landgrave of the capture of an entire congregation of Anabaptists. Thirty of them had been found meeting in an abandoned forest church. Their four leaders, George Schnabel, Hermann Bastian, Peter Lose, and Leonhard Faelber, had been brought to Kolmatsch. The first three had been banished from Hesse earlier. Kolmatsch sent them to Marburg, where all but Bastian were immediately sent to prison. Bastian would follow them later. With the Anabaptist leaders in prison, how should Philipp now proceed?

In a document dated May 20, 1536, Marburg officials suggested that a new order should be composed saying Philipp should expel all obstinate

Anabaptists. Three days later, Philipp sent a request to Duke Ernst of Lüneburg, the magistrates and council of Strassburg, and the Wittenberg theologians. He described his situation, shared his personal convictions, and asked for their considered opinions after they had given the matter proper attention.

In June 1536, Kolmatsch wrote Philipp a third time. By then he was distressed by the numbers of Anabaptists being found. Philipp appointed a committee to look into the matter. The committee was made up of Kolmatsch, scholars from Marburg University, and the mayors and councilmen of major Hessian cities. The committee drew up articles with a long list of requirements for the Anabaptists. Rather than withdraw from their congregation, they were to help defend the land in battle when it was attacked, attend the Protestant church services in Hesse, and take their complaints to the proper authorities.

Philipp also solicited the advice of his Hessian theologians. Adam Krafft was the first to respond. He was in favor of coercion. He was convinced that Anabaptists should be punished for obstinate separation. He advised Philipp that Anabaptists from other lands should be sent home, and Hessian Anabaptists who refused to return to the Church should be imprisoned for life.

Replies to Philipp's request began to arrive from neighboring princes and theologians. The opinion of the Wittenberg theologians was dated June 5. They divided Anabaptist teaching into two categories, one concerning physical order resulting in sedition, and the other concerning spiritual matters resulting in false doctrine, blasphemy, and heresy. Both categories were to be punished by death.

Luther revealed a lingering reservation, writing above his signature that the Wittenberg decision was a general rule. He recognized that Philipp might act with discretion regarding punishment, taking into account the local circumstances.

The Lüneburg document stated that Philipp was obliged to follow the command "Compel them to come in" of Luke 14:23. The Tübingen faculty wrote that those who erred and influenced others to follow them should be punished "in body and life." The mayor and council of Ulm stated that they knew of no law denying a prince the right to kill a person because of his heretical faith. The clergy of Ulm told Philipp to instruct with the word and, if that failed, to punish with the sword. Only one reply, that from Strassburg, most likely written by Martin Bucer, encouraged Philipp to persevere in his tolerant treatment of his Anabaptists.

Early in August 1536, a diet was convened in Homberg on the Efze River. There, major attention was given to the Anabaptist issue. Philipp appointed a committee and instructed it to meet in Kassel on August 7. The committee met and recommended that if all else failed, obstinate Anabaptists should be executed. Chancellor Feige agreed that action should be more severe than it had been. He stated that in his opinion foreign Anabaptists who returned after being banished three times should be executed. Philipp's counselors Riedesel and Boyneburg agreed.

Adam Krafft and Dionysius Melander (1486–1561) took more moderate positions. They sought reasons behind the Anabaptists' separation, evaluation of these reasons, and making right any wrongs in the Hessian church that might have contributed to their separation.

Philipp was under extreme pressure, and his important 1537 territorial ordinance that became known as his "Harsh Ordinance" followed the suggestions of his correspondents. In its preface, Philipp wrote that he recognized he was a Christian civil authority responsible to God for his office.

In point 15 of this ordinance, Philipp outlined procedures for dealing with the Anabaptists' erroneous beliefs. Hearing centers were to be set up in Marburg, Kassel, Eschwege, Darmstadt, and St. Goar. The local pastors would publicly examine the arrested Anabaptists, point out their errors, and do their best to lead them back to the Church. Foreign offenders who remained obstinate could be branded on the cheek and banished from Hesse forever. If any should return to Hesse, the civil authority would be permitted to execute them.

Three punishments—beating with a rod, branding on the face, and execution—were to be handled by the superintendents and the local governor. Philipp never took advantage of the extreme measures provided for in his Harsh Ordinance of 1537.

PHILIPP EMPLOYS MARTIN BUCER

Early in 1538, Martin Bucer of Strassburg had dealt successfully with his own Anabaptist problem. Afterward, he wrote and published his thoughts about the Church, which Philipp read. I have translated the original German title of Bucer's writing to *Pastoral Theology: Genuine Care of Souls and Effective Shepherding*. In it he states that Christians have complete and perfect unity among themselves. They are one body, living by one Spirit. They acknowledge one Lord and have one faith. It followed for Bucer that the Church is to be the most perfect, friendliest, and most faithful fellowship community, in unity with one another.

Also, according to Bucer, the Church is a community of love and service in which the original order of creation is being restored. Those who are banned are not to be completely shunned. They are excluded from the Christian community but not the civil. They are not to be denied the natural necessities from their relatives and civil authorities.[114]

Philipp was confident Bucer shared his tolerant concerns. He invited him to come to Hesse to help him solve his festering Anabaptist problem. At Speyer I in 1526, Philipp had become friends with Jakob Sturm of Strassburg. Sturm now convinced Bucer to accept Philipp's invitation, go to Marburg, and meet with the leaders of the Hessian Anabaptists. On August 23, 1538, Bucer accepted Philipp's invitation.

On October 1, Philipp received a letter from Otto Hunt, an official in Schönstein, 23 miles (37 km) northeast of Marburg. Hunt wrote that Anabaptists were becoming a growing problem in his area. Philipp recognized that his problem was acute, possibly because Schönstein was located midway between Marburg and Kassel, his two seats of power. He knew he had to act quickly.

Philipp wrote a personal letter, preserved in his own hand, to the four Anabaptist leaders. He told them he was very angry about how they had abused his lenient treatment of them in prison. Not only had he allowed them writing materials, but they had widened the hole through which they were served meals until it was large enough for them to crawl out, win converts in the area, and return to their cells, believing their absence had gone unnoticed.

Philipp knew that a letter from another Anabaptist leader, Peter Tasch (dates unknown), written earlier that summer, had been found in Schnabel's cell. In it Tasch revealed the inroads Anabaptism was making in England. The letter was forwarded to Melanchthon, and in September, Philipp and John Frederick took quick action. They wrote to Henry VIII, advising him to beware of the "Anabaptist pest." Henry did not hesitate. On October 1, he ordered his archbishop of Canterbury, Thomas Cranmer, to search out and examine the Anabaptists. On November 29, three of them were burned at the stake.

THE MARBURG DISPUTATION

Philipp had revealed in his Harsh Ordinance of 1537 that his patience was about to run out. Now in his letter to the four in prison, he revealed his final plan, namely for them to meet with his representative, Martin Bucer. He described Bucer as a pious, God-fearing, scripturally learned man, and assured them that Bucer would listen carefully to their concerns.

This meeting would become known as the Marburg Disputation. Nine years earlier, the Marburg Colloquy had been a gathering of four major theologians for a discussion of their differences. This meeting would be a disputation, meaning that one theologian and four laymen would meet to listen to one another in a civil manner, and the theologian would decide what action should be taken regarding their conflicting points of dispute.

The four Anabaptist leaders had one advantage few Anabaptists of that day enjoyed: they were relatively well educated and knew the Bible quite well. This disputation promised to be an intelligent meeting of minds, with Bucer and Philipp in total control.

A large audience turned out for the first session on Wednesday afternoon, September 30. Philipp insisted that special efforts be made to include only those suspected of being sympathetic to the Anabaptist cause. One of these was Peter Tasch. Though converted by the revolutionary Hoffmann, Tasch would turn out to be a surprisingly moderate figure, contributing much toward the success and lasting influence of the Marburg Disputation.

Philipp commissioned Valentin Bruel to record the proceedings. Dr. John Eisermann, a Marburg jurist and professor of law in the university, was asked to open with a review of Philipp's previous treatment of his Anabaptist subjects. He said that Philipp recognized their treatment might have created some bad feelings. He assured them that Martin Bucer had been invited to lead the discussion because of his piety, learning, and impressive experience with the Anabaptists in Strassburg.

Eisermann was chosen also to be the moderator. His experience prepared him well for that role. Five years earlier he had published a work touching on church discipline. It had been received well by some influential Anabaptists. George Schnabel had quoted it in a publication he wrote from prison.

Eisermann also stated that he and Philipp hoped Bucer could instruct them successfully and relieve them of any hard feelings they might have against the landgrave. He instructed them to speak when called upon, but only one at a time. The others were to wait in silence until it was their turn to speak.

Philipp knew his Anabaptists were more peaceful than many in other lands. He knew they would obey the civil authority they judged to be just. They would help defend the land should it be attacked. They would willingly pay necessary taxes. Still, he had watched in dismay as radical Anabaptists entered his lands following the fall of Münster three years earlier.

What troubled Philipp most was watching his Anabaptists abandon his Protestant Church. Eisermann addressed this issue directly. He simply asked them why they and their friends had separated from the Lutheran Church.

Schnabel responded by repeating his own story in more detail than he had done previously. He had been the treasurer of the congregation of his birth in Allendorf. There he was deeply troubled by what he judged to be the unbiblical spirit of his former pastor. He had witnessed how prosperous members of the congregation extracted exorbitant rates of interest on contracts for loans they signed with the poor (usury). Schnabel concluded that those who exploit the poor should be banned from the Church. He had made his concerns known to his pastor, but he felt he had been ignored. He decided a stricter form of church discipline was needed. The righteous life, he claimed, could best be served within a small, self-recruiting, self-disciplining church made up of believers independent of prince and magistrate.

Schnabel's fellow prisoners spoke up, each in his own turn. They addressed the standard Anabaptist points of concern: believer's baptism; the call and office of pastors who, in their opinion, were incompetent; and usury. They made their strongest case in connection with Baptism, arguing for instruction and a personal statement of faith as a prerequisite for Baptism. They added that church discipline was needed to enforce this instruction and to assure the purity of the congregation. Hermann Bastian declared he was willing to return to the Hessian church if only Philipp would satisfy these concerns. Peter Lose remained obstinate, refusing to accept any reconciliation.

The full plenary session continued for all of Thursday and into Friday morning. Bruel stopped recording his minutes at that time, stating that when Lose was given a chance to speak his mind, his attitude was so contemptuous that Bucer found it impossible to discuss any serious matters with him.

On Friday afternoon and Saturday, private meetings were held in the presence of Philipp's delegates and the Marburg city council. In this setting, George Schnabel assumed leadership again. Hermann Bastian remained firm in his willingness to return to the Lutheran congregation. Lose remained obstinate, refusing to relent.

The adoption of three closely related matters brought the disputation to a successful close. Following any infant Baptism, the growing child would be instructed in the Christian faith. Then, to confirm the effectiveness of this instruction, a rite would be created that would include the repetition of the Apostles' Creed and the child's promise to grow in the Christian faith and lead a godly life. Finally, the congregation would practice a more effective use of the ban than the ineffective ban of the state, administered by Philipp and in general use in Hesse.

On Sunday morning, after Bucer had preached a sermon on church unity, Hermann Bastian stood up and asked permission to confess his sin of separation and return to the fellowship of the church. He also sought the forgiveness of the congregation and asked that he might be invited to take Holy Communion. Many in the congregation wept tears of joy upon hearing Bastian speak so contritely.

On Monday, November 4, Bucer was told that Lose had decided to follow Bastian's lead. Bucer was so pleased that he apologized to Philipp for Lose's bad behavior. On that same day, Peter Tasch impressed Bucer with a constructive plan of his own. This convinced Bucer to write him a letter of introduction to Philipp in which he asked the landgrave to listen to Tasch's plan and consider it carefully. Tasch was offering to serve as a mediator. He had already told his Hessian friends his plan for rejoining the Hessian Church. Bucer added that if the Lord would help them through their leader himself (i.e., Tasch), something good should be accomplished. He also added that Tasch had already approached Bastian and Lose and talked with them about the wickedness of separation. On December 11, Tasch wrote a confession of faith to the other Anabaptists still imprisoned in Marburg.

On December 26, Philipp endorsed Tasch's confession in a letter to the mayor of Marburg. He ordered that all imprisoned Anabaptists who would accept Tasch's confession and promise to act accordingly should be released.

THE ZIEGENHAIN CHURCH ORDER

At the close of November 1538, a committee led by Martin Bucer met in the Hessian town of Ziegenhain. The meeting's purpose was to devise a workable means of discipline for the Hessian Church and to produce a Church Order that would be completed and published early in 1539. By December 1, Philipp received the *Ziegenhain Order*. He studied it and sent his written opinion to Chancellor Feige, the mayor, and the city council of Kassel. Philipp's opinion reveals his intelligence, sensitivity, and understanding.

Philipp found certain points in the order to be partly disproportionate and partly impractical. He found two matters that he felt were impractical. First, he was concerned about placing the children of wicked parents in other homes. What complications might develop, especially with those placements involving women and young maidens? Second—and Philipp's main concern—it would be impractical to expect all the Hessian pastors to immediately exercise the ban, for not all pastors were equally well trained.

Concerning the punishment of obstinate Anabaptists, Philipp asked Chancellor Feige to put both the *Ziegenhain Order* and his *Order of 1537* into language naming specific penalties for specific acts. He wished to avoid giving obstinate Anabaptists the opportunity to embitter the people against his government by claiming they had suffered innocently for faith and righteousness.

Philipp added that death sentences were to be passed only in Kassel and Marburg and, most important, he must always be informed. The specific violation for which an Anabaptist was to be condemned should be announced publicly. In the event of obstinate disobedience and other excesses, Philipp hoped to clear the way for future expulsions and imprisonments. Not every Anabaptist in Hesse was won over, but in the hard times that followed, Philipp continued to care for his people, especially his converted Anabaptists.

On June 1, 1542, Philipp wrote to his superintendents noting how many of the Hessian preachers were not behaving properly. He said that the superintendents should replace them with God-fearing men even if they were not as learned as the ones they replaced.

Philipp closed his heroic decade of the 1530s with his masterpiece of personal diplomacy, the Marburg Disputation. He had begun the decade by treating his Anabaptists with extraordinary kindness. In 1537, as the situation grew more threatening, he announced that if matters did not improve, he would be forced to bow to foreign pressure and execute radical Anabaptists found guilty of sedition. Finally, Philipp had called in expert assistance. Martin Bucer was aware of the pressure on Philipp to use the death penalty against obstinate Anabaptists. Still, Bucer achieved the goal Philipp set for him and returned Philipp's wandering Anabaptist sheep to the fold of the Protestant Church of Hesse.

Philipp was now at the top of his game. What could possibly go wrong?

Chapter 13

SCANDAL 1539–40
A Death in the Family

Philipp's father-in-law, Duke George of Albertine Saxony, died on April 17, 1539. A cause-and-effect relationship developed between George's death and Philipp's scandalous behavior later.

Philipp had lived with his father-in-law's critical mental image for at least fourteen years. George knew from the start that the marriage of Philipp and his daughter, Christine, was not built on mutual love. It was built on a legal contract George and Philipp's father had signed in March 1505, when Philipp was four months old and his future wife had not yet been born. Two years into their marriage, in the spring of 1525, George learned, possibly for the first time, that his son-in-law enjoyed visiting prostitutes in the evenings after he and Philipp had spent their day slaughtering rebellious peasants. George kept his suspicious eye on Philipp. George's wife, Barbara, died in 1535. With his father-in-law's death in 1539, Philipp felt free to indulge himself with the power he possessed as the landgrave of Hesse. How tragic that the scandalous acts Philipp performed in 1539 and 1540 became his undoing and dealt a serious blow to the Reformation!

Within the eleven months following Duke George's death, Philipp committed two scandalous acts that all but destroyed his heroic reputation. First, he scattered the bones of his ancestor St. Elizabeth. Then he nearly submerged the Reformation ship by entering a bigamous marriage, a rash act that had been declared punishable by death earlier in the decade.

SCATTERING ST. ELIZABETH'S BONES

For the first thirty-five years of his life, Philipp watched from his castle window as pilgrims poured into St. Elizabeth's Church below. They came to venerate the relics of St. Elizabeth and to pray, asking her to intercede for them with the Almighty. Philipp had learned from the Wittenberg reformers that such pious activity was a form of idolatry. It was one thing to simply venerate a saint; Martin Luther himself venerated the Virgin Mary. But to pray for a saint's intercession was idolatry for Luther and the landgrave. Within a month of Duke George's death, Philipp put a violent end to those pilgrimages.

Since its completion in the mid-thirteenth century, St. Elizabeth's Church had been owned and administered by the Order of Teutonic Knights. Now Philipp ordered his men to overwhelm those guardian knights, break into the saint's glorious tomb, and scatter her bones so they would never be completely regathered.[115]

When he scattered the saint's bones, Philipp had more in mind than putting an end to pilgrimages. He was determined to change the focus of his ancestry from the Thuringian line of St. Elizabeth to the Brabant line of the saint's grandson, Henry the Child, who was the first landgrave of independent Hesse. Doing so, he felt, would extend his heritage from the thirteenth century back to Emperor Charlemagne in the ninth century and replace Philipp's feminine heritage with his masculine heritage.[116] To confirm his purpose, years later, Philipp directed in his last will and testament of 1562 that upon his death, Christine's body and his own should be interred in Kassel, far from the saint's empty tomb in Marburg.

Even before 1539, Philipp was no stranger to controversy. In 1528, his preemptive strike against neighboring Catholic princes had created a scandal among his Lutheran friends as well as his Catholic foes. Six years later, his brilliant two-day military restoration of Württemberg to his cousin, Duke Ulrich, was a serious offense in the eyes of his Catholic opponents.

These two public scandals brought Philipp into the emperor's sharp focus. They caused Charles V to start planning how he might bring down this powerful, threatening Protestant prince. Rumors had been repeated in Hesse of Philipp's fascination with biblical precedents for bigamy. In the early 1530s, in response to Melanchthon's advice to King Henry VIII of England to take a second wife rather than divorcing his first, the emperor declared bigamy a crime punishable by death in an edict that became known as "the Carolina."

Bigamy had not caused much scandal until the emperor's edict was published in 1532. Legalized bigamous marriages had been judged a necessity following the decimation of the population in times of great plagues or war. In the wake of the Thirty Years' War, a century later, the city of Nürnberg allowed its surviving men to take a second wife to replenish its population.

BIGAMOUS MARRIAGES IN THE BIBLE

Philipp's crime of bigamy was scandalous, selfish, illegal, foolish, and most hurtful to those he loved most. It becomes, however, somewhat more understandable when considering the influence of Martin Luther's German Bible, a best seller of his day.

Germany was a surprisingly literate land. When reading Luther's German Bible, the average person could learn how God had allowed Jacob to take Rachel as his second wife. King David took at least a half dozen wives, and Solomon his son, known for his great wisdom, was also known for taking far more wives and concubines than his father.

Childbirth is a great blessing, and we rejoice when a child is born into this world. In the sixteenth century, bearing as many children as possible was seen as being obedient to God's will. Childlessness was believed to be a punishment from God. The command to be fruitful and multiply appears at least twice in the opening chapters of the Bible. In Philipp's day, this command was taken very seriously. When a couple was childless, someone—usually thought to be the wife—was believed to have done something wrong. Sarah, the wife of the revered patriarch Abraham, encouraged her husband to take a second wife when it appeared she would be forever childless. Philipp's literate neighbors could read about bigamous marriages in Luther's German Bible and draw their own conclusions.

There is, from a generation before Philipp, at least one example of a work of art portraying a bigamous marriage in the Bible. It is the marriage of Elkanah, the father of the prophet Samuel, as told in I Samuel 1. Elkanah is the last common man recorded in the Bible to have entered a bigamous marriage believing he was obeying God's command to be fruitful and multiply. Elkanah's first wife, Hannah, had borne him no children, so he took a second wife, Peninnah. Later, Samuel was born to Hannah. In the mid-fifteenth century, the Dutch artist Meister van de Vederwalken portrayed Elkanah and his two wives traveling to Shiloh to worship. Here was, and still is, visual evidence that even before Luther's Bible was published, a bigamous marriage was considered an acceptable way to fulfill the command to be fruitful and multiply.

THE COST OF LUTHER'S HATRED OF DIVORCE

Divorce in Luther's day often left the wife forsaken and her children destitute. In his 1520 treatise *The Babylonian Captivity of the Church*, Luther declared how much he hated divorce: "I would counsel her to contract a marriage with another . . . for my part I so greatly detest divorce that I should prefer bigamy to it."[117]

Late in the summer of 1531, King Henry VIII of England sought Luther and Melanchthon's support to divorce his wife, Catherine of Aragon, who happened to be the emperor's aunt. Melanchthon advised Henry to solve his problem by taking a second wife. He wrote, "It is certain that polygamy is not prohibited by divine law, nor is it unprecedented." He listed as precedents Abraham, David, and other holy men. He added that Emperor Valentinian had enacted a law allowing two wives and he married Justina without casting off Severa, his first wife. Melanchthon concluded, "The Popes too have formerly granted such permission, as to one George, an Englishman."[118] The emperor learned about Melanchthon's advice and declared bigamy a crime punishable by death. This put Philipp, who was known for his philandering, squarely in the emperor's crosshairs.

Charles's new law would later be aimed at Anabaptists as well, for in three years they would be practicing polygamy in Münster (as was told in chapter 11). This new law must have been a sober warning to Philipp. Martin Bucer would comment on rumors of bigamy he heard in Marburg in the 1530s. Philipp knew the emperor would look at any bigamous marriage as an insult to his dignity and power. How could Philipp dare insult the mighty Emperor Charles V? Apparently Philipp did not care about the risk he was taking. Philandering princes were common, even among the princes of the Church.

Four months after Duke George's death, Philipp visited his sister, Elizabeth, in the castle of Rochlitz, where she was living as a widow. There, one of the ladies-in-waiting, seventeen-year-old Margarethe von der Saale, caught Philipp's eye.

Margarethe's mother, Anna von der Saale, was the leader of the women of Elizabeth's court. When Philipp told Anna he was planning to marry her daughter, she was pleased. She believed Christine was grievously ill and Philipp was searching for a new mother to care for his children upon her death. When she learned Philipp's real intention, she was outraged and refused to allow her daughter to enter a bigamous marriage, even with the wealthy and powerful landgrave of Hesse. Philipp got his wish only by promising that the wedding would be private and witnessed by Protestant theologians.

Six months after Martin Bucer's successful service at the Marburg Disputation, Philipp sought his friend's help once again. He asked Bucer to secure

Luther's approval for his bigamous marriage. He sent Bucer to Wittenberg with Philipp's confessional memo and a cart full of Rhenish wine for the reformer. Bucer arrived in Wittenberg on December 9, 1539. On the following day, he met with Luther and Melanchthon.

In his memo, Philipp confessed how his conscience had always troubled him due to his unfaithfulness to Christine. He stated that because of this, he had not taken Holy Communion for fifteen years, since one month after their marriage. This made him despair over his eternal destiny. He added, "Since the very beginning, when I first took the Landgravine, I have had neither desire nor longing for her because of her unattractive appearance, her disposition, her smell, and also because she is often drunk as many of her ladies, maidens, and other people can attest. . . . But my physical constitution, as my doctors know, is such that I cannot live without a wife and so I have gone to many other women . . . I was unfaithful to my marriage just three weeks after getting married."[119] It seems likely Philipp might have been exaggerating to strengthen his appeal. Christine had already given birth to seven children, would bear him three more, and appears to have died in childbirth attempting to deliver their eleventh child while in her forties. Philipp's "problem" appears to have been more than his lack of desire for Christine.

Philipp ended his memo with a threat: should the reformers not cooperate, he would be forced to apply to the emperor and the pope for help. This was no empty threat in 1539. The Reformation scholar David M. Whitford concludes, "The defection of such a key member of the Schmalkaldic League would have been devastating to the League and to the fortunes of Luther personally and his reforms generally."[120]

Melanchthon had no problem with Philipp's request. Seven years earlier he had made his position on bigamy clear to Henry VIII. Luther gave Philipp his approval but added words of caution. Both Luther and Melanchthon stipulated that the wedding was to be kept secret. For them, it was a confessional situation. Philipp had confessed his sin, received absolution, and asked for their advice. Now he was to treat their permission with all the confidentiality of the confessional.

SECRET PREPARATIONS AND THE WEDDING

Until the wedding was performed, Philipp went to great extremes to keep his plan secret. This is evident from cryptic directions he gave his friend Martin

Bucer. They read like a treasure hunt. Bucer left Strassburg sometime before February 20, 1540, knowing nothing about a wedding.

Instead, the landgrave wrote to Bucer saying that he had important matters to discuss with him and to expect to meet him in Giessen, 172 miles (277 km) from Strassburg. Upon his arrival in Giessen, Bucer found that Philipp was not there. He was told to meet the landgrave in Ziegenhain in Hesse, 46 miles (75 km) from Giessen. The same thing happened there. Bucer was sent on to Friedewald, 35 miles (57 km) from Ziegenhain. On Wednesday, March 3, after traveling another 8 miles (13 km), Bucer stopped for the night in Hersfeld. There he learned that Philipp was in Rotenberg. Bucer decided he would go there in the morning, another 62 miles (100 km).

Rotenberg is 152 miles (244 km) from Marburg, far enough to offer Philipp the privacy he felt he needed to keep his bigamous wedding a secret. Rotenberg is 192 miles (308 km) from Strassburg. By following Philipp's treasure hunt directions, Bucer had traveled 323 miles (520 km), more than twice the distance he would have traveled had he simply gone directly from Strassburg to Rotenberg. That must have caused the Strassburg reformer some frustration.

When Bucer arrived in Rothenberg on the Fulda (spelled "Rotenberg" on modern maps) early on May 3, he found that Melanchthon had arrived the day before.[121] Two Hessian preachers, Melander and Lening, greeted him and revealed the purpose of Philipp's invitation. The wedding to Margarethe would be performed that afternoon. Bucer and Melanchthon were needed to serve as witnesses.

The rumors spread like wildfire. Philipp had dared to insult the emperor by ignoring his decree of death for anyone found guilty of bigamy. By his rash and insensitive act, Philipp had put both himself and the future of the Reformation in great danger.

Still, Philipp did not fear rumors. Once it was an accomplished deed, he took little effort to keep this marriage a secret. Fifteen days after the wedding, he wrote to Bucer, "I have no timidity about recognizing it openly, for I have done it before God with a good conscience."[122]

Philipp's sister, Elizabeth, had not been invited to the wedding. She was among the first to learn of it from Anna, the mother of the bride. Elizabeth was outraged and spread the disturbing news far enough to reach Elector Henry, Duke George's surviving brother, who was now ruling Albertine Saxony. Henry had no interest in keeping Philipp's bigamous marriage a secret. When he heard the scandalous news, he had the bride's mother arrested and held her captive for several hours until she willingly shared her full account of the wedding.

The news continued to spread. By early June 1540, Philipp's son-in-law, Duke Maurice of Saxony, heard of it. By the end of July, it had spread all the way to France, England, the ear of the emperor, and to the Roman Curia.

In a world in which the rich and the powerful lived by a double standard of their own choosing, Philipp may have been the rare one whose conscience troubled him for being unfaithful to Christine. It seems remarkable that Margarethe stayed with Philipp until she died eight months before his own death. Separation or divorce would have been relatively simple since theirs was a bigamous union. Could it be they enjoyed a genuine love match? Though Philipp hurt Christine deeply, in the end, the person he hurt most was himself, as we shall see in the remaining chapters.

HOW PHILIPP'S CULTURE MIGHT HAVE INFLUENCED HIS BIGAMY

It is not easy to account for Philipp's irrational behavior. Still, we may shed some light on his bigamy by considering both the "physical constitution" he referred to in his memo to Luther and Melanchthon and some of the sexual ideas from the ancient world that remained current in Philipp's day.

Philipp was born with a condition which the medical profession calls "triorchidism." Shortly after his birth, his attendants pointed out to the new father that his son had a third testicle. Landgrave Wilhelm II replied that if his son had not been born with that third testicle, he would not be his son, for he, too, was so gifted.

Sexuality was a popular topic in the literature and conversation of the sixteenth century, even as it is today. Vows of celibacy did little to stop some of the most pious men and women of the Church from enjoying the forbidden pleasures of sex. Even some popes had fathered children without enjoying the benefits of marriage.[123]

By 2005, the medical profession had studied 200 cases of triorchidism and declared that on the basis of that small sample, triorchidism is a relatively rare asymptomatic phenomenon, meaning that triorchidism, estimated to occur today in about 1 of every 500,000 male births, has little if any effect on one's sexual desire. That, however, is not what was commonly believed in the sixteenth century.

In Philipp's lifetime, it was thought that a son born with triorchidism was guaranteed to become a strong man, mighty in battle and in love. One primary source for this belief may have been the family circle itself. It is reasonable to assume that boys born with a third testicle might have asked their mother, "Why am I different from all my friends?" What loving mother would not have replied, "My son, God gave you a third testicle as a special gift to promise you will grow up to be a big strong man"? Mothers might have sown the seed with unintended consequences, but there is more to this story.

Observations about the power of the number of one's testicles to influence the adult male personality are preserved in ancient sources, especially by the philosopher Aristotle, of whose influence at Philipp's time the historian Dr. Robert Fischer writes, "All the major systems were grounded in the analytical philosophy of Aristotle."[124] Also included were two physicians, Hippocrates and Galen, who noted the effect castration had on the eunuchs they observed.[125]

Hippocrates, in the seventh century BC, noted the changes in the voices of eunuchs when castrated. Aristotle, who died in 322 BC, remarked about the testicles of male animals, "When they are missing, the animal is weak, and when they are present, they are a source of power." He added, "If the heart grants life, the testicles provide good life." He asked, "So, why is it that when these [testicles] are removed, the vigor of the body is also removed?" Aristotle concludes, "Hence, this excision [of the testicles] is unsafe, severing, together with the testicles, the power from the entire body."

In the second century AD, Galen, a Greek physician living in Rome, agreed with Aristotle, adding, "This force is the cause of vigor and virility, and for that reason, if a male is castrated by removal of the testicles, the male becomes similar to the female."

The article adds, "While monorchids [those with only one testicle] are considered only half-men, there is nevertheless one reference to a case of triorchidism, Agothoclese of Syracuse [fourth century BC]. During his youth he was a pervert, always prepared for debauchery, offering himself to all carnals, scurrilous, *having three testicles* (italics added)."

Whitford[126] relates briefly the example of one of the great warriors of the fifteenth century, Bartolomeo Colleoni, who was also a famous triorchid. Colleoni relished the fact that he possessed a third testicle, and he had his coat of arms fashioned with an artistic likeness of his three testicles engraved upon it. It was widely believed that by rubbing these graven testicles, young men could enhance their own military strength and sexual potency.

Pilgrimages in the late fifteenth century were quite common. With pilgrimages came messages from faraway places. On a pilgrimage to Rome in 1475, King Christian I of Denmark made a special point of meeting with Colleoni. Meeting with the king upon his return were some German princes, including Duke Magnus II of Mecklenburg, Philipp's maternal grandfather. Anna, Philipp's mother, was born ten years after this meeting. Fifteen years later, having married a man with triorchidism herself and having given birth to a son with the same condition, it is quite likely that Anna shared stories with Philipp she had heard in her childhood about the "heroic" Colleoni and his triorchidism, like that of her husband and her son.

We may never satisfy our need to adequately explain Philipp's scandalous behavior. Martin Luther said of him, "He is a divine wonder and heroic man; although a weak leader, he is still formidable."[127] We can only hope that once Philipp's story is better known, he might regain his well-earned place among other great, but seriously flawed, scandalous heroes of history.

Chapter 14

SERVITUDE 1540–46
Philipp's French Support Destroyed by the Truce of Nice

For twenty years, from 1519 to 1539, protracted and costly wars with his brother-in-law, French King Francis I, distracted Emperor Charles V from personally attending to his German problem. In June 1538, Pope Paul III concluded the Truce of Nice, declaring peace between Charles, King Francis, and the pope.

Word of this peace spread quickly through Europe to Germany and the members of the Schmalkald League. Four years earlier, King Francis had helped finance Philipp's restoration of the Duchy of Württemberg to Duke Ulrich, its legitimate ruler. Now the French king would be powerless to assist the league should the emperor attack it.

CHARLES V RETURNS DETERMINED TO SOLVE HIS GERMAN PROBLEM

Charles's wife, Isabella of Portugal (1504–39), died in childbirth on May 1, 1539, eleven months after the Truce of Nice was signed. In a letter Charles wrote to his brother Ferdinand, his words provide insight to the depth of his love for Isabella, his personal faith, and his frame of mind at the time when he was planning how he might handle his German problem. "The emperor declared that, in his great sorrow, he had no other comfort but the thought of his deceased wife's virtuous and devout life and her saintly death. He claimed that he had nothing left but to submit himself to God's will and pray to have Isabella taken to him in Paradise."[128]

The Truce of Nice followed by the death of Isabella freed Charles to tend to family matters in the Netherlands on his way to Germany. He turned over the regency of Spain and Milan to his teenage son, Philipp, and prepared for a long, tiring trip to the Netherlands.[129] There he planned to meet with his sister, the widowed Queen Mary of Hungary (1505–58), whom he had named the Regent of the Netherlands.

THE EMPEROR AFFIRMS HIS AUTHORITY IN NEARBY GHENT

Charles had last been in the Netherlands in 1530, following the death of his aunt Margaret of Austria (1480–1530), the daughter of Emperor Maximilian I, guardian of their childhood, and Charles's lifelong trusted counselor. Now Charles would need his sister's consolation. Still, his visit was more political than personal. Mary had endured two years of rebellion by Ghent, the city of their birth. Charles's decisive handling of this rebellion would spread fear throughout northern Germany, reaching Hesse at just the time the scandalous news of Philipp's bigamous marriage was spreading throughout the empire.

For centuries Ghent had been the dominant city of Flanders, an important area of the Netherlands. In 1499, the court of the Netherlands was established in Ghent. In the following year, the future emperor was born there. On February 14, 1540, just over two weeks before Philipp married Margarethe, Charles entered Ghent. The procession lasted five hours. It included cavalry, five thousand infantry troops, baggage, and a train of followers. Reports of Charles's procession and his quick takeover struck fear in the hearts of Schmalkald League members.

Charles put a swift end to Ghent's rebellion by executing nineteen rebel leaders, tearing down a full section of the city, replacing it with a garrison for his troops and supplies, and installing a new city constitution. Charles was declaring medieval Ghent dead and confirming his sister's rule. He did this in eighty-three days, from February 14 to May 6.

Jülich, a neighboring city of Hesse, is centrally located, about 142 miles (229 km) west of Marburg. The leaders of Jülich feared that it and Trier would be the first to be attacked by Charles, and they appealed to the Schmalkald League for membership and its protection.

Their fear was well-founded. The dukes of Jülich-Cleves-Berg and Trier, claiming to be loyal Catholics, were also on friendly terms with Elector John Frederick of Saxony, for on February 9, 1527, he had married Sybille (1512–54), the sister of Duke Wilhelm of Jülich-Cleves (1516–92). By 1540, John Frederick had served for five years as a co-leader of the Schmalkald League with Philipp.

In addition to his bigamy, Philipp had another reason to fear he might be targeted by the emperor, namely the important part he had played in the marriage of King Henry VIII of England. Henry had annulled his first marriage to the emperor's aunt Catherine of Aragon and married Anne Boleyn. After executing her, he married Anne of Cleves (1515–57), another sister of Duke Wilhelm of Jülich-Cleves. Their marriage was performed in January, one month before Charles entered Ghent and two months before Philipp's bigamous marriage. Philipp and Thomas Cromwell, Henry's Chancellor of the Exchequer,[130] had served as the royal couple's matchmakers.

Meanwhile, Philipp devoted himself to diplomatic business for the Schmalkald League. He was determined not to be distracted from important business by the uproar he knew would soon be caused by his own bigamous marriage.

In November 1539, the chancellor of Trier had proposed a meeting with Philipp. He sought a religious understanding that would allow Trier and Jülich-Cleves the protection of the Schmalkald League. Philipp quickly shared this news with Martin Bucer and the members of the league. In December, Bucer asked Philipp to arrange an interview with a Catholic councilor of Trier. The three met in Marburg on Christmas and the following day. They found agreement on justification, the Mass, and the liturgy. The negotiations, however, proved futile after Philipp unwisely remarked that one could hardly expect to achieve agreement with Catholics when Protestants themselves were divided over religious matters.

PHILIPP REFUSES TO CONCEAL
HIS SECOND MARRIAGE

Philipp had read about the bigamous marriages in the Bible that apparently had not been condemned as sinful. He had sought and received the support of Bucer, Melanchthon, and Luther. Now he refused to let anyone call his marriage to Margarethe immoral or unchristian. He also did little to contain the rumors. Yet he was aware that the emperor had the legal power to arrest him and seriously obstruct the progress of the Reformation. Philipp called for a conference of Hessian and Saxon representatives to meet in Eisenach in July 1540. He would need the military aid of Elector John Frederick should the emperor attack him.

The sessions opened on July 15 with a speech by Luther. The four-day discussion was filled with heated recriminations. Philipp defended his marriage to Margarethe, making it clear he would never recognize it as adultery or fornication. He also refused to lie about it.

Luther and the Saxon representatives would only agree to hold to their previous agreement requiring Philipp to keep the marriage a secret. They demanded that Philipp should not defend his bigamy in public. They recommended he should rely on a strong denial and ambiguous language. Philipp should also show more affection for Christine in public and conceal the second marriage contract in a safe hiding place. Hastings Eells, a historian of the bigamy, concludes, "From this moment Philipp drew further away from his religious allies and nearer to Charles V."[131]

Philipp was bitter about Luther's refusal to support him. He felt he had followed Luther's well-known advice published twenty years earlier when he wrote that he hated divorce and counseled bigamy in special cases. Furthermore, a decade later, Melanchthon had confirmed Luther's controversial counsel, advising King Henry VIII not to divorce Catherine of Aragon but to take a second wife for the good of the country and the king's conscience. Melanchthon had also served as a witness at the wedding that he and Luther were now rejecting as immoral. Philipp felt abandoned. Even Ulrich, whom Philipp had hosted in Marburg for seven years and who owed Philipp his swift return to rule in Württemberg, now refused to support his cousin![132]

PHILIPP APPEALS TO THE EMPEROR

Philipp felt he had no choice but to offer support to the emperor if, in return, he would be exempted from prosecution. He knew that in the eyes of many, this would be seen as his betrayal of the Reformation, but he could see no other choice.

On March 28, three weeks after the bigamous wedding, Philipp sent an emissary to meet with Charles in Ghent. Charles's earlier overtures had convinced Philipp that the emperor genuinely desired peace. On October 28, Charles assured Philipp that he had always desired peace and had never intended to use force against the Protestants. The emperor also reminded Philipp that he had recently sent Nicolas Perrenot de Granvelle (1486–1550, hereafter Granvelle)[133] to Worms with full power to make peace among the Germans.

Philipp's timing could not have been better. Now the emperor welcomed him not as a condemned criminal but as a trusted ally. But Philipp soon would find he had entered six unpleasant years of voluntary servitude to the emperor.

Charles wrote to his brother Ferdinand on June 17, 1540, that he was in no position to use force in Germany. On July 2, he wrote to Ferdinand again. This time he enthusiastically agreed with Ferdinand's idea of distancing Elector John Frederick and the northern Protestants from Philipp and the southern Protestants.

Religious talks continued between the representatives of the emperor and the Schmalkald League. Brandi tells of another source of pressure on Charles V: "One of his cleverest servants, Johann von Weeze, archbishop of Lund [in Sweden in office 1537–51, hereafter Lund], who was at this time acting as the ambassador to Ferdinand . . . deluged Charles with memoranda and reports, in which he even suggested that he would himself re-conquer Denmark if Charles would not." [134]

RELIGIOUS COLLOQUIES INVOLVING PHILIPP

Recognizing he could do more with diplomacy than with force, Charles focused on a series of religious colloquies, which were theological conversations between supposed equals. The first colloquy scheduled to meet in Speyer was canceled due to a plague in the area. It was rescheduled to open on June 12, 1540, in Hagenau, 60 miles (99 km) farther south. At Charles's request, Pope Paul III appointed Cardinal Giovanni Morone (1509–80) to represent him in Hagenau. There were voices in the Vatican willing to compromise on Communion wine for the laity and tolerance of married priests. Still, the orders given to Morone dated May 15, 1540, gave the cardinal little room for compromise.

Charles would not allow Morone and conservative Bavarian Catholics to wreck his colloquy. However, its results were little more than procedural. Six theologians were appointed to represent the Protestants. Ferdinand made certain his own theologians dominated the Catholic group. John Eck, Luther's opponent at the Leipzig Debate of 1519, was added later. A second colloquy, scheduled to meet in Worms, was announced.

Granvelle opened that colloquy on November 25, 1540. He communicated with Philipp throughout the discussions. Gradually Granvelle won individual Protestants to the emperor's side. Still, he noted that the Protestant party was growing. "The Protestants were friendly and the emperor's immediate political future seemed to lie in an alliance with them. The Catholics, on the other hand, displayed a desire for war which was highly undesirable at the present moment, and [they] were coolly indifferent to all attempts at mediation."[135]

Meanwhile, Philipp helped Granvelle organize some important private conferences. From Strassburg, Bucer and Capito represented the Protestants. The Catholics were represented by Johann Gropper of Cologne (1503–59) and Gerard Veltwick (dates unknown).

During these discussions, Granvelle met with Philipp's chancellor, John Feige. In January 1541, Granvelle promised Philipp the emperor's pardon for taking the Duchy of Württemberg from Ferdinand seven years earlier. In February, the emperor made a short visit to Heidelberg. Granvelle met with him there and was told the good news that Philipp had accepted all the terms he and Feige had worked out.

Cardinal-legate Marcellino Cervino was unable to resist the emperor's sincerity and intention. He was recalled, and his successor furthered the colloquy, which, by now, was supported by the papacy.[136]

At Worms, the basis for religious discussion was Melanchthon's Confession at the Diet of Augsburg in 1530 and his Apology, meaning his defense, of that Confession. In November, Granvelle announced that the colloquy was being transferred to Regensburg to meet there during the imperial diet. More advance preparations would be needed for this colloquy, and the basis for discussion would be a new document drawn up by a committee representing both sides.

Regensburg had been a free imperial city since 1245. The city is centrally located in the heartland of Bavaria, 223 miles (359 km) east of Worms and 248 miles (400 km) west of Ferdinand's residence, Vienna.

During the month of December, four theologians met in secret. Again, the Protestants were represented by Bucer and Capito and the Catholics were represented by Gropper and Veltwick. The new document they drew up became known as *The Regensburg Book*. A first draft was completed by January 10, 1541. Bucer gave a copy to Philipp, who sent it to the Wittenberg reformers. Melanchthon called it "fictional" and wrote on the first page, "*politia platonic*" ("platonic politics"), a not very complimentary note. At this point, Luther offered no opinion.

The diet opened on April 4. The emperor, knowing how easily the discussion could become bogged down with minutiae, appointed Julius Pflug (1499–1564), who was the last Catholic bishop of the Diocese of Naumburg, along with

Eck and Gropper to speak for the Catholics. For the Lutherans, he appointed Melanchthon, Bucer, and Johann Pistorius (1504–83), who was Philipp's super-intendent for the church in Nidda, Hesse. They were instructed not to try to cover everything. They were to explore only the conflicting doctrinal state-ments that they believed could most likely be reconciled.

The colloquy began on April 27, 1541, three weeks following the opening of the diet. Neither the Protestant Melanchthon nor the Catholic Eck approved the first draft on justification. They demanded a second and then a third draft. The third draft was accepted on May 2. Two days later, disagreement arose over the matter of the procession and veneration of the consecrated host.

The discussions became heated. At one point, even diplomatic Granvelle lost his temper, but he apologized later. At other times, the emperor felt com-pelled to intervene. Each side attempted to win over the other, even during social events. The elector of Brandenburg invited Philipp to dinner one evening. In the course of the evening, Catholic guests tried unsuccessfully to convince Philipp of the truth of the Catholic doctrine of the Holy Sacrament.

The reading of the *Regensburg Book* was completed on May 22 and was sub-mitted to the emperor on May 31. He transmitted it to the estates on June 8. A copy had been sent to Luther earlier, possibly by Philipp but more likely by Bucer. He received it on June 9. Luther accused Bucer of surrendering too much to the Catholics and rejected even some articles they had agreed upon earlier. Before Luther's response made its way to Regensburg, the Catholic estates also rejected the *Regensburg Book*, destroying Charles's hope for reunion.

In June, Charles succumbed to the Catholic clamor for the use of force against the Protestants. He grew ever more secretive and decided to tempt to his side important wavering Protestant princes.

Brandi writes:

> He first gave clear expression to this new policy in the final form of his treaty with the Landgrave of Hesse, on June 13th. The Landgrave undertook to enter into no alliance with the King of France or other foreign ruler, to make clear excep-tions in favour of imperial authority in each renewal of the Schmalkaldic League and to prevent the inclusion of the duke of Cleves among its members. He agreed also "to enter into no private treaty with the said Duke of Cleves"; rather he would support the imperial claims in Zutphen and Gelderland if the other Estates would undertake to do the same. In any case

he swore to stand by the emperor in a war against France, both he himself and his son-in-law Maurice of Saxony. In return for all these promises Charles declared that "out of particular grace and favour we have taken His Excellency into our especial protection and forgiven everything, of whatsoever kind, which he may previously have attempted or done, openly or secretly, against ourselves and our brother [Ferdinand], against imperial law and justice and the laws of the Empire." To this treaty a significant stipulation was added. The Landgrave was to stand by the Emperor in the event of a war against the Protestants in the name of religion.[137]

Albrecht, the archbishop of Mainz (1490–1545), Philipp's neighbor and antagonist, urged the emperor to attack the Protestants. The recess of the diet on June 29 dictated that the 1539 Peace of Frankfurt, stating that the emperor would not take up arms against the Schmalkald League, should be observed. On July 5, the Catholic estates decisively rejected Charles's efforts for reunion. Enraged, Charles left Regensburg on July 29, 1541.

In 1544 and 1546, Regensburg would again be the location of two more diets and religious colloquies. It was already evident by June 1541 that Charles had lost patience and would appear at those later meetings only to keep his support close and his opposition closer. Continued appeals for peace became Charles's way of distracting the Schmalkald League from preparing for the war that, by now, was becoming inevitable.

FAMILY LIFE IN HESSE

Meanwhile, in Marburg, Philipp's family was growing. Before she would accept Philipp's bigamous marriage, Christine had convinced Philipp not to bring his new bride or her children into their household in Marburg. She also made him agree that only her sons would inherit the land. As a result, Philipp housed Margarethe and their children in a large, patrician house on the market of Spangenberg, near his hunting lodge, at the corner of Burgstrasse and Klosterstrasse. When Philipp was in Hesse, he divided his time and attention between his two wives and their children.

At the time of his second wedding in March 1540, Philipp's household in Marburg included seven living children by Christine. In the following year, when Philipp returned from Regensburg, both wives conceived and gave birth nine months later to healthy sons. Margarethe was now nineteen. Her son was born on March 12, 1542. Christine was now thirty-five. Her son was born forty-two days later, on April 22. Both sons were named Philipp.

Philipp, the landgrave of Hesse, was now the father of nine. In the years to come, Christine would give birth to two more children. Margarethe would bring eight more into the world. By the time of his death in 1567, Philipp had fathered nineteen children, ten with Christine and nine with Margarethe. It is estimated that 30 percent of the children born in the sixteenth century did not survive to adulthood. By that statistic, Philipp would have lost six of his children before they reached adulthood. That makes it all the more remarkable that only two of Philipp's children, one from each wife, died before reaching maturity. Philipp must have seen to it that both wives had the best care available for their children.

DUKE MAURICE'S RISE TO POWER

Duke George's death in 1539 had dire consequences for the two Saxonies as well as for Hesse. George died without leaving an heir. Only Christine survived her father, and daughters could not inherit their father's rule. The only candidate qualified to rule Albertine Saxony was George's brother, sixty-six-year-old Henry (1473–1541).

There were two problems with Henry as George's successor: Henry was old and Henry was Lutheran. George might have preferred to have his nephew Maurice inherit the rule, for he was youthfully bold and decisive, and he appeared more flexible in his Lutheran faith than his father. But Maurice was only eighteen—in George's mind, too young to rule such an important duchy as Albertine Saxony. So Luther's bitter opponent had no choice but to bequeath his land to his Lutheran brother.

Henry immediately declared Albertine Saxony Lutheran and initiated a three-week visitation for introducing Luther's teachings in the land. Three weeks was not enough. On Pentecost Sunday, 1539, Luther came to Henry's aid, preaching in St. Thomas Church of Leipzig. Still, centers of Catholic devotion continued to dot Henry's land.

Henry's rule was short, only twenty-eight months. Upon his death, Maurice, now twenty and Lutheran like his father, was the only qualified heir. Maurice was known for aggressive behavior. He hated his cousin John Frederick and coveted his power as the elector of Saxony.[138]

Protecting the wealthy diocese of Meissen was the joint responsibility of Duke Maurice and Elector John Frederick. Wurzen was a town in that diocese. John Frederick wanted the tax raised for defense against the Turks to be paid directly to him so he could make certain it did not wind up in Catholic hands. In March 1542, when the bishop of Meissen refused to cooperate, John Frederick entered the area and collected the tax. Maurice could not allow his cousin to secure a foothold in his duchy. He prepared to attack John Frederick and drive him out of Wurzen.

Luther entered the scene. Though communication between Luther and Philipp had broken down earlier over Philipp's refusal to keep his bigamy a secret, he now urged Philipp to quickly mediate the dispute between the two Protestant princes. He also convinced John Frederick to allow Maurice safe passage through Wurzen. Finally, Luther lectured Philipp, urging him to convince Maurice that it was not responsible for the young duke to use armed force against his family members. On April 9, 1542, Philipp assured Luther there was hope for an end to the controversy.

PHILIPP CAPTURES DUKE HENRY OF BRAUNSCHWEIG-LÜNEBURG

In the summer of 1540, Duke Henry of Braunschweig-Lüneburg (1489–1568) attacked Philipp, most likely believing that Philipp had been weakened by the controversy surrounding his bigamous marriage. Henry and Philipp had once been friends. At the Diet of Augsburg of 1530, Henry supported parts of Melanchthon's Augsburg Confession. However, by 1541, Henry had cast his lot with the emperor and the pope. Duke Henry's attack on Philipp played a part in causing the scandalous news of Philipp's bigamy to spread quickly throughout the empire.

Duke Henry faced a serious problem. He ruled a land that was primarily Lutheran. That religious change took place in 1527 while Henry was absent, leading his army in support of the emperor's sack of Rome. Taking advantage of Henry's absence, Luther sent his pastor, John Bugenhagen, to establish the Reformation in Henry's duchy.[139]

Now Duke Henry committed the serious mistake of attacking John Frederick in writing. He claimed the elector was undermining the emperor politically. John Frederick denied Henry's charge. The charges and countercharges grew ever more personal and insulting. Henry labeled John Frederick "the drunkard of Saxony." Then he made a most serious mistake that drew Luther into the war of words. Henry wrote calling John Frederick the one "whom Martin Luther has called his dear and revered Hanswurst."[140] Hanswurst was a coarse comic character of Middle Low German theater introduced by Sebastian Brant in his satire *The Ship of Fools*.

Now Luther could not remain silent. Henry had publicly accused him of insulting his own sovereign. In February 1542, he published his most bitter treatise, titled *Against Hanswurst*, and addressed it to Henry.

Duke Henry took to arms, another most serious mistake. He attacked the Protestant imperial city of Goslar, which was located in his territory but independent. Facing their common enemy, Philipp and John Frederick united against Henry. They did not stop with recapturing Goslar. They occupied Henry's entire land, and captured and imprisoned the duke himself.

By 1542, the emperor had spent two years in what was to him a most frigid foreign land. Not only were the winters cold in Germany, but the theological attitudes Charles encountered on both sides were frozen harder than the North Sea ice in winter near Ghent, his birthplace. Charles had tried every plan he could dream up. Still he was opposed. On one side were radical Bavarian Catholics calling for war, supported by the Roman Curia. On the other side were Protestants opposing him over doctrinal matters.

Charles decided he would let the Bavarians have their way. He would continue his diplomatic efforts, but from then on, the Bavarians would have his sympathy. And as we shall see in the following chapter, his search for peace became only a ruse to keep the Protestants from arming for war.

Chapter 15

WAR 1546–47

Councils and Wars, Popes and Emperors

The call for an ecumenical council was complicated by competing calls for war. Martin Luther wished he might change that. The Fifth Lateran Council had adjourned on March 16, 1517. Luther posted his Ninety-five Theses eight months later. Thirteen months after that, he called for another council to consider issues raised by his teaching. Pressure for another council continued to build and accelerated for nearly three decades until the Council of Trent finally convened in 1545, followed by the Schmalkald War of 1546–1547.

The idea of holding an ecumenical council on German soil was discussed at the two Diets of Nürnberg in 1523 and 1524. Emperor Charles V rejected the idea but notified Pope Clement VII (1478–1534) that another council might be expedient. From then on, calls for a reform council became routine.

June 2, 1536, was set as the date for that council, but Pope Paul III postponed it three times. For the pope, the prospect of calling another council posed a threat to his authority. The emperor saw another council as his opportunity to settle the German problem and avoid resorting to force.[141]

The popes of the time had other good reasons to resist calling an ecumenical council. From the third through the fifteenth centuries, popes were confronted by at least forty anti-popes, men who had a pretense of being lawfully elected. Others, perhaps more threatening, simply appointed themselves as pope, claiming they had received a divine revelation.

The Conciliar Movement arose in the fourteenth century, asserting that supreme authority in spiritual matters resided in the ecumenical councils of the Church, not in the papal office. The Fifth Lateran Council of 1511–1517 declared the Conciliar Movement heretical, but its challenge to the power of the papacy could not be ignored. It is little wonder the popes of Philipp's day delayed calling councils.

The emperor, on the other hand, had strong precedent for calling an ecumenical council on his own, for eight councils had been called by the emperor, beginning with Constantine in AD 325.

PHILIPP'S WORKING RELATIONSHIP WITH CHARLES V

By 1542, Philipp was in voluntary servitude to the emperor. His conscience allowed this since Charles did not require him to renounce his Protestant faith or stop dealing with other Protestant princes. Philipp convinced himself that the emperor had no plan to attack the Protestants.

It appears that Charles and Philipp were able to converse in German—something that had not been possible in Worms in 1521—for Martin Bucer wrote that by then, the emperor was fluent in German.[142] However, it may be more likely that they conversed in Latin. Philipp supported the emperor's claim to be a peacemaker and lost valuable time failing to arm the Schmalkald League for war.

The emperor would put Philipp's loyalty to a test on the eastern border of the Netherlands. In doing this, he would at the same time strengthen his position in northwestern Germany. In the spring of 1543, his imperial army attacked the Duchy of Gelderland. The estates of Gelderland had chosen Duke William II (1516–92) of neighboring Jülich-Cleves to rule their land. William was Elector John Frederick's brother-in-law. Upon getting word of the emperor's advance, William took Communion in both kinds as a demonstration of his Protestant faith. The Schmalkald League was not involved in the brief military encounter. Philipp honored his commitment to the emperor not to interfere. Charles declared victory and added Gelderland to the Netherlands, governed by his sister, Queen Mary.

Why did John Frederick not use his superior power to come to the aid of his brother-in-law? Two factors were involved. First, John Frederick was no warrior. He revealed his timidity in 1534 when he appealed to Philipp not to attack Archduke Ferdinand. Second, John Frederick was not as powerful politically as his uncle, Frederick the Wise, had been.

What Philipp observed in the three years 1543–1546 provided him opportunity to broaden his vision of the empire, the papacy, and France. He learned as an eyewitness how futile it would be for the league to attack the emperor. He also observed how Pope Paul III, King Francis I, and Emperor Charles V were his deceitful, dangerous foes.

PAPAL AND IMPERIAL AFFAIRS BY 1544

Pope Paul III was born Alesandro Farnese on February 29, 1468. He ascended the papal throne on October 13, 1534. In his earlier years as a cardinal, he became known for promoting his own version of reform. When he was elected to be pope ten years later, he was seventy-six and showing the effects of age.

The pope chose his grandson, Cardinal Farnese, to serve as his legate to Emperor Charles V. Brandi describes the scene when Charles received the cardinal on January 21, 1544: "The Emperor had not directly asked for him, but had got Madruzzo to hint that he ought to come. Farnese's pretext for coming was that he brought subsidies against the Turk. He did in fact bring with him, to everyone's amazement, 100,000 ducats which were to be bestowed at Augsburg for the time being. For what purpose the money was intended was still in doubt. But the immense subsidy assured him a favourable reception."[143]

The fourth Diet of Speyer convened in the spring of 1544. Philipp arrived early, on February 8. "Charles had forbidden Protestant services in the church of the Dominicans, but he gave the Landgrave permission to use the church choir as he wished and the Landgrave took him at his word."[144]

John Frederick arrived in Speyer on February 18. Two days later, the emperor opened the diet. He asked for the Schmalkald League to support his plans to attack the king of France. Philipp spoke so persuasively for the support of the league that the bishop of Augsburg claimed Philipp appeared to be inspired by the Holy Spirit.[145] His appeal was well rewarded. The members of the league agreed that the emperor was to have 24,000 troops and 4,000 cavalry for six months. With this decision, the league cut all its support from France.

The diet adjourned on May 24, 1544. On June 10, the recess of the diet was published with the agreement of the league to support Charles against Francis. The pope was enraged when he read this. On August 24, he wrote condemning the recess. Thirty-five-year-old John Calvin and sixty-two-year-old Martin Luther both condemned the pope's condemnation.

Following that diet, Charles's first move was to drive the French king far from German soil. The times were in his favor. The Turks were not threatening. Francis had emptied his treasury in a futile attempt to regain control of Milan. Henry VIII was preparing to attack Francis. Charles planned to take Luxembourg from the French, gather troops in Metz, and march on to capture

Francis in Paris. This, in Brandi's words, would prove to be "his final and greatest war with King Francis."[146]

Charles's troops had taken Luxembourg by June 6, 1544. He arrived in Metz on June 17 and stayed there for nineteen days, raising more troops. Then he marched his army out of Metz on July 6. They advanced 60 miles toward Paris, meeting no opposition.

Charles's army laid siege to St. Dizier, 82 miles (132 km) southwest of Metz. During his twenty-seven-day siege, a garrison from the neighboring community of Vitry harassed the emperor's troops. Charles sent Philipp's son-in-law, Duke Maurice of Saxony, to capture Vitry. St. Dizier surrendered on August 17. Charles advanced, reaching Meaux, 34 miles (55km) from the French capital.

Panic broke out in Paris. The Treaty of Crepy affirming King Francis's surrender had been drawn up in early September 1544. Francis did not sign it until he learned on September 19 that Boulogne had fallen to Henry VIII.

NO HELP FROM FRANCE FOR PHILIPP

Now Francis would not be able to help the Schmalkald League, for he was committed to serve at the emperor's pleasure. The only thing Charles still needed was the pope's support for an attack he was planning on the league.

By a clause Charles inserted in the treaty, he made certain the pope would agree not only to his request for support against the league but also to his request for a council. There the emperor had required that King Francis should write Pope Paul to request a council. When the king's request arrived, the pope was prepared, having learned earlier how the treaty favored Charles. On November 19, 1544, Pope Paul set March 15, 1545, as the date to convene the Council of Trent.

A Diet of Worms opened one month later, on April 14, 1545. The emperor promised Philipp and the league that he would resolve their religious differences. His promise was only a smokescreen. By now, he was fully committed to war. He arrived in Worms on May 16, 1545. The papal legate arrived soon after. The legate brought 100,000 ducats to be kept in Augsburg and put to whatever use the emperor desired. This gift smoothed the way for the emperor and the legate to discuss their war plans against the Schmalkald League.

Charles complained about the stubborn Protestants. Then he confessed how he feared the league might attack him. He reminded the legate of Philipp's well-known military victories. Soon the emperor and the legate had worked themselves into an intense war fever. For five days, they laid out plans for attack. The legate disappeared, then reappeared in Rome on June 8.

It did not take long for the Vatican to make its decision. It was believed that war against the Protestants would make short work of the council feared by the pope. Furthermore, the emperor would be occupied in Germany, and the Farnese family, the family of the pope, would gather immense wealth from the spoils of the war in Germany.

By June 17, Pope Paul offered the emperor another 100,000 ducats, 12,000 troops, and 500 cavalry. In addition, he granted Charles 500,000 ducats in church lands in Spain with another 500,000 ducats in revenue. There would be no more talk of reform from Emperor Charles V.

Though the emperor was enjoying his victory over King Francis and a time of relative peace with the Turks, he still did not feel he was prepared to attack the Protestants. His decision to use force was firm, but he felt the time was not right. It was too late in the season to risk fighting in bad weather. His brother Ferdinand and sister Mary were also apprehensive. The emperor decided to put his war plans on hold until 1546. In doing so, Charles lost his chance to stage a surprise attack on the Schmalkald League.

Now the emperor asked Pope Paul to draw up a formal treaty declaring war on the league. The Vatican took months to prepare it. When the pope's treaty reached Charles, he rejected it and took six months more to write his own treaty, which was then accepted by the Vatican.

THE EMPEROR'S SECRET MEETING WITH PHILIPP

During the years Charles was in Germany, he did much traveling. He met with his brother Ferdinand in southern Germany, then with his sister Mary nearly 500 miles (805 km) north in the Netherlands. We have seen how in 1543 he traveled to win the Gelderland for Mary, then moved on to Metz and into France to put an end to years of warfare with Francis I.

Trips to engage in war were exceptional for the emperor. Most of his trips were in peace. When people feared he was coming to attack them, he simply told them to look and see how he was traveling unarmed, with only his supplies and a few armed troops to protect him.

Following a stay in the Netherlands in 1545, Charles left the following January, planning to be in Regensburg by Lent. He took advantage of the secure route through Luxembourg, now controlled by his sister. Word spread quickly that the emperor might be planning an attack. Philipp and the Schmalkald League began recruiting troops.

Crossing the Rhine into Germany was a fearful event, even for the emperor and his troops. Emissaries were sent to convince Charles not to cross into Germany. Charles simply pointed to the evidence that he was traveling in peace, not war.

In the dark of night, Charles sent a contingent of his troops over the river at Speyer. They stood guard as the remainder crossed in safety. He spent five days in Speyer planning his attack on the league with the elector of Mainz and the bishop of Speyer.

Then the emperor made a surprising 120-mile (193 km) detour to meet with Philipp in Hesse. They met in the countryside south of Marburg. Philipp came in peace, unarmed, wearing not a helmet but a plumed hat, with a falcon perched on his wrist. He was, however, protected by two hundred armed guards.

Philipp may have brought the falcon to suggest the pleasure of a hunt. The emperor's gout was under control for a time, so they decided to do some hunting. The hunt may have been enjoyable, but their talk no longer was friendly.

Philipp spoke with confidence, having raised an army large enough to seriously challenge the emperor. He asked for concessions, but Charles refused and countered with a demand that they talk about Duke Henry of Braunschweig, whom Philipp was holding prisoner. That Philipp refused to talk about. The emperor could see he was dealing with the bold Philipp of the past, Philipp the liberator of Württemberg.

The landgrave and the emperor parted, each one sobered by the experience. Philipp had urged Charles to study the Scriptures and lectured him on how little the empire was worth. This again was brash young Philipp of 1534. The emperor was not pleased.

PHILIPP AND THE LEAGUE
ABANDON HOPE FOR PEACE

The fourth and final religious colloquy of the decade opened in Regensburg on February 5, 1546.[147] Little was accomplished and it was adjourned after only one month. The emperor arrived for the Diet of Regensburg, which had been scheduled to follow that colloquy.

Hate filled the atmosphere at this diet. A month before it was convened, a shocking fratricidal murder had been committed. Juan Diaz, a Spanish theologian and former student at Wittenberg, arrived at the colloquy with Martin Bucer. His Catholic brother, Alfonso, was also in Regensburg. Following the colloquy, Juan returned to Neuburg on the Danube. Alfonso followed him there. On March 26, Alfonso had Juan murdered in his bed. Charles did nothing about it. He ignored the outraged Protestants. There would be no justice for Protestants in the divided city of Regensburg.[148]

Cardinal Madruzzo arrived in Regensburg on May 21. A treaty declaring war was drawn up and signed on June 7. The cardinal took it to Rome, arriving there on June 19. The following day the pope met with him and presented the treaty to the cardinals. It was signed and confirmed by the pope on June 26.[149]

Charles now waited in vain for the arrival of the Protestant electors. His gout was under control, and he passed his time hunting and partying. Ladies of the city were pleased to entertain him. One lady, Barbara Blomberg, conceived the emperor's child. He was named Don Juan of Austria. Years later, on October 7, 1571, as the commander-in-chief of the allied Christian fleets on the Mediterranean, he would destroy the Ottoman fleet at the Battle of Lepanto.

The diet opened on June 6. The sessions sounded peaceful enough, but both sides were recruiting troops. Philipp feared a treaty worked out between the kings of France and England would mean that more troops would join the emperor. The question was on everyone's lips: "Where will the emperor attack first?"

Charles formally ratified a treaty between the Wittelsbachs of Bavaria and the Hapsburgs of Austria on June 11. For a generation they had been foes. With this treaty, the way was cleared for the emperor and the pope to confirm their declaration of war.

On June 16, Charles showed his hand by asking the Catholic bishops to melt down and donate all their precious metal to help pay for his war against Saxony. It was clear that a religious war was on the horizon. Charles dissolved the diet on July 24.

On June 6, the same day that the diet was convened, Henry VIII and Francis I signed a treaty of alliance. Fear abounded. Philipp feared this treaty would free troops to support the emperor, and Charles feared the same troops would join the Protestants.

While all this was happening, "On June 19th Maurice of Saxony entered into a pact with the Emperor. . . . He undertook to respect the decisions made by the council, and Charles in return agreed to keep the council under control. Furthermore, Maurice was promised that he might have any of the lands belonging to the Ernestine branch of the Wettin Family, if he should conquer them in the course of the War."[150]

Charles wrote to his sister Queen Mary, describing the situation on June 9: "All my efforts on my journey here, and the Regensburg conference itself, have come to nothing. . . . Unless we take immediate action, all the estates of Germany may lose their faith and the Netherlands may follow. . . . I decided to begin by levying war on Hesse and Saxony as disturbers of the peace."[151]

Brandi writes:

> That same July 4th which saw the celebration of the Austro-Bavarian Marriage at Regensburg, and the proclamation of Ottavio Farnese as Captain-general of the papal auxilaries at Rome, saw also a meeting of the Schmalkaldic League at Ichtershausen, a little to the south of Erfurt. The Landgrave and the Elector here bound themselves to raise an army of 8000 infantry and 2500 cavalry each. On the same day they completed their credentials and instructions for ambassadors to France and England. Later on they were to send pressing and detailed letters to reinforce their instructions, but all to no purpose. The following night the army raised by the Swabian towns marched from Augsburg, to break up the rendezvous of the imperial troops at Nesselwant and Fuessen. On both sides, war had begun.[152]

To follow the action, one must know the players. In addition to the three princely leaders, Landgrave Philipp, Elector John Frederick, and Emperor Charles V, each side had its own military leader whom we might compare to a general. The emperor had Maximilian of Egmont, Count of Buren and Leerdam (1509–48, hereafter Buren). He had been distinguished as a member of the Order of the Golden Fleece for his service as a commander of the Dutch army in its wars against the French.

Philipp and John Frederick had as their military leader Sebastian Schertlin von Burtenbach (1496–1577, hereafter Schertlin). He had distinguished himself earlier by his service to the emperor. For example, he supported the Swabian League in 1519 when ownership of Württemberg was transferred to Charles V. Eight years later, in 1527, he earned his claim to distinguished service by supporting the emperor when he sacked Rome and held Pope Clement VII hostage. Nineteen years later, Schertlin entered the service of the Schmalkald League.

PHILIPP BOMBARDS THE EMPEROR'S CAMP

When the Schmalkald War is dated 1546–1547, it is natural to assume it lasted two years. That is technically correct, but it is misleading. German wars in the sixteenth century were seldom fought in the cold of winter. They were generally fought from March until November.

For that reason, it is more precise to speak of two campaigns, or theaters,[153] of the war, the Danube theater in the autumn of 1546, and the Saxon theater in the spring of 1547. The issues at stake, not the time spent in battle, made the Schmalkald War one of the great military events of modern history.

Schertlin knew the value of good intelligence and the wisdom of listening carefully to all reports, the bad as well as the good. He was often frustrated by the pointless bickering between John Frederick and Philipp. In July, he learned that armies of the Vatican were fast approaching, bearing the pope's financial support. Schertlin knew they would have to cross the Alps. Schertlin also knew about the Fern Pass.

A huge mountain collapsed in 2200 BC (as dated in 2006 by carbon 14 testing). This collapse formed the twelve-mile-long Fern Pass. A Roman road through the pass was completed by Emperor Claudius in the first century AD. By 1546, the Fern Pass was still the quickest and easiest route from Italy to Germany and Austria.

Before the first shot was fired in anger, Schertlin led a contingent of troops to seal off the Fern Pass. This delayed the emperor, but only for a time. Now the Vatican's men and money had to travel a longer, more difficult route. Before the papal reinforcements arrived, the two armies were equally matched in manpower. Schertlin's delay of the papal reinforcements gave Philipp and John Frederick an opportunity to attack. But they squandered this gift by quarreling over tactical matters.

For a time, the emperor was defenseless. Later he described the league's failure to attack as their mistake; but attacking Charles would have meant risking attack on the defenses of Regensburg, where the emperor was being protected.

On August 3, Charles's troops started to march from Regensburg to Innsbruck, a distance of 182 miles (293 km). Ten days later, at Landshut, he was reinforced by the papal troops. Now Charles was fully prepared to attack.

Still, Charles feared he did not have manifestly superior forces to engage the league. The armies were still quite evenly matched, and those of the league had the advantage of morale, being filled with the expectation of victory.

Now was the worst possible time for Philipp and John Frederick to delay. The duke of Bavaria was claiming neutrality. Charles was in the duke's land. Philipp and John Frederick decided not to enter that land without the duke's permission. They negotiated with him for a full week, giving Charles time to escape to the Danube.

In the north by July 31, the league had 15,000 troops to defend the Rhine. The emperor's troops, led by Buren, had the advantage with 5,000 cavalry, but he faced the dangerous crossing of the Rhine into hostile territory. Under the cover of darkness, he crossed safely in the night of August 20–21.[154]

In addition to bringing reinforcements for Charles, Buren was bringing much-needed cash. His progress was reported to John Frederick and Philipp. Again, the two could not agree. John Frederick felt Buren could be stopped. Philipp wanted to attack Charles. More days were wasted in foolish debate until Buren arrived on the scene, between Regensburg and Ingolstadt.

"On August 31 the first clash took place. The Protestants bombarded the imperial camp. . . . They waited too long and missed their best moment. . . . When they returned to attack on September 2nd the imperial troops had long since dug themselves in."[155]

Buren joined the emperor near Ingolstadt on September 15. Two days earlier Philipp's troops had been reinforced by the Rhenish troops under Oldenburg, Reiffenburg, and Beichlingen—reinforcements almost as large as those brought to Charles by Buren.[156]

The emperor's troops stumbled upon Philipp's flank on October 4. Buren ordered an attack, but thick fog allowed Philipp's army to withdraw. Philipp was also "well defended by marshy ground" that caused Buren to mire down and draw back. This was a serious reverse for Charles.[157]

Something similar happened on October 14, but this time it was Philipp's troops that happened upon Charles's flank, as he was marching to Ulm. Philipp failed to pursue Charles and lost another opportunity.

"On the 18th Cardinal Farnese took his leave. It was said that thousands of the Italians went with him. This was not for fear of the battle, for which all were longing but for fear of the rain and cold of the fast approaching winter, which caused untold suffering to the southern troops. From October 24th onwards the roads became very bad, the camps cold and dank, both intolerably muddy. Disease soon broke out. The imperial army was alleged to have dwindled to half its size."[158] Philipp was expected to take in stride the discomforts of late autumn and early winter. "But Charles had one advantage: his staying power was greater than that of the Schmalkaldic League."[159] The strong morale of Charles's men is evident from their song that has survived.

> The Emperor is a man of honor.
> He marches in the foremost rank
> On horse or on foot.
> Take heed, all ye bold *knights of the land*
> For the Emperor himself has said:
> "We shall not yield!"[160]

In the night of November 8–9, Charles received the news that Maurice of Saxony and Ferdinand had decided to invade the lands of John Frederick. As Charles expected, John Frederick ignored Philipp's need for support and marched north to defend his land.

Now the emperor was clearly in control of the situation, and he refused to negotiate with Philipp. "The morale of the League forces weakened under the double pressure of weariness and lack of funds."[161] Philipp marched his troops off on November 21 and returned to spend Christmas with his growing families in Hesse. "Charles was master of the field. He was now undisputed lord of southern Germany." The ultimate showdown with Saxony would come the following spring. Charles had been on the defense all through the Danube campaign. He played defense brilliantly, and he succeeded.[162]

ELECTOR JOHN FREDERICK ATTEMPTS TO REGAIN HIS LAND

On February 2, Charles began planning how he would join forces with Maurice and Ferdinand in Saxony. In March, he announced his decision to Mary and Ferdinand. The year 1547 would be Charles's year of victory over the Protestants.

In Saxony, Maurice's councilors were overwhelmingly imperialist. Maurice let his greed for his cousin's land and electoral status control him. He is still known today as a traitor to the Reformation, called "the Judas of Meissen." Fellow Protestants tried to persuade Maurice not to abandon his Protestant friends. Members of his family tried as well, including his wife, Agnes, and Philipp's sister, Elizabeth, who had loved and cared for Maurice in his childhood as if he were the son she never could have. Blinded by ambition, however, Maurice disregarded all appeals.

Still, it might not be right to call Maurice a traitor. He did not disavow his Protestant faith. In time he came to his senses. One day his father-in-law, Philipp, would owe him his freedom, possibly his life. Furthermore, Maurice was not the only Lutheran leader with feet of clay.

Maurice's attack on Saxony succeeded, but perhaps because they were near Hesse, he did not take Gotha, Eisenach, and Coburg, three Thuringian towns in western Saxony. He gave religious concessions in every district he occupied. In the end, he prepared to lay siege to Wittenberg.[163] The emperor declared in private that Maurice was the elector of Saxony.

Experience had taught John Frederick to be bolder and more skillful. He did not invade his lands to win them back from Maurice. Instead, on December 23, ignoring the bitter cold of winter, he attacked Maurice's original lands. John Frederick was joyfully received in Halle. But when he attacked Leipzig, the city held out valiantly. In the night of January 26, John Frederick was forced to withdraw for lack of funds.

Maurice pleaded for help from the Bohemians on the eastern border of Saxony. They refused to send troops, for earlier Maurice had mocked them as poor warriors. The emperor promised to send reinforcements with Margrave Albrecht Alcibiades. The margrave was at Zwickau by January 26. He advanced to capture the castle of Rochlitz, the dowry of Philipp's sister, Elizabeth. John Frederick learned of this, probably in a letter from Elizabeth, who was well known for posting messages during the war. Early on the morning of March 2, John Frederick took Alcibiades prisoner and rescued Elizabeth.

The former elector was now welcomed in the area, but he was still too cautious to take advantage of the opportunity the people's goodwill might have provided him. For the rest of March, he remained idle near Rochlitz.

The emperor left Nürnberg on March 28. He reached Wieden by April 8, having traveled a distance of 88 miles (142 km). In the next few days, he joined Maurice and Ferdinand on the edge of the Bohemian forest, about 100 miles (161 km) north of Wieden. They headed for John Frederick's headquarters on the Mulde River. It was well known that the emperor was coming. Thinking he would be safe on the far side of the Elbe River, John Frederick crossed over and marched his troops toward Wittenberg. Poorly defended Mühlberg was on the way.[164]

EMPEROR CHARLES V CAPTURES JOHN FREDERICK

John Frederick felt secure in Mühlberg. That was a mistake, but it was also understandable. The Elbe River is 200 feet wide at that point. It was spring-time and the river was swollen with waters from melting snow. There was no bridge, and Charles had no material to build one. He did not have enough boats to carry his army across the Elbe to John Frederick's side.

Brandi's description of the emperor's victory is so vivid, it is worth quoting verbatim:

> It was Sunday and the Elector was in church. When, between ten and eleven o'clock, both sides became aware of the presence of the enemy across the river, the Elector still thought he was safe on the far bank of the Elbe, and continued his march. The Emperor decided to lead the attack. Still the Elector, unaware of his danger, made no effort to fortify his bank of the Elbe, but sent all his artillery on ahead [for he knew how much it had cost him]. His only precaution was to lower some of the boats for making bridges into the water and to put a few troops on them. Charles determined to seize these ships for himself, and soon a violent battle was raging about them. The Emperor himself was present in person, encouraging his Spanish soldiers to incredible deeds of valour. The gunners advanced, up to the armpits in water, to reply to the enemy's fire and if possible to silence it. The most determined threw themselves into the water, stripped, with knives between their teeth, to attack the ships at close quarters. Horsemen swam across the river. At length the defensive fire ceased and a peasant showed the Emperor where the ford actually was, so that he could cross.[165] But in the meantime the Elector of Saxony's captured ships had been put to use, and the greater part of Charles's baggage and infantry went over dry-shod.[166]

There was no fight. In the chaos, John Frederick was slightly wounded and taken prisoner.

PHILIPP RETURNS TO HESSE
AND MAURICE IS DECLARED ELECTOR

The emperor declared that April 24, 1547, the day of John Frederick's capture, was the happiest day of his life.[167] Though his gout had returned and he had to be carried, he commissioned the artist Titian to paint him as the victor of Mühlberg, fully armed, astride his warhorse.[168] John Frederick surrendered on May 19 and signed the Wittenberg Capitulation.

The previous October, Maurice had decided he would not publicly announce his appointment as the elector of Saxony. Now, on June 4, the emperor solemnly invested him in public with the electorate and its lands.[169]

Philipp had returned to Hesse the previous November. In Hesse, his responsibilities as the husband of two wives and head of two families was increasing. In mid-January, both Christine and Margarethe conceived. George was born to Christine on September 10 and Philipp Konrad was born to Margarethe nineteen days later, on September 29.

Now, what might the victorious emperor do next?

Chapter 16

HUMILIATION 1547–52
Home in Hesse but Still a Threat to the Emperor

Philipp had chosen not to fight, but Emperor Charles V knew he was still a serious threat to the peace of the land and the future of Catholicism in Germany. He set out to devise ways to humiliate the proud and resourceful landgrave. Before he could do that, however, the emperor had another problem to solve.[170]

THE SIEGE OF BREMEN

The imperial army, commanded by Josse van Cruningen, was on its way to attack Bremen, the foremost Protestant city in northern Germany. Cruningen laid siege to Bremen on February 27 and waited for the city to surrender until March 19. By then, he was running out of gunpowder, and by March 30 he had no money to pay his troops, who were threatening mutiny.[171]

Charles ordered Cruningen to leave Bremen and march to Hamburg. The emperor gave the command to a young prince, Erich of Calenberg (hereafter Calenberg). Calenberg left Bremen, though it had not been conquered, and moved the army to Drakenburg on the Weser River.[172]

There, on May 23, the Protestants would enjoy an impressive victory, just three days after John Frederick's surrender to the emperor. The Protestant leaders of Drakenburg gathered their troops to pray and sing psalms. After enlisting local pastors as chaplains, they attacked Calenberg's troops. The young prince was caught by surprise and saved himself by jumping into the river and swimming to the other shore. His men were either drowned, killed, or taken captive. The bad news reached Charles. It angered him, for he still had many items on his agenda. At the top of his list was the humiliation of Landgrave Philipp, now at home in Hesse.[173]

MAURICE CONVINCES PHILIPP TO SURRENDER

Meanwhile, newly declared Elector Maurice of Saxony decided to convince his father-in-law, Philipp, to surrender. He assured Philipp that the emperor was his friend and would agree to generous terms if he surrendered voluntarily. Maurice corresponded with Ferdinand about reasonable conditions the emperor might offer. Both Ferdinand and Charles encouraged Maurice to continue negotiating with Philipp. They knew that as long as the landgrave was talking, he was not gathering troops to attack them.[174]

Philipp knew well that Maurice could not be speaking for the emperor. He tried unsuccessfully to convince Maurice to ask Charles to extend generous terms to all Protestant leaders, but Philipp knew that would not happen. Maurice wrote Ferdinand a second time, asking for his advice. Ferdinand replied that the emperor would yield, but only on the harshest of terms.

In April, Philipp felt more hopeful that Charles might spare his life, for he believed the emperor might still value his cooperation. He expressed pride to Maurice over his part in the Protestant cause and pointed out how, even when cooperating with Charles, he had refused to fight against John Frederick.[175] Maurice had hated John Frederick since his childhood, when he felt he had been mistreated by him. He suggested that Philipp should attack the elector to win the emperor's favor, but Philipp refused.

In the Wittenberg Capitulation of May 18–19, John Frederick ceded most of Ernestine Saxony and his office as the elector to Maurice. Maurice's cousin Joachim Hector II,[176] the elector of Brandenburg, joined the effort to convince Philipp to surrender. By the spring of 1547, the emperor and his army were approaching Kassel, where Philipp was still pondering his options. Charles commanded Philipp to surrender within three days. A courier reported that the emperor was only a four-day march from Kassel.

The two electors asked for and received a letter of safe conduct from Charles so they could travel safely to and from the imperial camp. They worked out a first draft of a reconciliation document they hoped Philipp would sign. It appealed to Charles for mercy by including the words "submission at mercy." "Philipp crossed out 'at mercy' but agreed to discuss submission on terms. . . . [The emperor] refused all terms."[177]

Philipp made offers, which were read to the emperor. The two electors delivered their own document seeking Charles's assurance that should Philipp surrender, he would not be executed or sentenced to captivity for life. The emperor approved this document.

When signing that document, Charles meant one thing, but the electors intended something else. Their difference depended on spelling. Charles meant that Philipp would not be submitted to eternal captivity, *ewige*. Maurice and Joachim believed Charles meant he would only hold Philipp captive for a short time, *einige*. They assured Philipp that he need not fear a life sentence or death. With this document signed, Charles marched his troops back to Halle and Philipp followed, anticipating the reality of his humiliation.

PHILIPP ENTERS FIVE AND A HALF YEARS OF HUMILIATION

June 19, 1547, was a full and fateful day for Philipp. It would begin his years of humiliation. That morning he had an interview with the bishop of Arras, a representative of the emperor, who came with the bad news of the emperor's real intention. Philipp had come in good faith. The two electors, Maurice and Joachim, had acted deceptively. They knew the intense anger the emperor held against Philipp.[178] When planning Philipp's surrender with the emperor, they asked Charles simply to give Philipp his hand when he kneeled before him. Charles refused even that small gesture. Still, the two electors twisted the emperor's signature to mean what they wanted it to mean. Philipp, on the other hand, had no illusions. He knew the emperor's terms would be harsh. Still, Maurice and Joachim did what they could to calm the landgrave's fears.

On June 19, the stage was set for the emperor's grand moment of triumph and the start of Philipp's years of humiliation. Philipp's enemies had been invited as witnesses, including Duke Henry of Braunschweig, whom Philipp had captured and held prisoner, and a Hessian who held a responsible position and hated Philipp for breaking into the tomb of St. Elizabeth, scattering her bones, and putting an end to three centuries of lucrative pilgrimages to her tomb.

Philipp was brought into a long hall. The emperor was enthroned at the far end of that hall, surrounded by luxuriously robed nobles.[179] The emperor commanded Philipp to walk through the steely stares of the vengeful guests lining the walls. They were expecting him to walk with head bowed, possibly weeping, in the fashion of a penitent sinner seeking absolution. Philipp would have nothing to do with such a false show of humility. He composed himself, stood tall, and, looking straight ahead, he allowed a sneer to appear on his face. The emperor took Philipp's look as an insult, convincing him all the more to humiliate Philipp. He would drag the proud landgrave as his trophy, that those in the valley of the Danube who had supported him might see how their hero was doing now.

When he reached the emperor, Philipp was commanded to kneel, and he obeyed. The Hessian chancellor[180] read a printed apology that included Philipp's promise to destroy his fortifications and artillery storage parks in Hesse. The emperor remained silent. His answer, read by the imperial chancellor, clearly stated that Philipp would not suffer death or lifelong imprisonment. It was read loudly for everyone present to hear. The emperor watched, unmoved, as Philipp struggled to rise; at age 43, he perhaps was afflicted with premature arthritis, especially given what he had gone through.[181] But the emperor refused to offer his hand; in fact, he refused to allow anyone to give Philipp a hand as Maurice had requested.

Then came a brief interlude in Philipp's first day of humiliation. Later in the evening, the duke of Alva invited Philipp, Maurice, and Joachim to dine with him. At midnight, when the dinner and entertainment were over, Philipp was taken to a separate room. Fearing foul play, the two electors objected that the landgrave should not be left alone. Maurice insisted on spending the night with Philipp, but in vain.[182]

On June 21, the emperor raised the fears of Philipp's supporters when he announced that he considered the landgrave's body to be the only adequate hostage to assure him that his peace plans could succeed.[183] With this statement, it was obvious Philipp's years of public humiliation had begun.

Charles decided not to bother attacking any of the remaining Protestant areas in northern Germany. The booty he could take there would not cover his expenses. He had plans to create his own league to raise the money he needed and keep peace in the land at the expense of the Protestants.

The emperor planned that Philipp's captivity would be much more humiliating than that of John Frederick. Charles would hold them both for the same period of approximately five years. John Frederick would be treated with respect, but not Philipp. Still, on one very important point, Philipp was the fortunate one: he would keep approximately 75 percent of his land and retain his title as the landgrave of Hesse. John Frederick would lose at least 75 percent of Ernestine Saxony and his title as well.

PHILIPP IS WATCHED BY SPANISH GUARDS

A company of Spanish armed guards was assigned to watch Philipp around the clock every day of his captivity. Their commander was Don Juan de Guevara. He would remain Philipp's chief guard for the first three and a half years.

In the night, at unpredictable intervals, Granvelle, the president of the imperial council, would have Philipp brought to him. His purpose was to wear down Philipp's resolve by promising that if he would renounce his Protestant faith, he would be set free. Philipp refused to cooperate. Throughout their years of captivity, both of these Reformation heroes, Philipp of Hesse and John Frederick of Saxony, remained committed to the Augsburg Confession. This earned them the respect of their contemporaries and their shared title "Magnanimous."

Charles had ten weeks to parade his princely trophies in public. The Diet of Augsburg would convene on September 1. It would be called "the Armed Diet," for Charles would dominate it as the victor of the Schmalkald War. In the weeks remaining leading up to the diet, Charles took Philipp and John Frederick through the South German lands bordering the Danube River, where they had nearly captured their emperor the year before.

In Naumburg, on June 23, John Frederick was housed in a patrician house on the market square, while Philipp was quartered in a small house at the foot of the city wall. They were in Jena on June 24 and Kahla on June 25. In both communities, Philipp was compelled to remain in the field camp, sleeping uncomfortably in a military tent, while John Frederick was given more-comfortable accommodations.

As they moved on, Philipp had to ride in a miserable cart while John Frederick was treated to the comforts of a coach. Philipp slept in stinking houses, a reference to farmhouses in which the cattle were housed on the ground floor and the family slept above. John Frederick spent his nights in more patrician houses on town market squares.

The Diet of Augsburg met for nearly a year, from July 23, 1547, until late June the following year. During much of that time, Philipp was held captive in Donauwörth,[184] a community located where the Danube and Wörnitz Rivers meet, about 28 miles (46 km) north of Augsburg. There Philipp could recall how, in the war, Charles's troops had encountered the flank of his army near Donauwörth and only a dense fog had allowed Philipp to escape.

Again, John Frederick was housed in a patrician house of Donauwörth and Philipp was kept under guard in a hostel named The Golden Lion. He was watched over by the Spanish guards, who were instructed not to use any princely titles when addressing him.

There was more than one reason the presence of Spanish guards in Philipp's small room was humiliating. There was the problem of communication, for the guards knew only Spanish. Every night at the changing of the guard, the new guards ripped Philipp's bedcovers off him to make certain he had not escaped. Finally, the cold weather and a diet that was foreign to the guards afflicted them with disgusting colds and diarrhea.

Charles feared a conspiracy to free Philipp and tightly controlled his correspondence. Even Guevara was not allowed to approve Philipp's correspondence. That approval had to come from higher up the chain of command.

Again, Maurice and Joachim negotiated for Philipp's release. Meanwhile, Philipp authorized the destruction of his fortresses and artillery parks as he had promised Charles in Halle. Philipp's fifteen-year-old son, Wilhelm, now acting as the landgrave, could do little more than watch as the destruction progressed. At the same time, the emperor's commissioners restored what they could of the sequestered church wealth, including a few of St. Elizabeth's bones. Among the most lasting and dire consequences for Philipp, they awarded the dukes of Nassau the prize Hessian territory of Katzenelnbogen that had been the possession of the Hessian landgraves since the 1470s.

Philipp was hopeful that if he cooperated with the emperor, he might be released by the close of the diet. Granvelle dashed that hope. He declared that any trust the emperor might ever have put in Philipp was now destroyed. To make communication more difficult, Philipp was moved from Donauwörth to Nördlingen, about 18 miles (31 km) farther from Augsburg.

In February 1548, a supplicant from Hesse appeared in Augsburg. This time it was not a learned councilor or jurist, but Philipp's wife Christine. Other noblewomen also were present. Among them was Queen Mary,[185] sister of the emperor. She was there to mediate a disagreement between her brothers, a role she played often throughout her life. Christine requested an audience with the emperor. Kneeling, she pleaded for the release of her husband, but Charles refused.

Still hopeful of securing Philipp's release, Maurice mobilized high-ranking persons to serve as translators. An oral agreement with Ferdinand and his son Maximilian was to be confirmed in writing by July 1548. By then, however, Philipp was on his way to the Netherlands.

PHILIPP SUPPORTS THE *INTERIM*

The emperor had learned he could not win the hearts of his people by using force. Compromise became more attractive. He called the Diet of Augsburg for the express purpose of drawing up and adopting a compromise document that would address both Catholic and Lutheran concerns and serve for the interim until the Council of Trent took action. A first draft composed only by Catholics was rejected by both the Protestants and the Catholics. For the second draft, Charles enlisted a Protestant theologian, John Agricola.[186] This draft was adopted by the diet and was named simply the *Interim*.

The *Interim* was published on May 15, 1548. Philipp wrote to the emperor on June 22 telling him he had read it and found it to be Christian. He swore he would devote heart and soul [*Fleiss und Ernst*] for its adoption in Hesse. That was not to happen. The pastors of Hesse rejected the *Interim*, convinced it surrendered too much to Rome. They felt that even the privileges allowed, like married priests and Communion wine for the laity, could be taken back quickly by a negative decision of the Council of Trent. Some Hessians also believed that Philipp's letter approving the *Interim* was a forgery.

CHARLES'S MOVEMENT WITH PHILIPP TO THE NETHERLANDS

Philipp was moved still farther from Augsburg, to Heilbronn. The diet was adjourned by the end of June. In July, Christine was allowed to visit her husband in Heilbronn. Nine months later Christine died. The coincidence is too great not to conclude that she died delivering their eleventh child. No records would have been kept of a stillbirth. Christine was forty-three at the time of her death.

On August 20, 1548, Philipp's hopes to be freed were dashed as the emperor ordered his troops to march north toward the Netherlands. Philipp appealed not to be taken there. Charles did not reply.

The emperor broke up his army in the city of Ulm. Two days later, he ordered Don Juan de Guevara to bring both captives to him in Cannstatt, near Stuttgart. From there Charles took Philipp on a detour of about 40 miles (64 km) east to Schwäbisch Hall of Württemberg. Since 1522, that city had been the center for the spread of Lutheranism in Württemberg. Since that year, John Brentz, a student of Luther, had served as the pastor of St. Mark's there. In

1534, Duke Ulrich and Brentz had introduced a thorough program of Lutheran reform. The object lesson of Charles's detour with humiliated Philipp would not be lost on the Lutherans of Schwäbisch Hall.

At the end of August, they stopped for several days at Speyer. Landgravine Christine appeared again, requesting another audience with the emperor to plead for Philipp's release, but her plea was denied. The march continued, past Worms to Mainz. Mainz is located near the southern border of Hesse. Since the thirteenth century, there had been animosity between Mainz and Hesse. No doubt the emperor remembered how, at the climax of the Pack Affair in 1528 (treated in chapter 7), Philipp had confiscated Hessian land governed by Albrecht, the archbishop of Mainz. A stop in Mainz provided Charles yet another opportunity to humiliate Philipp.

On September 10, the emperor took Philipp by riverboat to Cologne. Six years earlier, Archbishop Wied had invited Martin Bucer to come to neighboring Bonn to assist him in drafting a document for reformation in Cologne. Wied was later deposed by the Cathedral Chapter of Cologne. Philipp's presence under armed guard in Cologne was also an object lesson to those who might still harbor sympathetic feelings for the Reformation.

PHILIPP IS TAKEN TO THE NETHERLANDS

Fear spread in Hesse over the destiny of their landgrave. It was obvious to them that Charles was taking his two captives to the Netherlands. The rumors in Kassel grew ominous. The fear was that the emperor might send Philipp from the Netherlands to Spain, never to return and probably to be executed there.

Philipp was in the Netherlands when a message arrived in Kassel on September 16. All it said was that Philipp would soon be taken from Brussels to Ghent. This news stoked the fears of the residents of Kassel, for it meant Philipp would be 37 miles (60 km) from the harbor of Antwerp. Many wondered whether their landgrave might already be aboard ship to Spain. The emperor remained in Brussels for twenty months, from September 1548 to May 1550. It seems likely he feared a rescue attempt by the Hessians and remained there to keep a close eye on Philipp. At the very least, he was vividly displaying his humiliation of Philipp to the local population.

By the beginning of October 1548, more messages had arrived in Kassel. They offered some relief from the fears about Spain. According to information from Philipp's guard Guevara, the chamberlain of the mayor of Brussels had informed Maurice that Philipp would be kept in Oudenaarde, about 300 miles (483 km) due west of Kassel and 51 miles (82 kg) from Antwerp. On October 19, another message arrived. Philipp had written in his own hand on an undated table napkin, "I sit here [in Oudenaarde] in a small house. I have the use of only one room. I and Reinhard Abel [his paymaster] are not allowed to write. Our captor [the emperor] is a false and horrible man."[187]

Philipp's quarters in Oudenaarde, though below the dignity of a prince of his status, were actually quite comfortable, compared with what he had endured in Germany. Could that be due to Queen Mary's influence? Philipp's "small house" was a Burgundian castle built in the previous century. Besides the room Philipp mentioned in his letter, he was allowed to use a second room, which served as his dining room, writing room, meeting room, and lounge. It also provided space for the Spanish guards. A serving staff were hired as day laborers from the city. They included a physician, a paymaster, a cook, a bartender, and a barber. A fool was also included, possibly to harass Philipp with the emperor's threats. Only two chambermaids spent their nights in the castle. Here Philipp's correspondence was censored by Granvelle.

No further news was received in Kassel until mid-November. Konrad Zolner, Philipp's secretary in Heilbronn, reached Oudenaarde and reported, "God be praised I have finally found him in good bodily health and reasonably happy, which we had not expected after such a long time, but he is kept in hard and close quarters."[188]

Philipp was burdened with dozens of problems and was allowed to continue some of his governmental business. He attempted to set up a small Hessian consulate. Several assistants were brought in from Oudenaarde. They were allowed to handle Philipp's business only under close observation by the Spaniards.

MAURICE IS ASKED TO INTERVENE FOR PHILIPP

Another imperial diet was scheduled for 1550, raising Philipp's hopes that he might be freed. His son Wilhelm asked the electors Maurice and Joachim II of Brandenburg to appeal once again for Philipp's release. Philipp offered to hand over the rule of Hesse to his son, keeping for himself only Kassel and two hunting lodges, Friedewald and Spangenberg. He also offered to submit to the decisions of the Council of Trent. Finally, he promised to fulfill all the stipulations of the Capitulation he had signed in Halle, should these stipulations only be clarified.

Philipp knew all his offers would be in vain. The emperor would never free him as long as conditions in Germany remained as they were and Lutheran pastors and princes continued to reject the *Interim*. Philipp's appeals would only be answered with more humiliation. By the end of 1549, Philipp decided he must take a new approach. Should the efforts of the electors fail, Philipp felt only one way to freedom remained. Someone must break him out of prison.

He had entertained fleeting thoughts of escape earlier, when the emperor was parading him and John Frederick through the Danube lands. As long as he felt some glimmer of hope, he had put those thoughts aside. Now Philipp felt hopeless. In the autumn of 1549, others in Oudenaarde attempted to free him legally, but they failed. The emperor learned about their attempt, and it only made him angrier.

In May 1550, the emperor prepared to return to Germany to chair another Diet of Augsburg that summer. That diet was of so little note to historians that one is at a loss today to find more than passing references to it. The Protestant princes appeared, but only to complain about the *Interim*. They made no appeal for Philipp's release.

On May 29, when the emperor was about to leave the Netherlands for the diet, he had Philipp moved to more-restrictive quarters in Mechelen, about 15 miles (24 km) south of the harbor of Antwerp. By June, the emperor was back in Germany. Philipp feared he would be taken to Spain soon. The suggestion that the Council of Trent might free him only filled him with scorn.

PHILIPP JUMPS FROM THE FRYING PAN INTO THE FIRE

Maurice changed his course of action.[189] He contacted King Henry II of France, who assured him that Landgrave Wilhelm IV, Philipp's son, would be given asylum in France should the emperor attack Hesse. In Kassel, the idea was circulated that Landgrave Philipp might be rescued by a bold commando raid by Hessian troops provided by the mayor of Kassel. Maurice feared this might result in a bloodbath, but since the mayor was offering to cover the cost, Maurice knew he must be patient.

This high-risk operation was carried out on December 22, 1550. It did end in a bloodbath, just as Maurice had feared. Once it was over, Philipp was found alive and well in his room. Nothing was touched in the tumult.

Outraged, the emperor now judged his captive guilty of more than the already serious crime of disrupting the peace of the land. Philipp was now judged guilty of high treason. More than ever, the new year 1551 threatened to be the year Philipp would be shipped off to Spain and be executed. Due to the commando raid, Philipp had leaped from the frying pan of the emperor's displeasure into the raging fire of his wrath.

Now the emperor decided there was no need for him to comply with the terms of the Capitulation he had signed four years earlier in Halle. He appointed the president of the city council of Brussels to lead an investigation. He commanded the use of careful attention to detail, including the use of torture. He ordered Philipp's living conditions to be made still more harsh. Philipp was forced to sit in virtual darkness in a narrow chamber of less than 20 square meters (65.5 square feet, perhaps 8 x 8 or 9 x 7 feet). The windows let in no light, for they were nailed shut with boards. These boards were removed only for him to witness the execution on the street outside of the surviving men who had come to rescue him.

Though all conversation with Germans or even Netherlanders was now forbidden, Philipp's German service staff, except for those who had successfully escaped, were now relocated to Vilvoorde, near Brussels. Surprisingly, in spite of the strong security measures, or perhaps because of them, secret correspondence continued with the help of some citizens of Mechelen and bribes for the Spanish guards.

The guards still remained with Philipp. The leader of the guards, Guevara, had been promoted to camp major over the emperor's Spanish troops in Württemberg. In January 1551, Don Sancho Mardones succeeded Guevara. He served several months and was replaced by Antonio de Esquivel. Each one treated the landgrave more harshly than the last.

In time, Philipp's release did take place, but it was not by his own initiative. Only the diplomatic and military efforts of Maurice finally succeeded in freeing him.

THOSE OPPOSED TO THE *INTERIM* CONTRIBUTE TO PHILIPP'S RELEASE

Three cities stood out in their opposition to the *Interim*: Hamburg, Bremen, and most important, Magdeburg, which was the hotbed of opposition, not only to the *Interim*, but also to Philipp Melanchthon's compromise document known as the *Leipzig Interim*. The fourth Diet of Augsburg in 1550 placed a ban on Magdeburg and commissioned Maurice to enforce this ban. Charles also agreed to finance Maurice generously for the recruitment of an army strong enough to capture the city.

Maurice agreed to enforce the ban. To all appearances, Maurice was still in full support of the emperor. By February 26, three Protestant princes formed a league and began raising their own army to stop Maurice when they learned he was laying siege to Magdeburg. As soon as Maurice heard about this, he stopped them, added as many of their troops as he could to his own army, and dispersed the rest.

In the meantime, all Germany was astonished to learn how well the citizens of Magdeburg were defending their city. It was a carefully guarded secret that Maurice's siege was intentionally half-hearted, for every day that he delayed taking Magdeburg was another day he was paid by the emperor. Maurice's plan was to raise enough money to build an army that would challenge the emperor.

Soon Maurice's army did become the strongest army in Germany. He knew, however, that to conquer the emperor it would take more than his wages earned laying siege to Magdeburg. Early in October 1550, an ambassador from King Henry II of France met with Maurice on the same Lochau Heath near Mühlberg where the emperor had defeated John Frederick. Now the French ambassador signed a treaty promising that the French king would pay Maurice 70,000 crowns per month with 240,000 added for him to use raising more troops during the first three months. In return, King Henry was to receive Kammerich, Toul, Metz, and Verdun, cities on or near the Lower Rhine River.[190]

Maurice's plan in offering these towns to the French was to cut the emperor off from his sister Mary in the Netherlands. King Henry personally visited these towns in February 1552 and realized their strategic value. The decisions made on the Lochau Heath would be ratified by the Treaty of Chambord on July 15, 1552.

This treaty was little more than a formality since Maurice had completed his negotiations with the German princes and the French king by November 17 the previous year. At that time, he issued his last direct appeal to Charles for Philipp's release, but Charles refused.[191] The emperor had no idea of the danger in which he was putting himself by his refusal. On February 25, 1552, Maurice refused the emperor's invitation to come to negotiate with him. The emperor wrote again on March 4, promising that if Maurice would come, everything could be worked out. Two weeks later, Maurice declined that invitation.[192]

Finally, the emperor agreed to release Philipp, but he insisted that Maurice break up his army two weeks before Philipp's release. Maurice demanded that Philipp's release and the breaking up of his army happen at the same time. The two were still at an impasse when Maurice commanded his army to march south to attack Charles at Innsbruck. Charles explored the possibility of escaping to the Netherlands, but he was told that French troops were garrisoned on the Lower Rhine to block his retreat. He appealed to the city of Augsburg for financial help, but they refused. Now the emperor knew that Maurice had strong backing from most of the German people.

Charles sent one of his couriers to seek the aid and advice of his brother, Ferdinand, but at the same time, he feared that Ferdinand might be in sympathy with Maurice, for he did not know that on March 4 Ferdinand had admonished Maurice to keep the peace. Now the emperor sent the chancellor of Bohemia to meet with Maurice. On March 16, they met in Leipzig and arranged for a conference at Linz.[193] On his way to Linz, Ferdinand wrote to Charles asking him to release John Frederick. One month later, John Frederick was a free man.

Negotiations at Linz opened on Easter Tuesday, April 19, 1552. Those present were Ferdinand and his sons, the duke of Bavaria, the bishop of Passau, Charles's two representatives, and Maurice. Maurice held back while encouraging his allies and the French to speak for him. A second meeting was scheduled for Passau on May 26. Charles made many demands that could not be met. The preliminaries that had been signed at Linz on May 6 now meant little.[194] Maurice made certain his troops were well prepared for an attack on Innsbruck.

THE IMPASSE IS BROKEN IN PASSAU

Maurice knew "he could not hope to eradicate all fear of the emperor in Germany, nor to check the violence of the emperor's soldiers unless," once and for all, he put Charles "out of action" in Germany. The risk Maurice was about to take was immense. Still distrusted by the Lutherans as the Judas of Meissen, he would need to strain his credibility with the French to the breaking point. In the opinion of Karl Brandi, only a complex personality like Maurice could have handled this situation successfully.[195] Above all, Maurice needed to act quickly to enhance his credibility.

Maurice's army entered Innsbruck on May 23, but the emperor escaped. By May 27, Charles was at Villach, where he made his own plans for war. Should he attack, hoping to prevent the meeting in Passau? The emperor knew that would be of no help for himself or his brother. He decided to bide his time, hoping he might win some freedom of action at Passau.[196]

Brandi was an ardent admirer of the emperor, which makes remarkable the words of commendation for Maurice he expressed when describing what happened at Passau. He wrote: "Maurice's action now underwent a significant change. He stepped forward openly as the champion of the most urgent demands of his allies. He defended the claims of the Landgrave and the French, refused to yield over the demobilization of the army and voiced the general complaints of the princes in questions of political and religious liberty. *This step converted him from a mere ambitious dilettante into an historic figure. He it was who, standing forth at Passau, gave the final form to the Reformation settlement. He it was who laid down the preliminaries, which were to be permanently enshrined three years later in the Peace of Augsburg.*"[197]

PHILIPP'S RELEASE[198]

John Frederick was already a free man. Now, at Passau, Philipp would also be freed. No one was happy with the treaty struck at Passau. It was agreed that Philipp be released only if Maurice agreed to use his army to support Ferdinand's defense against the Turks. On August 3, 1552, Maurice struck camp. When his soldiers protested, he set the camp on fire. Then he marched his army off to join Ferdinand's army. On August 15, Charles ratified the treaty.[199] Philipp was now a free man—or was he?

On August 9, emissaries from Hesse had finally been able to greet Philipp. It was expected that he would be released on August 11 or 12, he would spend a few days in Rheinfels Castle in St. Goar, and soon after that, he would be greeted in Marburg. But these plans were dashed. Their journey home was halted.

The emperor had arranged a few more stumbling blocks that again left the landgrave in serious doubt of release. Philipp would have to return to the castle of Tervuren, near Brussels. There he would no longer be held in a wretched chamber. He would be the personal guest of the mayor, waiting for more of the emperor's tactics of delay to play out.

First, they had to wait for the imperial ratification of the Passau Treaty, which arrived on August 15. Then, there was a delay caused by a mutiny of the Hessian regiment. Finally, Philipp's guard, Don Esquivel, refused to give up his prisoner without a written order from the emperor.

Only on September 5 could Philipp finally leave Tervuren. Abandoning their planned route, his party traveled through Jülich, Cologne, and Siegen, and from there to Hesse. On September 10, 1552, joyful crowds welcomed their landgrave in Marburg.

Chapter 17

RETIREMENT 1552–67
Philipp Returns Unbroken

What was Philipp's mental state when he returned to Hesse after five and a half years of humiliation by the emperor? Celebrating the 500th anniversary of the landgrave's birth in 2004, Dr. Fritz Wolff addressed this question.[200]

Wolff quotes Karl-Hermann Wegner, who, five years earlier, had written that Philipp returned home a broken man. Wolff asks, "Is this often read formula really true?" He responds with two words: "Well hardly!" Then he lays out evidence of Philipp's sound mind upon returning home to retirement in Hesse.

Certainly Philipp had aged rapidly in captivity. He was no longer the good-looking man he had been in 1538. Ten years later, the Saxon ambassador Kram visited Philipp in captivity and reported, "He is quite gray and unattractive, has put on some weight, but apparently he is well."[201]

Philipp had not aged nearly as much as Emperor Charles V, who was only four years older than Philipp. A portrait of Charles V done in 1555 shows a consumed old man who, a year later, would have to be supported while standing and could not hold a piece of paper in his fingers. He died in 1558. Philipp, on the other hand, enjoyed robust health to the end of his life fifteen years after his release. He enjoyed hunting big game, and he begot three more children by his second wife, Margarethe.

Of Philipp's mental state of mind, Wolff wrote that if in the time of his captivity he often complained, dwelt sometimes upon his health problems, or feared that he might lose his mind, all that cannot be affirmed by inactivity on his part. Even in the last few months as he sat in the gravest danger, he marched every day for a couple of hours back and forth in his small chamber. He sang and, when he could get his hands on a book, he read. When he could procure writing utensils, he wrote home. All of this proves he did not sink into silent resignation or deep sadness. Philipp refused to be defeated.

During his captivity, Philipp was subjected to the most severe physical and psychological stress under physical conditions beyond description. In August 1551, Philipp wrote, "To think how by now I have sat in misery four years and several months. What sarcasm, scorn, and complaints I have suffered with no woman to go to."[202] Added to this was the persistent uncertainty over his fate, sorrow for his land and family, even the fear that his son-in-law, Elector Maurice, might be playing him a false hand.

Philipp repeatedly sought courage from his son and councilors, writing, "Don't be smug. Don't be frightened. Persevere even if they take me to Spain and you never hear from me again."[203] With astounding willpower, Philipp persevered and carried out an enormous amount of work.

Upon his return to Hesse, "Philipp immediately mounted the horse of domestic and foreign policy. He was no longer the hotheaded young politician of his twenties and thirties. That change was not only due to changed circumstances. It was also due to Philipp's changed personality. He was older. Because of his experience, he was wiser. He was even more cautious. Sometimes, since he was now approaching the sixth decade of his life, he was also weary. But broken? Certainly not!"[204]

Upon his surrender to Emperor Charles V in June 1548, Philipp left behind his two wives and fourteen children in Hesse. His oldest child at the time was Agnes, twenty-one, married to her father's future liberator, Maurice, the elector of Saxony. The youngest child, Philipp Konrad, was three months old. Wilhelm IV was the oldest son, who at age 16 took his father's place as the landgrave of Hesse. His mother, Christine, age 42, supported her son, as her mother-in-law, Anna of Mecklenburg, had supported her thirteen-year-old son, Philipp, thirty years earlier.

PHILIPP'S FAMILY UPON HIS RETURN

Upon his return on September 10, 1552, Philipp was welcomed by one wife, Margarethe. Christine had died on April 15, 1549. Upon his capitulation at Halle in 1548, Philipp had entrusted the day-to-day rule of Hesse to his oldest son, Wilhelm IV. Now, upon his return in 1552, Philipp was still the head of the household and could not delegate his personal responsibilities. Margarethe would give birth to three more children. One, named after Maurice, was born on June 8, 1553, nine months after Philipp's return and a month before his son-in-law and rescuer's death in battle. Fourteen months later, Ernst would be born, on August 12, 1554. Anna was born in 1558, but she died later that year.

DUTY CALLS, MAURICE RESPONDS

Philipp's liberation, described in the previous chapter, was not of his own doing. He was freed due to the inspired effort of Maurice, the elector of Saxony, his son-in-law. Lacking Maurice's intervention, Philipp most likely would have been taken off to Spain, never to be seen or heard from again. Maurice was aware that what he needed to do to free Philipp would cost him the emperor's goodwill, but he trusted that Charles would keep his word and not hold Philipp captive for life.

From his childhood, Maurice had admired Philipp. In Marburg on January 9, 1541, he married Philipp and Christine's oldest child, Agnes. They lived in Dresden, where Agnes gave birth to Philipp's first two grandchildren. Anna, who was eight years old at the time of Philipp's return, was born on December 23, 1544. A grandson, Albert, was born in 1545, but he died the following year. From then on, Agnes was unable to conceive, though the couple never lost hope for a surviving son and heir.

Maurice was a military genius of insatiable ambition who proved his skill in the Schmalkald War. In 1552, he led his army into Hungary to attack the Turks threatening Archduke Ferdinand's eastern lands. He withdrew only when he was stopped by the Black Plague ravaging the land. When Maurice returned to Dresden, Agnes told him she feared he might be killed in battle. There is no reason to conclude that Maurice did not intend to keep his promise to retire for good from military activity. Anja Zimmer, the author of the two-volume biography of Philipp's sister, Elizabeth, told me she has read in Maurice's letters to Agnes on the way to the battlefield his promise that he would return to give her a little "bump," which was his affectionate way of promising her another child. Then duty called. The empire needed Maurice's help once again.

Margrave Albrecht Alcibiades of Brandenburg-Kulmbach (1522–57) and Maurice had been comrades in arms in the Schmalkald War. But Albrecht refused to support the Peace of Passau, the new foundation of peace in the empire. By September 1552, the emperor was faced with two enemies. On the one hand, there was the French King Henry II (1519–59), the son of the deceased King Francis I. On the other was Albrecht Alcibiades, demanding that the emperor should confirm the notorious treaties he had forced upon Würzburg and Bamberg in 1551.[205]

The French king was the emperor's major concern. French possession of the fortress of Metz protecting the Lower Rhine River meant French troops were able to block Charles's way to the Netherlands to seek counsel from his sister, Queen Mary. Earlier, Charles had canceled Albrecht's notorious treaties. Now he agreed to do as Albrecht was requesting, and he confirmed the treaties. He did this to secure the margrave's support for his attack on Metz. In November 1552, Albrecht brought 15,000 troops to the emperor's support.[206]

By Christmas, it was evident Charles could not prevail against the superior defenses of Metz. His men threatened mutiny. Charles was forced to retreat, and this would turn out to be the final battle of his life. Albrecht's military power was enhanced in the process. Ferdinand's alarming message in early 1553 told Maurice that Albrecht was by then powerful enough to threaten the peace of the land, a serious imperial crime. It was obvious Albrecht needed to be stopped.

Maurice reluctantly left Agnes and Anna, promising this would be his last battle. This time Maurice kept his promise, but not in the way he intended. Maurice was by far the superior warrior. His troops outnumbered those of Albrecht, were better equipped and well trained. Still, Albrecht succeeded in setting an ambush for Maurice, luring the elector and his cavalry into a wooded glen where, unknown to Maurice, Albrecht had positioned snipers in the trees armed with the primitive but effective guns of the period.

Racing forward, mounted in full field armor, leading his cavalry, and confident of victory, Maurice suddenly felt a sharp pain in his lower back. Ignoring the pain, he continued his chase and defeated Albrecht's army before falling from his horse, weak from loss of blood. He lingered two days before he died on July 9, 1553.

In the mid to upper back, the field armor Maurice wore could not protect him against bullets,. for it was made of leather. The bullet fatally pierced his bladder. The joy of Philipp's return ten months earlier was now overshadowed by Maurice's untimely death at age 32.

THE 1555 RELIGIOUS PEACE OF AUGSBURG

In the years of Philipp's retirement, the event of greatest importance for both the Church and the empire, and which influenced the scope of Philipp's continuing reform efforts, was the Religious Peace of Augsburg of 1555. It provided that rulers could choose either Catholicism or Lutheranism as their religion and that of their people. Those subjects that refused to accept their ruler's religion were free to move to a land where the ruler was committed to their choice of faith. Only Catholicism and Lutheranism were recognized in 1555. Anabaptists and Zwinglians were excluded, and the Reformed movement was not strong enough to be recognized at the time.

SOME PERSONAL LOSSES PHILIPP FACED

Each day Philipp faced the urgent concern of how he might secure Hesse's economic strength and provide for his growing family of seventeen. Much of Philipp's wealth had come from Katzenelnbogen, which provided him with direct access to the Middle Rhine River, a world market for his goods, tax revenue from the sale of Rhenish wine, and tolls extracted from the Rhine River traffic. Upon his return, Philipp learned that all this income was lost; Katzenelnbogen had been confiscated by the emperor and given to the dukes of Nassau.

Philipp also faced great personal losses during his fifteen years of retirement following his return from captivity. Ulrich von Württemberg, his cousin and beneficiary, died on November 6, 1550. Martin Bucer, his close friend and theological confidant, died in exile in England on February 28, 1551.

Philipp would be saddened by the deaths of others he loved and respected. Duke John Frederick of Saxony died on March 3, 1554. Agnes, Philipp's widowed daughter, married Duke John Frederick II of Saxony on May 26, 1555. She suffered a miscarriage and died in November. Philipp's sister, Elizabeth, died on December 6, 1557. Melanchthon, who had influenced Philipp to accept the Lutheran faith thirty-six years earlier, died on April 19, 1560, and Philipp's second wife, Margarethe, died on July 6, 1566, just eight months before Philipp's own death.

PHILIPP'S INVOLVEMENT IN EUROPEAN POLITICS

Throughout the fifteen years of his retirement, Philipp was involved in European politics, but his political activities no longer involved seeking German Protestant alliances. The Peace of Augsburg had put that need to rest. Now Philipp focused on assisting the Protestants of France, the Netherlands, and some Hapsburg lands.[207]

By 1560, Philipp was in close correspondence with Louis, the Bourbon Prince of Conde, and the brothers de Coligny of France, who were leaders of the Protestant Huguenots. In the summer of 1566, one year before Philipp died, Conde referred to him as "one who from his youth until now was as a father and protector of the Christian religion."[208] Ten years earlier, Admiral Coligny had asked Philipp to invite the French Protestants to talks for mediation between French followers of Luther and Calvin scheduled to meet in Erfurt.

Despite his age, personal losses, and responsibilities, Philipp nevertheless was able to lend considerable support to the Huguenots, intervening with the French court on their behalf, and arranging loans and bonds for them. He always took great care, however, not to take on any contractual obligations for Hesse, and he avoided becoming involved in disputes that threatened war. At the same time, he worked to improve relations with the French crown.

Philipp carried on similar correspondence with William of Orange in the Netherlands, who, in November 1566, four months before Philipp's death, recognized Philipp's "sole commitment to the true religion and the glory of God."[209] The duke sent two ambassadors to Philipp, asking his opinion on whether the Netherlands should adopt the Lutheran or the Calvinist confession. His request was urgent, for the Catholic soldier Fernando Alvarez de Toledo and his troops were approaching; they would take control of the Netherlands in 1567 and rule it for five years. By then, death had taken Philipp from the scene.

Philipp also supported the Protestants in some Hapsburg hereditary lands. Hans Ungnad of Sonneck, the head of state in Styria, had adopted Luther's teachings at the Diet of Augsburg in 1530. In 1555, he was sent into exile and was given permanent asylum in Württemberg. Ungnad brought Philipp letters of recommendation from landlords of Carinthia, Krain, and Styria. Ungnad found a fellow worker, the reformer of Croatia, Primus Truber, and together they were able to translate the New Testament and writings of Luther into Croatian and Slovenian. Philipp covered the cost of new presses.

WEDDING ARRANGEMENTS

From 1555 to 1566, Philipp was involved in wedding arrangements for six of Christine's surviving children.[210] On May 26, 1555, two years after the death of her husband Maurice, Agnes married Duke John Frederick II of Saxony. In September of that year, Barbara married Duke George of Württemberg. He died on July 18, 1558.

A hiatus of five years passed with no weddings for Philipp. Then, on July 8, 1560, he faced four weddings in quick succession. On that day, his daughter Elizabeth married Ludwig VI von Zweibruecken/der Pfalz. Philipp's son Ludwig would marry Duchess Hedwig von Württemberg on May 10, 1563. His daughter Christine would choose Duke Adolph von Holstein-Gottorp on December 16, 1564. The last marriage in Philipp's lifetime was that of Wilhelm IV, his oldest male heir, on February 11, 1566.

Of Philipp and Margarethe's eight surviving children, only one married. Their daughter Margarethe married Johann Bernhard von Eberstein on December 31, 1567, eight months after Philipp's death.

Of all the marriages in Philipp's household, we have the most information about Wilhelm's marriage to Duchess Sabine of Württemberg. Wilhelm was thirty-five, more than twice the age of seventeen-year-old Sabine. Due in large part to the high mortality rate of the day, wedding protocol in the sixteenth century involved impressive care to secure the bride's financial future. This was especially important when the bride was much younger than the groom, as Sabine was. Reading the nuptial arrangements for their wedding, one feels that money was more important than love at the time.

Marriages by the second half of the sixteenth century were not generally arranged by the parents early in their children's lives, as Philipp's marriage to Christine had been. One wonders, however, what role Philipp played in choosing partners for his children. The spouses for half of his children were from Württemberg, the area so very important to Philipp (see chapter 9). Regardless of Philipp's likely role in choosing mates for his children, Wilhelm and Sabine's marriage, like that of Agnes and Maurice twenty years earlier, was a love match.

Aging Philipp insisted on knowing that the guest list was not too long and the celebration not too expensive. None of Margarethe's children were tolerated at any of the weddings. Wilhelm was responsible for the preparations for his own wedding. That meant he saw to it that enough food and drinks were purchased and there would be no shortage of crockery and table utensils. Guest accommodations had to be provided, including stalls for their horses and parking places for their carriages and wagons. Invitations to the tournament, an expected event at the wedding of a prince, needed to be sent out on time. Even choosing the wedding clothing of the bride and her bridesmaids was Wilhelm's responsibility.

Added to the many logistical problems and unusual tasks preparing for the wedding, the start of this week of celebration was visited by sickness. Through it all, Wilhelm proved to be a good organizer. Following the wedding, Philipp reflected that the celebration was satisfactory. The guests had been happy and well behaved.

William of Orange sought to marry Philipp's granddaughter Anna, the only surviving child of his daughter Agnes and Maurice. Anna had been through much as a young child. Her father, Maurice, died when she was nine. Her mother, Agnes, died two years later. At that time, she was taken to Dresden to be cared for by Elector August I, Maurice's younger brother. She was not happy there. By the time she reached adulthood, she had grown mentally unstable. Philipp felt that since William of Orange already had a male heir by his previous marriage, he only wanted Anna for her money, of which she had much, and should William of Orange die early, she would be burdened with great debt. He delayed the marriage for a full year before Anna and William were married in Leipzig, on August 24, 1561.

PHILIPP, THE PASSIONATE GAME HUNTER

Philipp, like many princes of his day, was a passionate game hunter.[211] Throughout his captivity, he had been haunted by the thought of never again being able to hunt and tend to the tasks associated with hunting. Upon his release, he returned to his passion, game hunting.

Philipp's journeys through his land were for hunting as well as administrative tasks. He had met Philipp Melanchthon on the road to a crossbow competition in 1524, a meeting that led to his turn to Lutheranism and his introduction of reform in Hesse two years later. In his capitulation at Halle, Philipp won the emperor's concession for him to keep possession of one castle in Kassel and two hunting lodges[212] for his hunting pleasure. Unlike Emperor Charles V, who in his retirement died in monastic solitude, Philipp was no loner in his retirement. He was a passionate game hunter, and hunting was a social sport back then, as it still is today.

Being a game hunter involved many concerns for a prince, chief of which was careful wildlife management. Upon his return, Philipp ordered the construction of high fences to surround villages as well as the borders of his fields. This he did to protect the wild animals from injuring themselves when jumping over the lower fences already in place. In cold winters with heavy snowfalls, additional feed was needed, especially for the big game animals

Philipp preferred to hunt, like wild pigs and deer, which were abundant in the area and still appear to be today.[213]

Philipp claimed the larger game for himself. The lower nobility were allowed smaller game, which included foxes, rabbits, and pheasants. This, of course, did not go down well with members of the lower nobility. Disputes arose in which Philipp did not always get his way.

Poachers were a serious problem that Philipp took responsibility for handling. Thieves caught stealing wildlife as small and seemingly insignificant as fish and crabs were interrogated. This might include torture and threats of execution, which might sound ironic for a ruler as tolerant of religious dissent as Philipp was.

Hired men and their dogs drove the large game to the point of exhaustion or into an ambush where Philipp could dispatch them with spears, a crossbow, or his primitive gun. Falcons were used to bring down birds and small game.

The destruction of farmland by inconsiderate princes on their hunts was one of the long-standing grievances that led to the Peasants' War of 1525.

DEATH ON EASTER MONDAY

In the last years of Philipp's life, Calvinists were challenging their exclusion from the Peace of Augsburg. Philipp's neighbor and close friend Frederick III, Count Palatine of the Rhine, accepted the Calvinist faith in 1559. Philipp had named his second son after the count and that son married the count's daughter. The count was called to give an account for his change of faith at the imperial diet of 1566. He asked Philipp to speak for him. By then Philipp was too feeble to attend, and he sent his son Wilhelm IV in his place. The diet convened in March and Margarethe died in July. Her declining health may have played a part in Philipp's decision not to attend.

Philipp of Hesse, the scandalous hero of the Reformation, received Holy Communion in the chapel of his castle on Maundy Thursday, March 27, 1567. He died four days later, on Easter Monday, March 31, 1567. He was sixty-two years, four months, and eighteen days old. Margarethe, the love of his life for whom he had sacrificed much, including his role as a well-known hero of the Reformation, remained by his side until her death on July 6, 1566, only eight months before Philipp's death.

Upon Philipp's death, Christine's children ordered the construction of an impressive monument to their parents in St. Martin Church of Kassel. It was damaged by British bombing in World War II and was restored to its original condition for Philipp's 500th birthday in 2004. In his last will and testament, Philipp admonished his children to remain Protestant, and he divided his land among his four sons by Christine.

Epilogue

1830–THE PRESENT

Philipp of Hesse wrote his last will and testament in 1562, five years before he died. In it he divided his land among his four sons by Christine. Wilhelm IV was to receive northern Hesse surrounding Kassel. The area of Marburg was given to Louis IV. Philipp II received Rheinfels of St. Goar. George I inherited southern Hesse surrounding Darmstadt. The terms of Philipp's will were executed following its reading on March 31, 1567.

Though Philipp may always be remembered by his people as magnanimous, the partition of his land was neither wise nor magnanimous. It started a rivalry between the brothers that was continued by their heirs. This rivalry resulted in a virtual blackout of iconography, including paintings, statues, and plaques honoring Philipp's contribution to the Reformation. This appears to be the result not only of the competitiveness of the four but also their lingering embarrassment and mutual animosity caused at least in part by their father's bigamy.

The court archivist and historian of Kassel, Christoph von Rommel (1781–1859), challenged that artistic blackout in his 1830 publication of a six-volume biography of Philipp. Rommel listed nineteen possible pictorial themes from the life and reign of Philipp for a total cycle of ninety-one picture titles.

Three decades later, in 1862, Max Schasler (1819–1903) wrote in *Dioscuri*, a German art newspaper, his passionate appeal entitled, "What Does German Historical Painting Need?" (*Was thut der deutchen Historienmalerei Noth?*). In 2004, writing for the celebration of the 400th anniversary of Philipp's birth, Dr. Holger Th. Gräf of Philipps University in Marburg reflected that the visual artists of 1862 were prepared for Schasler's challenge. Seeing personal opportunity to prosper, they "demanded an increased commitment of the state to their implementation."[214]

The first modern emperor of Germany, Kaiser Wilhelm I (1797–1888), was crowned king of Prussia on October 18, 1861, a year before Schasler wrote. He ruled for twenty-seven years and died on March 9, 1888. That year became known as "the year of the three emperors." Friedrich (1831–88), Kaiser Wilhelm's son, was fighting cancer when his father died and made him the German emperor. He was named Kaiser Frederick III, though he ruled for only ninety-nine days. He died on June 15, 1888. At age 29, Kaiser Frederick's son was crowned Kaiser Wilhelm II (1859–1941). The year 1888 was indeed the year of the three emperors.

Both kaisers, Wilhelm I and his grandson Wilhelm II, appreciated the political potential for increasing their popularity by heeding the calls of Rommel and Schasler. Artists were contracted, and statues, paintings, and murals appeared in some Reformation sites of Germany.

First, however, Kaiser Wilhelm I had a serious score to settle with France. In Wilhelm's youth, the French general Napoleon had subjugated Germany. In the Franco-Prussian War of 1871, Kaiser Wilhelm I captured Napoleon III and put an end to the Second French Empire. Five years earlier, in 1866, the kaiser had annexed Hesse to his empire. This annexation provided Wilhelm access to France, but the imperial couple also recognized something special about the land and chose it for their summer retreat. There they were exposed to popular lore about Philipp.

Dr. Gräf writes about the famous Luther monument in Worms: "With the beginning of the Philipp iconography of history belongs one of the most prominent examples of such memorial culture of the 19th century, the Luther monument of Worms designed by Ernst Rietschel (1804–1861)."[215] This monument was dedicated seven years after Rietschel's death and was completed by three of his students. A century and a half later, it is still a popular site, visited by thousands each year. A statue of Martin Luther stands in the center. In front are Luther's two protectors. On his right hand is Elector Frederick the Wise of Saxony, the protector of Luther's early years. On his left is Philipp of Hesse, honored as the protector of Luther's later years.

Following the monument in Worms, works of art appeared throughout the Prussian Empire. They may be found in Marburg, Speyer, Wittenberg, and Berlin. In the *aula* (large auditorium) of the Old University of Marburg, murals adorn the walls featuring highlights of Hessian history. They include St. Elizabeth's humble service to the sick and the dying in Marburg, her daughter Sophie of Brabant's formation of independent Hesse, Philipp's welcome of Martin Luther to the Marburg Colloquy of 1529, and the retreat of the Dominicans from their monastery following Philipp's formation of his university.

In the *aula* of the Melanchthon Gymnasium (i.e., high school) in Wittenberg, we find an impressive—though inaccurate—mural of sixteen-year-old
Philipp greeting Martin Luther at the Diet of Worms soon after the reformer
made his bold stand and when the emperor had left the scene in anger. The
mural, while impressive, is probably inaccurate, for I have found no evidence
that Philipp personally witnessed Luther's famous stand; but as I stated in
chapter one, they met in Luther's apartment the day after Luther arrived in
Worms.

Finally, in the Berlin Cathedral, built from 1894 to 1905, we find an impres-
sive statue of Philipp in the company of Frederick the Wise of Saxony, Joachim
II of Brandenburg, Albrecht of Prussia, and four reformers, Luther, Zwingli,
Calvin, and Melanchthon.

In time, Kaiser Wilhelm II's attention was distracted from art to warfare.
After leading his people through the First World War, Kaiser Wilhelm II went
into exile on November 9, 1918, forty-eight hours before the armistice was
signed, and abdicated on November 28. On that day, he escaped to the Netherlands, and he died there in 1941. Today, with the celebration of the 400th
anniversary of Philipp's birth completed in 1904 and the two disastrous World
Wars that followed, emphasis on Philipp's iconography in Germany appears to
have vanished. German literary work on the landgrave, however, is alive and
well. Attention to Philipp in the English-speaking world shows promise but
still is lacking.

In conclusion, some readers may raise the question, "Do you love Philipp
after writing his life story?" My only reply must be, I am not certain about that.
I may not want him to be my next-door neighbor or a member of my church
council, but I certainly do want him to be recognized by everyone as heroic as
well as scandalous.

Appendix 1

PERSONALITY PROFILE
OF PHILIPP OF HESSE

William J. Wright, professor emeritus of the Department of History at the University of Tennessee in Chattanooga, published _Personality Profiles of the Four Leaders of the German Lutheran Reformation._[216] He selected for this study the well-known personality theory of Raymond B. Cattell, who identified sixteen primary traits and several secondary traits derived from the primaries.

Wright chose the Cattellian theory for three reasons. First, it takes a very comprehensive view of behavior. Second, Cattellian personality research has been quite exhaustive. Third, the Cattellian theory is a truly quantitative one, which has given major considerations to properly formulating experimental designs.

"Five Reformation historians who were knowledgeable about the four historical subjects were asked to rate them on the sixteen primary traits. The raters had all read the standard and latest biographical studies of Luther and Melanchthon, _though modern full-length biographies of Philipp and John Frederick are not available_ [italics mine]. Philip[217] of Hesse stood out as a militant activist who was the driving force behind the political moves that assured the independence of Protestantism during the first two crucial decades. His intelligence was above average. Like Luther, Philip was bold, impulsive, self-sufficient, and dominant. He was well-adapted to formulating his own policies and representing them among his colleagues (theologians as well as politicians).

"The results of the ratings also suggest Philip tended to be practical, concerning himself with immediate problems and issues. At the same time, he was probably well informed, innovative, and very flexible concerning traditional views. In small groups he was likely to be an especially effective problem solver. His personality seems well suited to putting new ideas into practice. Since Philip was not high on conformity, one may assume that he was more comfortable than the others in a revolutionary role.

"On the secondary traits and criterion scales, Philip was again similar to Luther. He was extroverted, independent, and above average on all three leadership scales. However, Philip seems to have lacked Luther's creativity. Since the Landgrave's behavior is sometimes seen as neurotic, it is important to note that, as with Luther, his score on the neuroticism scale was in the low average range, thus making it unlikely that neuroticism was a consistent characteristic of his behavior.

"From the early 1530s, Philip, John Frederick, and Luther may be conceived as an authoritative group for the Lutheran movement. . . . The basic task of this group was to insure the security of the Protestant movement. Each of the three men had a different idea about how this could be done.

"It is not surprising, then, to find energetic but uncoordinated, indeed divergent, activity coming out of this group. Philip of Hesse worked to broaden the defensive alliance as much as possible, even in the face of making doctrinal compromises, in order to prepare for war. When the three did cooperate, as in attacking Henry of Braunschweig, a leading anti-Protestant prince, they were efficient and successful. But even in success they could fall into disagreement, as when they captured Henry in the Second Braunschweig War but could not agree on what to do with him.

"More absurd is the picture of Philip and John Frederick on the battlefield of the Schmalkaldic War (August and September 1546, after Luther's death), trying to agree on what military strategy to pursue: they argued themselves into an unnecessary defeat. Philip of Hesse noted the defective synergy of the military leadership of the Schmalkaldic League, even if he did not understand it. Had he been alone, he claimed, he would have won the war, a claim consistent with an earlier assessment."

Appendix 2

TREATMENT OF STUDIES
OF PHILIPP OF HESSE

The following is from Gustav Wolf's "Treatment of Studies of Philipp of Hesse" in *Quellenkunde der deutschen Reformationsgeschichte*, Hildesheim, Georg Olms Verlagsbuchhandlung, vol. 2, pp. 527–37, translated by John E. Helmke in 1979. I am happy to comply with Dr. Robert Kolb's desire that this be included and updated.

Among all the Evangelical princes of the sixteenth century, Landgrave Philipp was the only one, who, as regent, lived through the Reformation from its beginning beyond the religious peace of Augsburg to the total outbreak of inner Protestant controversies, which his preeminent attributes also influenced. For forty years he took a significant part in nearly all the important events of imperial history. Few instructors of our time attempt to describe him exhaustively without consideration for his viewpoint and his significance. Still, while aside from the Landgrave almost all of his princely contemporaries were provided with posthumous fame, his reign is not commonly known even today.

Already at the height of his work the memory of his dominion would be interrupted. Although he energetically took control in the churchly organization, his domestic aides stood behind the Wittenbergers and the Swiss, even the Strassburgers, and raised trivial considerations. Philipp attacked militarily only occasionally and at great intervals. Of high politics, his main concern, we learn the least and these also are most piecemeal. Sleidan (1506–1556), sooner than anyone else, called for Philipp's vindication, often made a genuine critical use of his material, and remained unmoved by the conflict between the great princes and imperial estates in the Schmalcald Union. The Landgrave returned from his five-year imprisonment as a broken man [!], and his later resolutions frequently rebounded against his own interests. For he was still spiritually and politically in the antiquated perspective of the period of the

Schmalcald Union. Above all he wanted to prevent a feared international Catholic conspiracy by a close association of German and non-German Protestants and judge and control the Evangelical infighting in the light of higher political horizons. Yet these two paramount wishes found no fruitful ground and found even less response in contemporary historical events.

Therefore, even when Wigand Lauze's [1495–1570] biography of the Landgrave followed and was about to be published, it had difficulty influencing the tradition of following past generations in Philipp's favor. The passing of time damaged the understanding of his religious and political outlook. The Elector of Saxony [i.e., August I] with whose predecessor [i.e., Maurice] Philipp fought many battles, took the position of the Protestant princes, their opponent [in Hesse] turned to the Reformed faith, for among the German Lutheran theologians a hostile attitude toward the Landgrave prevailed, which found little to interest it in historical-political questions. But even in Hesse itself the recollection of Philipp would be distorted.

Yet among his followers a lively historical attitude arose. Also among his contemporaries and soon thereafter the survivors in the land gathered many materials and/or wrote down their experiences. Thus William Buch, whose father was invested by Philipp with an important position of trust and who himself served for a long time, first in Marburg then in Darmstadt courts, composed a *Chronicle*, which preserved many of his father's and his own recollections since the beginning of Philipp's reign. These recollections remained unused until the 18th century and even thereafter met an adverse fate. Even so, the *Acts of the History of the Church*, by Herman Habronius, which in the light of the accessible original are indeed worthless, was never printed. It is told of Landgrave George [of Hesse Darmstadt, 1547–96] that he gave Hortleder and Goldast free access to the archives. Influence upon the broad picture of Reformation history was not won by this work treating too much. Therefore, Landgrave George arranged a plan with his councilor Anton Wolf of Todterwait, a plan for a family history with complete or exerpted documents inserted. Among others, John Justus Winkelmann, the son of the strict Lutheran theologian of Gussen, would be named court historian by George. But before he was halfway prepared with gathering, travels, and note taking, he had changed his loyalties [*Verhaeltnisse*], and his interest in the Darmstadt court cooled down. His *Hessian Chronicle* published after a decade aroused only slight attention, although he claimed to have used new material for Philipp's history. Today that work has some value only as a source to the history of Hessian historical writing.

Historiographical sponsorship arose again with the reign of Landgrave Charles [1654–1730?]. The Marburg professor Johann Hermann Schminke [1684–1743] became his court historian in 1717. Until 1722 he was also librarian in Cassel. [As a result of] his friendship with Leibnitz and its strong influence, he gave the credit for his vital and critically trained mind for the source documents of Hessian historical knowledge, which he passed on to his son Fredrick Christopher. Indeed the father, like many predecessors, kept material of which his son used only the smallest part in the *Monuments of Hesse* (1747–65). Still, important sources, such as the *Reformatio of Hesse* of 1526 and the Hessian criminal code of 1535, were brought to light; letters on the history of the Reformation were offered as miscellaneous [matters], Lauze's *Chronicle* had known their worth and revealed their hiding place, though it did not publish them. After the two Schminkes, Sennkenberg and Ayrmann thoroughly studied the Kuchenberg *Chronicles and Acts*, and finally they left only splinters, yet many still today are worthy studies of Reformation history, like the last twelve volumes of the *Analecta Hesse* (1728–1742), the fruit of an untiring collector's zeal.

Surpassing all others is no doubt Helferich Bernard Wenck. While his predecessors did not comment with colorful compilations and critical essays, he was the first to write a *History of the Hessian Territory* (1783–1803) according to purposeful methodical principles. They remained the body and became, as it happened, essentially of great benefit to [the history of] the Middle Ages. Still today [1915] it is highly regarded in many ways. While they are the first among others to deal with a single part of the Hessian estates and various known parts, they still offered the most lasting visions, and won general and serious recognition for Reformation history, namely [of] the cultural and literary historians. Wenck followed particularly the history of the Landgraves of *Katzenelnbogen* to the 16th century and various intrigues among the Hessian nobility [*verschiedener hessischer Adelsgeschter*] until they died out. But above all, he systematically examined the printed and unprinted earlier works and produced in his first volume what is still today an indispensable Hessian historiography.

Still the need for a new *Hessian Chronicle* was not satisfied by Wenck. Christoph von Rommel was the first to attempt to fill this gap. His *History of Hesse* begun in 1829 and not completed until 1832 [an error in the German text has 1732], and his chief work, in which he boasted basic documents from the imperial archives of the 16th and 17th centuries, contains, even now [1915] the outstanding authentic representation of Landgrave Philipp. He particularly improved his portrait, not through the precise insight of an author, but through countless details which were first exploited by later studies and were more widely followed. In the footnotes and especially in the *Sourcebook for the History of Philipp the Magnanimous* (1830), a body of material too large to comprehend was piled up like cordwood whether it was complete or excerpted. Besides [this], his bias for union inspired many studies and reports on a documentary basis.

Memorials to Philipp were not enthusiastically received in earlier centuries, but double good fortune was his in the 19th century: namely the evangelical union movement, to which the humane Landgrave stood closer than the strict Lutherans or Reformed, and the relationship between church and political history promoted by Ranke. While earlier hardly any exceptional Hessian citizens or foreigners commissioned by Hessians had dealt with Philipp adequately, now his reign was to become a common subject of German studies. At the same time, there were new obstructions as a result of the Enlightenment. Already the *Hessian Acts* preserved in Marburg were inexhaustible; for the Landgrave had reigned a long time, [and] he corresponded with continuous zeal and applied himself tirelessly to the affairs of the day. Added to that there had been no adequate organization of the Marburg materials until shortly before that time. The *Acts of the Schmalcald Union* were in Ulm; other writings were surrendered to the Emperor [Charles V] by the Wittenberg capitulation [in 1548] and afterward were lost in Vienna. Many more distant questions were alluded to, in which the Landgrave took a part, numerous factors must be considered from all sides and very carefully, in light of the *Hessian Acts*. Since, with the taking up of such a special study, a feeling for such duties became sharpened, scholars did more and more research for a great biography of Philipp.

Thus we come to a noteworthy appearance. In the area of Church history where the need of a comprehensive biography was most urgent and other objections less significant, there appeared the great works of Hassencamp and Heppe. Beyond that, the research produced only symposia of essays or individual compositions.

Hassencamp and Heppe were closely related both in motive and in point of view. Both, well established with long years of archival research, conceived the contemporary Hessian Church as by nature and organization being more broadly conceived as a result of the Reformation. Both took special interests in the 16th century and wanted to break with a long and well-known tradition. They started with the idea that since the 16th century in the evangelical literature of Reformation history, the authority of the Elector of Saxony came to the written word and removed the Reformation predominantly from the horizon of the Landgrave. To that end not only were light and shadows made to appear as something else, since Philipp not only in theological outlook but also in practical zeal differed from the Elector of Saxony. Since at large the influence and competition from prince and theologian did not coincide in both lands, new problems came to light simultaneously. They intruded supervising the Counts [Grenzen] of Hesse and beyond.

It is not by accident that the basic lines of the Hessian Reformation History as drawn up by Heppe and Hassencamp appear to be essentially the same. On the contrary, our knowledge of the spirit of the Landgrave's politics and Philipp's foreign affairs was corrected and broadened. Both scholars carefully viewed Philipp's participation, but least of all did they care for all the early and quiet influences upon him. Also they did not need to study and relate his individuality. For them it was enough, since Philipp took part in widely different issues and events, to view the judgments he followed and which decisions he abandoned. To that end they consulted the archive about known problems and did not worry about others. Though important, for direct use they were deemed dispensable. The *Imperial Acts* alone, at that time practically the main source for the general political positions of the princes of that time, promised to offer only trifling benefits for Hesse and Hassencamp's special point of view. Above all they enriched themselves upon the unpublished *Hessian Acts*, in order to learn the motives of other parties. They enriched themselves in the published material from beyond the Marburg body of literature [Stoff].

According to one interpretation in particular, the apparent picture of Heppe and Hassencamp was off the mark. In their works Philipp appears, above all, as a mediator in the religious, inner Protestant controversies, at least as the methodical political thinker and promoter of general ecumenical relations [Bundnisbestrebungen], to this end the settlement of controversies served well. Therefore, Philipp's reign was divided by Heppe into two halves. Before the Schmalcaldic War [1547–48] he promoted the awakening of the domestic [Hessian] church. In that period Philipp took no personal interest in the theological battles among Evangelicals [according to Heppe]. After his imprisonment [1552–67] the era of domestic organization was essentially closed. The Landgrave's idea of union still arose from the same motive, followed the same good, but he remained in the role of mediator between the evangelical religious parties. In this the great importance of the Landgrave's influence was lost. Different events did not allow this *caesura* to be brought forward outwardly in Heppe and Hassencamp's works; but it is disclosed when one considers the points of agreement of both scholars. First, a predisposition for the statesmanly political motive of the Landgrave would be observed and his reign would receive a unifying character. His work [for them] of organizing the Church as a single special question would most likely be pushed into the background. The union politics of the first half becomes more than a practical necessity in the later years, to the degree that the unchanged conduct and meaning at the end of [Philipp's] life is explained in the light of the conditions of the earlier time.

The change is highlighted by the Political Correspondence of the City of Strassburg and the letters of Landgrave Philipp the Magnanimous with Bucer. The editor of the former, Max Lenz, saw his publication through several editions, and among the scholars he followed Heidenhein above all. He with his broader view examined the last years of the reign against the standards of his [Philipp's] earlier goals. Thereby, new materials came to light and our knowledge today is established on a broader base.

Also, among the prevailing conditions at the time of the anniversary of 1904 was the fact that the desired biography of Philipp had still not appeared, still many worthy building stones had been left [uncovered]. A standard work is found among them, viz. the *Political Archive of Landgrave Philipp the Magnanimous of Hesse* by Friedrich Kuech, technically a landmark in archival literature, issuing from long years of reorganization of the Landgrave's acts. To that point in time it was the one and only completely published archival repertory from the domestic bureau. Although it was only related to the Landgrave's papers in a very limited way, and justice, finance, and pure administrative acts were excerpted, everyone who would use the *Marburg Archives* for the time would have learned to know the work well. But scholars who do not study the acts in Marburg may not neglect the *Political Archives*. Business procedures came to light since the papers were organized according to the basic plan, to reestablish the old position of Chancellor [?], and to again unite the separated original fascicle.

In this way, the secretary of the chamber, Bing, whose trace one hardly finds in the published correspondence, but in foreign affairs was always active behind the scenes, won for himself in historical studies a blossoming position.

Besides the *Political Archives* there appeared in 1904 the *Memorials of the Society for Hessian History* and the *Historical Society for the Great Duchy of Hesse*. The first one is composed essentially of the essays of Marburg archivists and contains original communication of critical discussions over sources. The second is a more motley collection, the Darmstadt. After painstaking special labors, in which each was similar to the other, they found some interesting miscellaneous pieces which were not generally useful for Reformation history. Neither of the two collections of writings should or can establish a new interpretation of the man and his reign; but each one fills a gap, corrects false decisions on details, draws attention to an otherwise little-known time and describes it from good original spadework.

The most important monograph on Philipp from the anniversary year [of his birth 1904] is by Rockwell, *The Bigamy of Landgraph Philipp of Hesse*. Earlier works were for the main part concerned about whether and how far the Wittenberg reformers had sanctioned the step and what influence it had over the politics of the Landgrave. Rockwell's predecessors also had been satisfied essentially with the printed literature and the documents, which they had found in other collections; in addition, the *Marburg Acts* were still unorganized. Rockwell attacked the subject with the broadest archival principles. The political results he gave only fleeting attention. The main emphasis he placed upon the history of the bigamy itself, the real position of the reformers, and what was the general Catholic and evangelical view on polygamy at that point in time. Although there remains no discussion that he also did research with much solid material which at the time had already been touched upon, he made possible for the user his individual judgment upon the standard of the sources. The basis for Philipp's approach to the Saales [the family of his second bride, Margarethe] does not appear in the *Acts* and only circumstantial proof was accessible; even so, the authors of Catholic literature pressed this question, making it a matter of principle. Unfortunately, we here again still see nothing of Philipp's family life as it was after the marriage to Margarethe and of the conflict between the children of both marriages.

After the bigamy, the craft focused on the Katzenelnbogen question. Philipp's power [and wealth] as a territorial prince was essentially dependent upon this land struggle, and since he survived through the Reformation to 1567 it claimed Philipp's interest for a decade [actually four decades since Worms in 1521; see chapter 2] and became a factor in imperial politics. As it was with most similar business affairs, this controversy is rich in legal documentation, which does not cease until his death. How he would be treated by the recital of history he considered to be nonessential. The motive, on account of which one took interest in the Landgrave in the 19th century, lay in other areas. Neither Lenz and his students nor Heppe (who just recently [in 1915] on account of his religious point of view, had thoroughly treated the sources on the divisive conflict at the meeting of princes in Frankfurt, but had avoided the Katzenelnbogen question) had taken any interest in the problem. Therefore, when Meinardus edited the letters of the Count of Nassau, he intuitively suggested this conclusion: that the true worth of a great question would not be unknown [therefore Katzenelnbogen was not a great question]. On account of the relationships of so many different problems, Meinardus conceded a central position for the battle in Philipp's policy of unification and described the general political awakening against the background of the legal conflicts. Finally, he often exaggerates, when we may possibly find many threads of connection, but we thank him out of general appreciation for a worthwhile publication of the *Acts*.

Other areas are more fruitful than Meinardus's study of the Landgrave's unification policy. W. Diehl happened to "strike it rich" with the study of the Hessian school codes, until then neglected or, at least, not a historically oriented department of Hessian culture and public instruction. After his main work he achieved no greater work, such a variety of little [works] were required, painstaking studies of the acts continually satisfying the general interest. For example, the research of Lenz on the relationship between Philipp and Bucer was essentially completed and corrected, through the studies and sources of [the ceremony of] confirmation.

The military organization was closer at hand for the Landgrave personally. A prince, who believed in the security of his court and land when threatened and carrying on a strong foreign policy himself, would not be satisfied with the old establishment. Even if he raised no great standing army, he must still concern himself seriously with his need to lend assistance, preparing for the recruitment of troops and their support. He did not leave any well-established legal system. His concern was manifest in outstanding supervision and administration of details. The scholar often attempts to interpret these matters from the available circumstantial evidence. So [the scholar] Pactel advises studies of tiresome detailed work and broad research. These are an important building block in Philipp's biography and through these typical insights in the general range of military matters are discovered.

Pactel's work concentrates carefully on the relationship between the prince and the territorial business. *The Acts of the Hessian Diet* edited by [Hans] Glagau spans only the years 1508–1521 and provides an introduction to Philipp's reign. Still they are indispensable for understanding it. To that end the Landgrave's independence from the territorial Diets will be noted, which first made possible Philipp's resolute policy. Otherwise, the *Acts of the Hessian Parliament [Diets]* pass judgment upon Philipp's mother, Anna, who Glagau clearly idealized in a contemporaneous biography (see chapter 2).

Hessencamp and Heppe leave a serious gap in their church histories. According to their tendency they had to show which position the Landgrave and his religious renewal took in German Protestantism at least from which earlier starting point the Hessian reform was promoted. Hessencamp took the 16th century as the official starting point. Fundamentally Heppe was to take the Middle Ages; but as much unity as well as the plan of the work prevented him from proceeding to describe the pre-Reformation history. Steps back to earlier times were apparent, but only in very slight concern for details, and also in biased material and judgment. Where preference for the Landgrave was considered, he saw well the influence of the Reformation on him. But the controversy over Philipp's reprimands, the old relationships which they might be modeled around, appear superficially and in the wrong light. Through *The History of the Catholic Church in Hesse*, which Raich published from the papers left after death by Johan Bapt. Rady (1904), would also therefore balance out our view even if he depicted the Catholic times too idealistically.

In many ways for the first time the historical basis for Philipp's reform is clarified. Yet the main worth of the book rests on the fact that it is the only thing like it available, not in the fact that the author worked over the printed material conclusively for over a decade. Through years of collecting, Rady drew out piecemeal writings, laid aside building stones to the history of different Hessian parishes and towns, and mediated a completion of statistical knowledge.

Translator's note: For the 500th anniversary of Philipp of Hesse's birth in 2004, two works were published that bring Wolf's work in 1915 up to that year. From the footnotes and bibliography, it may be noted that we consulted all the English books written since 2004 and a sampling of those in German. *Untersuchungen und Materialien zer Verfassings und Landesgeschichte: herausgegeben von Hessischen Landesamt für geschichtliche Landeskunde*, Holger Th. Gräf und Anke Stoesser (Bearb. Und Hrsg.), *Philipp der Grossmütige, Landgraf von Hessen (1504–1567): Eine Bibliographie zu Person und Territorium im Reformationszeitalter* (Marburg: 2004). *Landgraf Philipp der Grossmütige 1504–1567: Hessen im Zentrum der Reform*, Begleitband zu einer Ausstellung des Landes Hessen, herausgegeben von Ursula Braasch-Schwersmann, Hans Schneider, und Wilhelm Ernst Winterhager in zusammenarbeit mit der Historischen Kommission für Hessen, (Marburg: Neustadt an der Aisch, 2004).

1 Hans J. Hillerbrand, *Landgrave Philipp of Hesse 1504–1567: Religion and Politics in the Reformation* (St. Louis: The Foundation for Reformation Research, 1967), 1.

2 William J. Wright, *Capitalism, the State, and the Lutheran Reformation: Sixteenth-Century Hesse* (Athens: Ohio University Press, 1988), 1. This book is one of the primary sources for this chapter.

3 The Teutonic Order was founded in 1190 to aid Christians on their pilgrimages and to establish hospitals.

4 The Third Order of St. Francis is believed to be the oldest of the three orders. It includes congregations of vowed men and women living standard lives in the world, most of the time married, who on account of circumstances cannot enter a religious order. Third Orders are also called "Tertiaries."

5 Elizabeth would become a prolific writer of personal correspondence, which is being collected and published in *Die Korrespondenz der Herzogin Elisabeth von Sachsen*, vol. 1: 1505–1532 (Leipzig: The University Press GMBH, 2010). Her story is told by Anja Zimmer.

6 Sam Wellman, *Frederick the Wise, Seen and Unseen Lives of Martin Luther's Protector* (St. Louis: Concordia Publishing House, 2015), 108.

7 Wellman, *Frederick the Wise*, 108.

8 Though he was not a military man, this was Luther's choice of military metaphor.

9 William John Wright, "Philipp of Hesse" in *The Oxford Encyclopedia of the Reformation*, vol. 3 (New York: Oxford University Press, 1996), 262.

10 Wright, *Capitalism, the State, and the Lutheran Reformation*, 65.

11 The English translation of the Epitome by Charles Leander Hill is published in *Melanchthon, Selected Writings*, eds. Elmer E. Flack and Lowell Satre (Minneapolis: Augsburg Fortress, 1962), 93–101.

12 *Melanchthon, Selected Writings*, 93.

13 *Melanchthon, Selected Writings*, 94.

14 *Melanchthon, Selected Writings*, 94.

15 *Melanchthon, Selected Writings*, 95.

16 *Melanchthon, Selected Writings*, 95.

17 *Melanchthon, Selected Writings*, 97.

18 *Melanchthon, Selected Writings*, 98.

19 *Melanchthon, Selected Writings*, 100.

20 Richard Andrew Cahill, *Philipp of Hesse and the Reformation* (Mainz: Verlag Philipp von Zabern, 2001), 189.

21 Cahill, *Philipp of Hesse and the Reformation*, 194ff.

22 Alton O. Hancock, *Church History*, vol. 35 (1936), 162. The tower was most likely the thirteenth-century "witch tower" (*Hexenturm*), which still stands in Fulda.

23 The name "Martinian" appears sporadically in the literature. It appears to have been a pejorative Catholic term for Luther's followers. Luther preferred to call his followers "Evangelicals." We have chosen the term "Lutheran" up to 1530 and "Protestant" thereafter.

24 Hancock, *Church History*, 163.

25 Anna was thirty-five at the time. The cause of her death has not been found. It seems likely she died in childbirth, since she was still able to correspond with Philipp in April, which appears to rule out an unknown lingering illness.

26 An excellent biography of Ferdinand and the Hapsburg Dynasty he founded is *Ferdinand of Austria: The Politics of Dynasticism in the Age of the Reformation* by Paula Sutter Fichtner (New York: Columbia University Press, 1982).

27 The term "Roman Catholic" was introduced in England late in the sixteenth century. It had a pejorative connotation, not the generic sense it has today. I choose not to use it here.

28 Hillerbrand, *Landgrave Philipp of Hesse*, 10.

29 Cahill, *Philipp of Hesse and the Reformation*, 132.

30 Cahill, *Philipp of Hesse and the Reformation*, 133.

31 Cahill, *Philipp of Hesse and the Reformation*, 137–38.

32 Cahill, *Philipp of Hesse and the Reformation*, 140.

33 Cahill, *Philipp of Hesse and the Reformation*, 140.

34 Cahill, *Philipp of Hesse and the Reformation*, 143.

35 Cahill, *Philipp of Hesse and the Reformation*, 144.

36 Cahill, *Philipp of Hesse and the Reformation*, 146.

37 Cahill, *Philipp of Hesse and the Reformation*, 148.

38 The four disciplines of theology—exegetical, historical, systematic, and practical—were not used in the sixteenth century. I use the term "systematic theologian" to distinguish the different roles of Adam Krafft, Philipp's more practical theologian, and Lambert of Avignon, his more systematic theologian.

39 Roy Lutz Winters, *Francis Lambert of Avignon: A Study in Reformation Origins* (Philadelphia: United Lutheran Publication House, 1938), 12. This is the only book on Lambert I could find in English. It is the source of my knowledge of Francis.

40 Winters, *Francis Lambert of Avignon*, 20.

41 Winters, *Francis Lambert of Avignon*, 32.

42 Winters, *Francis Lambert of Avignon*, 34.

43 Winters, *Francis Lambert of Avignon*, 143n2.

44 Martin Luther, *D. Martin Luthers Werke: Briefwechsel* (Weimar: H. Böhlau, 1930–, hereafter abbreviated as WA Br), III:30.

45 Winters, *Francis Lambert of Avignon*, 144n11.

46 WA Br III:30.

47 Winters, *Francis Lambert of Avignon*, 55.

48 Winters, *Francis Lambert of Avignon*, 56.

49 The original German text of Philipp's letter is 1035 in WA Br IV:112–15. This English translation is mine.

50 The primary source for knowledge of the Homberg Synod is Wilhelm Schmitt, *Die Synode zu Homberg und ihre Vorgeschichte* (Homberg: Selbstverlag der Evangelischen Kirchengemeinde, 1926). Quotations are my translation.

51 Schmitt, *Die Synode zu Homberg und ihre Vorgeschichte*, 71.

52 He may have been Philipp's confessor for two or three years, but it is unlikely he had been Philipp's teacher, for by the time Herborn arrived in Marburg in 1520, Philipp had already ruled for two years.

53 For an English translation of Herborn's letter and Philipp's response, see Cahill, *Philipp of Hesse and the Reformation*, 187–91.

54 "St. Isidore of Seville" in *The Catholic Encyclopedia*, https://www.catholic.org/encyclopedia/view. php?id=6199 (accessed May 2, 2018).

55 The complete document in both Latin and German is available with a detailed German introduction by the editor, Karl August Credner, in *Hessische Kirchenreformations–Ordnung* (Giessen: F. Rickersche Buchhandlung, 1852).

56 Credner, *Hessische Kirchenreformations–Ordnung*, sections 29–32, 104–107.

57 Wright, *Capitalism, the State, and the Lutheran Reformation*, 56.

58 Cahill, *Philipp of Hesse and the Reformation*, 179.

59 Small Catechism Preface 1 from Robert Kolb and Timothy J. Wengert, eds. *The Book of Concord: The Confessions of the Evangelical Lutheran Church* (Minneapolis: Fortress, 2000), 347ff.

60 Quoted from WA Br X:699, no. 4049, by Rudolf and Marilynn Markwald in *Katharina von Bora: A Reformation Life* (St. Louis: Concordia, 2002), 96.

61 Roland Bainton, *Here I Stand* (New York: Abingdon-Cokesbury Press, 1950), 42.

62 Kurt K. Hendel, *Johannes Bugenhagen: Selected Writings*, vol. 1 (Minneapolis: Fortress Press, 2015) 93–102.

63 The exact date of Luther's composition of "A Mighty Fortress" is unknown. It is known that it was not included on publishers' lists in 1525, but it was in 1529.

64 Coming from Pomerania, Bugenhagen spoke only Low German and Latin. Low German and High German are like our dialects; they could be understood when spoken, and Bugenhagen could have spoken with Luther and his congregation. When written, however, there was a problem.

65 Hendel, *Johannes Bugenhagen*, 80.

66 Martin Brecht, *Martin Luther*, vol. 2 (Minneapolis: Fortress Press, 1990), 357.

67 Kurt Dülfer, *Die Packishen Händel. Darstellung und Quellen, Veröffentlichngen der Historischen Kommission für Hessen und Waldeck 24,3* (Marburg: N.G. Elwert, 1958), letters 56–69, pp. 61–73.

68 Karl Brandi, *The Emperor Charles V* (London: Jonathan Cape, 1939), 297.

69 *The Augsburg Confession: A Collection of Sources with a Historical Introduction* (St. Louis: Concordia Publishing House, 2005), 12.

70 George Huntston Williams, *The Radical Reformation* (Philadelphia: The Westminster Press, 1962), 30–44. What follows is my summary. I will quote, for the reader's convenience, Williams's personal ideas and interpretations.

71 This treatise can be found in AE 40.

72 My source of information on Zwingli is Edward Peters's twenty-five-page introduction to *Ulrich Zwingli 1484–1531: Selected Works*, ed. Samuel Macauley Jackson (Philadelphia: University of Pennsylvania Press, 1972). I will give citation for Peters's ideas and interpretations.

73 AE 49:228–31. "Your Sovereign Grace" is capitalized because it was the normal address for a prince and normally abbreviated "YSG" or its German or Latin equivalent.

74 For an excellent account of the colloquy including transcripts of the discussions, read Hermann Sasse, *This Is My Body* (Adelaide, Australia: Lutheran Publishing House, 1977; rev. ed. Minneapolis: Augsburg Publishing House, 1957).

75 Sasse, *This Is My Body*, 174.

76 Sasse, *This Is My Body*, 174.

77 Sasse, *This Is My Body*, 175.

78 Sasse, *This Is My Body*, 105.

79 Bainton, *Here I Stand*, 316ff.

80 Mary was the wife of King Louis II of Hungary, who was killed in the Battle of Mohacs in 1526. She retained her title as Queen of Hungary for life.

81 Historians consistently use the German spelling Schmalkald. The English spelling Smalcald is used only for Luther's Smalcald Articles.

82 Thomas A. Brady Jr., *Protestant Politics: Jacob Sturm (1489–1553) and the German Reformation* (Boston: Humanities Press, 1995), 84.

83 Luther on duty for his Augustinian Order in Rome in 1510 found that Pope Julius was not there. As a warrior pope, he was off with his army, defending Rome against Maximilian.

84 Martin Brecht, *Martin Luther: The Preservation of the Church, 1532–1546*, vol. 3 (Minneapolis: Fortress Press, 1993), 39. Brecht is the major source for the historical facts I have written. For the reader's convenience, I will cite all his personal ideas and interpretations.

85 Jon Vieker, *Closed Communion* (St. Louis: Concordia Publishing House, 2017) 3–19.

86 Brecht, *Martin Luther: The Preservation of the Church*, 40.

87 Brecht, *Martin Luther: The Preservation of the Church*, 43.

88 *Tetrapolitana Confessio*, in the McClintock and Strong Biblical Cyclopedia, http://www.biblicalcyclopedia.com/T/tetrapolitana-confessio.html (accessed May 4, 2018).

89 Brecht, *Martin Luther: The Preservation of the Church*, 45. Brecht's source is WA Br VII:117–18.

90 Brecht, *Martin Luther: The Preservation of the Church*, 47.

91 Brecht, *Martin Luther: The Preservation of the Church*, 48. Brecht's note 31 gives as his source WA Br VII:727–28 and WA Br VII:353.

92 Brecht, *Martin Luther: the Preservation of the Church*, 51.

93 See note 81 above.

94 Wright, *Capitalism, the State, and the Lutheran Reformation*, 55. This is the best English-language account of Hessian economics and social welfare in the sixteenth century.

95 *Untersuchungen und Materialien zer Verfassungs und Landesgeschichte: herausgegeben von Hessischen Landesamt für geschichtliche Landeskunde.* Holger Th. Gräf und Anke Stoesser (Bearb. Und Hrsg.), *Philipp der Grossmütige, Landgraf von Hessen (1504–1567): Ene Bibliographie zu Person und Territorium im Reformationszeitalter* (Marburg: 2004).

96 Quoted by Wright, *Capitalism, the State, and the Lutheran Reformation*, 190.

97 Wright, *Capitalism, the State, and the Lutheran Reformation*, 192.

98 Wright, *Capitalism, the State, and the Lutheran Reformation*, 195.

99 Wright, *Capitalism, the State, and the Lutheran Reformation*, 189.

100 AE 44:206.

101 AE 45:350.

102 AE 40:314.

103 Quoted and translated by William J. Wright, "The Impact of the Reformation on Hessian Education," *Church History* 44, no. 2 (June 1975): 182.

104 Presumably the High German of Saxony and Hesse and influenced by Luther's Bible.

105 George Huntston Williams's *The Radical Reformation* is the main source for the information in this chapter. All quotes of the author's ideas or interpretations will be cited.

106 John Nicholas Lenker, ed., *The Precious and Sacred Writings of Martin Luther*, vol. 2 (Minneapolis: Lutherans in All Lands, 1903), 102.

107 Williams, *The Radical Reformation*, 364.

108 Williams, *The Radical Reformation*, 366.

109 Williams, *The Radical Reformation*, 371.

110 Williams, *The Radical Reformation*, 372.

111 Williams, *The Radical Reformation*, 371.

112 Harold J. Grimm, *The Reformation Era: 1500–1650* (New York: The Macmillan Company, 1954), 273.

113 Williams's *The Radical Reformation*, pp. 439–47, is the major source of my information in this chapter. I will report the historical facts in my own words.

114 Bucer's comments may sound congenial to us today. They were not, however, what Philipp had learned from Luther and Melanchthon, namely that the Church is not a community of love restoring the original order of creation; rather, it is the forward-looking community of Christ's redeemed, gathered in love to celebrate the resurrection of the body and the forgiveness of sin in Word and Sacraments.

115 We shall read in chapter 16 that in accord with papers of surrender Philipp signed in 1548, some of the saint's bones were returned to Hesse.

116 Rene Sommerfeldt, *Der Grossmuetige Hesse: Philipp von Hessen (1504–1567) Historisches Urteil und Erinnerungskultur* (Marburg: Tectum Verlag, 2007), 32ff.

117 Quoted from Theodore G. Tappert, ed., *Selected Writings of Martin Luther*, vol. 1 (Minneapolis: Fortress Press, 2007), 460.

118 Clyde Leonard Manschreck, *Melanchthon: The Quiet Reformer* (New York: Abingdon, 1958), 262–63.

119 For an analysis of Luther and Melanchthon's response, see Brecht's *Luther: The Preservation of the Church*, 205–7.

120 David M. Whitford, *A Reformation Life: The European Reformation through the Eyes of Philipp of Hesse* (Santa Barbara: Praeger Publishing, 2015), 117.

121 It would be interesting to learn if Philipp sent Melanchthon on a similar "treasure hunt" to Rotenberg on the Fulda. Unfortunately, Clyde Manschreck says only, "On some pretext he lured Malanchthon to Rotenberg on the Fulda" (*Melanchthon*, 267).

122 Hastings Eells, *The Attitude of Martin Bucer toward the Bigamy of Philipp of Hesse* (New Haven/London: Yale Historical Publications, 1924), 109.

123 Alexander VI, pope from 1492 to 1503, had at least seven and possibly as many as ten illegitimate children. Pope Leo X, who excommunicated Luther in 1520, was accused of homosexuality after his death.

124 Robert H. Fischer, *Luther* (Philadelphia: Lutheran Church Press), 66.

125 The examples they recorded are preserved in the article by Thanasosios Diamandopoulos, Pavlos Goudas, and Demetra Patsy, "The Ancient and medieval Greek writer's perceptions concerning the relationship between sexual characteristics and testicular volume," *Hormones* 4 no. 2 (2005): 117–20.

126 Whitford, *A Reformation Life*, 2.

127 Martin Luther, *D. Martin Luthers Werke: Tischreden* (Weimar: H. Böhlau, 1912–21), VI:634 (my translation).

128 Brandi, *The Emperor Charles V*, 421. Chapter 2, pp. 181–381, is the main source of information for this chapter. I will give citation for his ideas and/or interpretations that I quote. The telling of historical facts shall be in my own words.

129 The distance from Granada, Spain, to Ghent, Belgium, through France is approximately 1,227 miles (1,975 km).

130 Cromwell shared Anne Boleyn's fate; he was executed five months later, in June 1540.

131 Eells, *The Attitude of Martin Bucer Toward the Bigamy of Philipp of Hesse*, 120.

132 Eells, *The Attitude of Martin Bucer Toward the Bigamy of Philipp of Hesse*, 136.

133 Granvelle, like Lund and Burin later, are locations, not persons. Yet these two imperial officers are referred to in the literature simply as "Granvelle" and "Lund."

134 Eells, *The Attitude of Martin Bucer Toward the Bigamy of Philipp of Hesse*, 354.

135 Brandi, *The Emperor Charles V*, 442.

136 Brandi, *The Emperor Charles V*, 443.

137 Brandi, *The Emperor Charles V*, 451.

138 Details of the event that follows are given by Martin Brecht in *Martin Luther: The Preservation of the Church*, 290–95.

139 For the Braunschweig Church Order published by Bugenhagen in 1528, see Hendel, *Johannes Bugenhagen: Selected Writings*, 1181.

140 Brecht, *Martin Luther: The Preservation of the Church*, 219.

141 Brandi, *The Emperor Charles V*, 523–587. This volume is the source of many of the historical facts in this chapter. The telling of these facts shall be in my own words. I will give citation for the ideas and/or interpretations of other writers, including Brandi.

142 Brandi, *The Emperor Charles V*, 502.

143 Brandi, *The Emperor Charles V*, 527.

144 Brandi, *The Emperor Charles V*, 512. The choir is the altar area of a large church that can accompany two hundred or more with standing room only.

145 Brandi, *The Emperor Charles V*, 511.

146 Brandi, *The Emperor Charles V*, 516.

147 *Landgraf Philipp der Grossmütige 1504–1567: Hessen im Zentrum der Reform*, Begleitband zu einer Ausstellung des Landes Hessen, herausgegeben von Ursula Braasch-Schwersmann, Hans Schneider, und Wilhelm Ernst Winterhager in Zusammenarbeit mit der Historischen Kommission für Hessen (Marburg: Neustadt an der Aisch, 2004).

148 Brandi, *The Emperor Charles V*, 543.

149 Brandi, *The Emperor Charles V*, 545.

150 Brandi, *The Emperor Charles V*, 547.

151 Brandi, *The Emperor Charles V*, 548.

152 Brandi, *The Emperor Charles V*, 549.

153 Brandi's terms from *The Emperor Charles V*, 549–56.

154 Brandi, *The Emperor Charles V*, 552.

155 Brandi, *The Emperor Charles V*, 553–54.

156 Brandi, *The Emperor Charles V*, 554.

157 Brandi, *The Emperor Charles V*, 555.

158 Brandi, *The Emperor Charles V*, 555.

159 Brandi, *The Emperor Charles V*, 555.

160 Translation by Brandi, *The Emperor Charles V*, 553. He includes the original German wording:
Der Kaiser ist ein ehrlich Mann
allzeit ist er der vorderst dran,
zu Ross und auch zu Fussen.
Seint wohlgemut Ihr Lantzknecht gut,
da sprach der edle Kaiser gut:
"Wir wollin uns nit ergeben."

161 Brandi, *The Emperor Charles V*, 555.

162 Brandi, *The Emperor Charles V*, 556.

163 Brandi, *The Emperor Charles V*, 564.

164 Brandi, *The Emperor Charles V*, 567.

165 The historian Anja Zimmer has visited the area and was told the footprints and wheel ruts at the riverside would have quickly revealed the location of the ford.

166 Brandi, *The Emperor Charles V*, 567ff.

167 Brandi, *The Emperor Charles V*, 569.

168 Brandi, *The Emperor Charles V*, 567.

169 Brandi, *The Emperor Charles V*, 570.

170 Brandi, *The Emperor Charles V*, 571.

171 Brandi, *The Emperor Charles V*, 570.

172 Brandi, *The Emperor Charles V*, 571.

173 Brandi, *The Emperor Charles V*, 571.

174 Brandi, *The Emperor Charles V*, 571ff.

175 Brandi, *The Emperor Charles V*, 571ff.

176 Joachim Hector II had taken Communion in both kinds in 1539 indicating he was inclined to become a Protestant, but it would be 1555 before he would publicly announce his turn to Protestantism. The two electors were first cousins once removed, for Joachim's mother was the daughter of Maurice's uncle, Duke George the Bearded of Saxony. For interesting details of Joachim's parents' dysfunctional marriage involving Luther, see Brecht, *Martin Luther: Shaping and Defining the Reformation*, 356ff.

177 Brandi, *The Emperor Charles V*, 572.

178 Brandi, *The Emperor Charles V*, 572.

179 Brandi, *The Emperor Charles V*, 573.

180 His name is unknown. Chancellor Feige retired in 1541 after serving for twenty-seven years, and he died the following year.

181 Brandi, *The Emperor Charles V*, 573.

182 Brandi, *The Emperor Charles V*, 573.

183 Brandi, *The Emperor Charles V*, 573.

184 The name "Donauwörth" is a compound of *Donau*, the German word for the Danube River, and *wörth*, an apparent corruption of the Wörnitz River.

185 Mary was the regent, not the queen, of the Netherlands. She is rightfully called queen because she was the widow of King Louis of Hungary.

186 There were at least three Agricolas at the time. This was John Agricola, Luther's former student, who had been discredited for his Antinomian views and, though he lacked credibility to Protestants that either of the father and son Stephen Acrigolas of Augsburg might have brought, he was recommended by Elector Joachim II of Brandenburg. See Robert Kolb, *Luther's World of Wittenberg* (Minneapolis: Fortress, 2018), p. 128 for comments on the two Stephen Agricolas, and pp. 75–77, 85, 100, 188, 209, and 279 for comments on John Agricola.

187 Fritz Wolff, "Der Gefangene Landgraf: Der Wege in die Gefangenschaft" and "Gefangenschaft in Oudenaarde und Mecheln" in Ursula Braasch-Schwersmann, the *festschrift* for the 500th anniversary of Philipp's birth. Braasch-Schwersman et al., *Landgraf Philipp der Grossmütige*, 130.

188 Wolff, "Der Gefangene Landgraf," 130.

189 For more details of Maurice's successful efforts to have Philipp released, see Brandi, *The Emperor Charles V*, pp. 590–606.

190 Brandi, *The Emperor Charles V*, 603. I have been told that Metz is on a tributary a short distance from the Rhine.

191 Brandi, *The Emperor Charles V*, 605ff.

192 Brandi, *The Emperor Charles V*, 606.

193 Brandi, *The Emperor Charles V*, 608.

194 Brandi, *The Emperor Charles V*, 609.

195 Brandi, *The Emperor Charles V*, 612.

196 Brandi, *The Emperor Charles V*, 611.

197 Brandi, *The Emperor Charles V*, 612; emphasis added.

198 Information for the release of Philipp is from Fritz Wolff, "Der gefangene Landgraf: Der Wege in die Gefangenschaft" and "Gefangenschaft in Oudenaarde und Mecheln," originally published in *Landgraf Philipp der Grossmütige: 1504–1567*, Braasch-Schwersman et al., 123–39 and 274f.

199 Brandi, *The Emperor Charles V*, 614.

200 All the information for this section, "Philipp Returns Unbroken," is my translation of Wolff's article "Der Gefangene Landgraf: Der Weg in die Gegenwandschaft," originally published in *Landgraf Philipp der Grossmütige: 1504–1567*, Braasch-Schwersman et al., 133–34.

201 Wolff, "Der Gefangene Landgraf," 133. This book is very hard to find. Interlibrary loan searches turned up only two in the United States, both not to be borrowed. The German historian Anja Zimmer called it to my attention and showed me the copy she uses from the library in Bonn. She found online the copy I own, for which I am most grateful. It is a beautifully published treasury of information on Philipp.

202 Wolff, "Der Gefangene Landgraf," 133.

203 Wolff, "Der Gefangene Landgraf," 134.

204 Wolff, "Der Gefangene Landgraf," 134.

205 Brandi, *Emperor Charles V*, 619ff.

206 Brandi, *Emperor Charles V*, 619ff.

207 Wolff, "Der Gefangene Landgraf," 282.

208 Wolff, "Der Gefangene Landgraf," 282.

209 Wolff, "Der Gefangene Landgraf," 282.

210 Wolff, "Der Gefangene Landgraf," 278ff.

211 The source of my information for this section, "Philipp, the Passionate Game Hunter," is from "Jagt" by Dr. Uta Loewensteing of Marburg, originally published in *Landgraf Philipp der Grossmütige: 1504–1567*, Braasch-Schwersman et al., 281f.

212 I have not found which of his several hunting lodges Philipp was allowed to keep. I believe that one was Spangenberg Castle, in the shadow of which Philipp kept Margarethe. The castle had a long history of being used as a hunting lodge by Hessian landgraves. The other one may have been Friedewald, which is in the same general area. The castle mentioned was in Kassel while Philipp's son Wilhelm IV had possession of Marburg during Philipp's lifetime.

213 Last summer, our daughter Catherine watched a wild boar graze on the lawn behind our lodging in Eisenach.

214 The information for all but the final concluding paragraph is from Holger Th. Gräf and Andreas Tacke, ". . . dem Hessenvolk seinen Philipp, dem evangelischen Deutschland seinen schwertgewaltigen Helden der Reformation"? Ein Hessischer Beitrag zur preußisch-deutschen Erinnerungs Kultur, in *Landgraf Philipp der Grossmütige: 1504–1567*, Braasch-Schwersman et al., 169–74.

215 Gräf, "dem Hessenvolk seinen Philipp," 170.

216 The selections chosen from this study all deal with Philipp of Hesse. These selections are used with the permission of the author, Dr. William J. Wright.

217 Dr. Wright always uses the English spelling Philip.

Bibliography

Author's note: Normally a bibliography shows authors listed in alphabetical order, but William J. Wright's work on Hesse and Landgrave Philipp is too important to bury at the end.

Wright, William John. *Capitalism, the State, and the Lutheran Reformation: Sixteenth Century Hesse*. Athens, Ohio: Ohio University Press, 1988.

——. "Hesse." In *Encyclopedia of the Renaissance* 3:147–48. Edited by Erika Rummel and Paul Grendler. New York: Charles Scribner's Sons, 1999.

——. "Mainz versus Rome: Two Responses to Luther in the 1520s." *Archiv für Reformationsgeschichte* 82 (1991): 83–105.

——. "Evaluating the Results of Sixteenth Century Educational Policy: Some Hessian Data." *Sixteenth Century Journal* 18, no. 3 (Autumn 1987): 411–26.

——. "The Homberg Synod and Philip of Hesse's Plan for a New Church-State Settlement." *Sixteenth Century Journal* 1, no. 2 (October 1973): 23–48.

——. "The Impact of the Reformation on Hessian Education." *Church History* 44 (June 1975): 23–48.

——. "A Closer Look at House Poor Relief through the Common Chest and Indigence in Sixteenth Century Hesse." *Archive for Reformation History* 70 (1979): 225–38.

——. "Personality Profiles of Four Leaders of the German Lutheran Reformation." *The Psychohistory Review* 14, no. 1 (Fall 1985): 16–18.

——. "Hesse." In *The Oxford Encyclopedia of the Reformation* 2:235–37. Edited by Hans J. Hillerbrand. New York: Oxford University Press, 1996.

——. "Adam Krafft." In *The Oxford Encyclopedia of the Reformation* 2:382. Edited by Hans J. Hillerbrand. New York: Oxford University Press, 1996.

——. "Francois Lambert." In *The Oxford Encyclopedia of the Reformation* 2:187. Edited by Hans J. Hillerbrand. New York: Oxford University Press, 1996.

——. "Pack Affair." In *The Oxford Encyclopedia of the Reformation* 3:184. Edited by Hans J. Hillerbrand. New York: Oxford University Press, 1996.

——. "Philipp of Hesse." In *The Oxford Encyclopedia of the Reformation* 3:362–63. Edited by Hans J. Hillerbrand. New York: Oxford University Press, 1996.

Aland, Kurt. *Four Reformers*. Minneapolis: Augsburg Publishing House, 1979.

Bainton, Roland H. *Here I Stand: a Life of Martin Luther*. New York: Abingdon-Cokesbury Press, 1950.

Braasch-Schwersmann, Ursula, Hans Schneider, and Wilhelm Ernst Winterhager in zusammenarbeit mit der Historischen Kommission für Hessen. *Landgraf Philipp der Grossmütige 1504–1567: Hessen im Zentrum der Reform*, Begleitband zu einer Ausstellung des Landes Hessen. Marburg: Neustadt an der Aisch, 2004.

Brady, Thomas A., Jr. *Protestant Politics: Jacob Sturm (1489–1553) and the German Reformation.* Boston: Humanities Press, Inc., 1995.

Brandi, Karl. *The Emperor Charles V: the Growth and Destiny of a Man and of a World Empire*. Translated by C. V. Wedgwood (1939). Atlantic Highlands, N.J.: Humanities Press, 1980.

Brecht, Martin. *Martin Luther: Shaping and Defining the Reformation 1521–1532*. Translated by James L. Schaaf. Minneapolis: Fortress Press, 1987.

———. *Martin Luther: the Preservation of the Church 1532–1546*. Translated by James L. Schaaf. Minneapolis: Fortress Press, 1987.

Browning Oscar. *The Life of Bartolomeo Colleoni, of Anjou and Burgundy (1891)*. London: Forgotten Books, 2012.

Cahill, Richard Andrew. *Philipp of Hesse and the Reformation*. Mainz: Verlag Philipp von Zabern, 2001.

Edwards, Mark U., Jr. *Luther's Last Battles: Politics and Polemecs, 1531–46*. Minneapolis: Fortress Press, 1983.

Eells, Hastings. *The Attitude of Martin Bucer toward the Bigamy of Philipp of Hesse*. New Haven/London: Yale Historical Publications, 1924.

Estes, James Martin. *Christian Magistrate and State Church: the Reforming Career of Johannes Brenz*. Toronto: University of Toronto Press, 1982.

Fischer, Robert H. *Luther*. Philadelphia: Lutheran Church Press, 1966.

Franz, Guenther *Wiedertaeuferakten 1527–1626, Urkundlichen Quellen zur hessischen Reformationsgeschichte* vol. 4. Marburg: Elwert, 1951.

Gräf, Holger Th. und Anke Stoesser. *Philipp der Grossmütige, Landgraf von Hessen (1504–1567): Eine Bibliographie zu Person und Territorium im Reformationszeitalter*. Marburg: 2004.

Grimm, Harold J. *The Reformation Era 1500–1650*. New York: Macmillan Company, 1954.

Hancock, Alton Odell. "The Reformation in Hesse to 1538: A Study of the Encounter of Differing Reformation Points of View." Diss., Emory University, 1962.

Hendel, Kurt K. *Johannes Bugenhagen: Selected Writings in Two Volumes*. Minneapolis: Fortress Press, 2015.

——. "The Smalcald Articles." In *The Annotated Luther* vol. 2, *Word and Faith*. Edited by Kirsi I. Stjerna. Minneapolis: Fortress Press, 2015.

Hill, Charles Leander, trans. *Melanchthon: Selected Writings*. Edited by Elmer Ellsworth Flack and Lowell J. Satre. Minneapolis: Augsburg Publishing House, 1962.

Holborn, Hajo. *Ulrich von Hutten and the German Reformation*. Translated by Roland H. Bainton. New York: Harper Torchbooks, 1965.

Jackson, Samuel Macauley. *Ulrich Zwingli (1484–1531): Selected Works*, with introduction by Edward Peters (1972). Philadelphia: University of Pennsylvania Press, 1901.

Kolb, Robert. *Luther's World of Wittenberg*. Minneapolis: Fortress Press, 2018.

Kolb, Robert and Timothy J. Wengert, eds. *The Book of Concord: The Confessions of the Evangelical Lutheran Church*. Minneapolis: Fortress Press, 2000.

Loewenich, Walter. *Luther's Theology of the Cross*. Translated by Herbert J. A. Bouman. Minneapolis: Augsburg Publishing House, 1976.

Maltby, William. *The Reign of Charles V*. New York: Palgrave, 2002.

Manschreck, Clyde L. *Melanchthon on Christian Doctrine: Loci Communes 1555*. New York: Oxford University Press, 1965.

——. *Melanchthon: The Quiet Reformer*. New York: Abingdon Press, 1958.

Markwald, Rudolf K. and Marilynn Morris Markwald. *Katharina von Bora: a Reformation Life*. St. Louis: Concordia Publishing House, 2002.

Oyer, John S. *Lutheran Reformers against Anabaptists: Luther, Melandhthon and Menius and the Anabaptists of Central Germany*. The Hague: Martinus Mijhoff, 1964.

Ranke, Leopold. *Reformation in Germany*. London: Longman, Brown Green, and Longmans, 1845.

Schmidt-Pauli, Elizabeth. *Saint Elizabeth: Sister of Saint Francis*. New York: Henry Holt and Company, 1932.

Rait, Jill, ed. *Shapers of Religious Traditions in Germany, Switzerland, and Poland, 1560–1600*. New Haven: Yale University Press, 1981.

Reu, Johann Michael. *The Augsburg Confession: A Collection of Sources with a Historical Introduction*. St. Louis: Concordia Publishing House, 2005 (reprint of original 1930 edition).

Robeck, Nesta de. *Saint Elizabeth of Hungary: a Story of Twenty-four Years*. Milwaukee: The Bruce Publishing Company, 1953.

Rogness, Michael. *Philip Melanchthon: Reformer Without Honor*. Minneapolis: Augsburg Publishing House, 1969.

Sasse, Herman. *This Is My Body*. Adelaide: Lutheran Publishing House, 1977 (revised ed.).

Schwiebert, E. G. *Luther and His Times: The Reformation from a New Perspective*. St. Louis: Concordia Publishing House, 1950.

Sider, Ronald J. *Karlstadt's Battle with Luther*. Philadelphia: Fortress Press, 1978.

Smith, Preserved. *Luther's Correspondence: and Other Contemporary Letters* vol. 1, 1507–1521, and vol. 2, 1521–1530. Philadelphia: The Lutheran Publication Society, 1913.

——. *The Age of the Reformation*. New York: Henry Holt and Company, 1920.

Sommerfeldt, Rene. "Der Grossmuetige Hesse: Philipp von Hessen (1504–1567)." *Historisches Urteil und Erinnerungskultur*. Marburg: Tectum Verlag, 2007.

Wellman, Sam. *Frederick the Wise: Seen and Unseen Lives of Martin Luther's Protector*. St. Louis: Concordia Publishing House, 2011.

Whitford, David M. *A Reformation Life: The European Reformation through the Eyes of Philipp of Hesse*. Santa Barbara: Praeger, 2015.

Williams, George Huntston. *The Radical Reformation*. Philadelphia: Westminster Press, 1962.

Wolf, Gustaf. *Wuellenkunde der deutschen Reformationsgeschichte*. Hildesheim: Georg Olms Verlagsbuchhandlung, 1965.

Zuber, Janet W. and Emilie L. Z. Hoppe. *Inspired by God's Word*. Amana: Amana Church Society, 2013.

Index